LOVE YOU TO DEATH

Michael Clifford

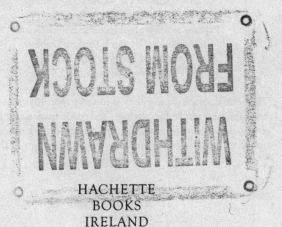
HACHETTE
BOOKS
IRELAND

Copyright © 2008 Michael Clifford

Published in 2008 by Hachette Books Ireland

The right of Michael Clifford to be identified as the Author of the Work
has been asserted by him in accordance with the Copyright, Designs and
Patents Act, 1988.

A CIP catalogue record for this title is available from the British Library.

ISBN 978 0 340 963 51 7

Typeset in Sabon by Hachette Books Ireland
Cover design by Sin É Design, Dublin
Printed and bound in the UK by,
CPI Mackays, Chatham ME5 8TD

Hachette Books Ireland policy is to use papers that are natural,
renewable and recyclable products and made from wood grown in
sustainable forests. The logging and manufacturing processes are
expected to conform to the environmental regulations of the country
of origin.

Hachette Books Ireland
8 Castlecourt Centre
Castleknock
Dublin 15
Ireland
A division of Hachette Livre UK Ltd, 338 Euston Road,
London NW1 3BH, England

CONTENTS

INTRODUCTION

The queue twisted like a human chain across the Round Hall of the Four Courts. It was 9.40 a.m., on 18 July 2007, and crowds were already gathering for the few seats available to the public in the trial of Joe O'Reilly for murdering his wife.

The O'Reilly case had hit a nerve in the public imagination. It had all the elements of a classic whodunnit. There had been extensive media coverage of the case before O'Reilly was charged. But one of the principal elements of interest to the public was that this was a case in which a man was accused of murdering his wife even though the couple and their two children had appeared from the outside to be an idyllic family.

The phenomenon of a man killing his partner, or ex-partner, is not a new one, but it elicits heightened emotions in the families left behind. Unlike other fatal crimes, this is one based on a relationship that was once intimate but has, for some reason, turned sour to the extent that the man feels moved to kill the person he once considered his life partner.

A few statistics put this crime into perspective. There has been little research in Ireland as to the prevalence of and factors involved in killings by partners or ex-partners. According to a report compiled in 2008 by the Dublin-based women and children's refuge, Aoibhneas, 140 Irish women were murdered between 1995 and 2007. Of these, 103 have been legally resolved. In 47 per cent of cases a husband, partner or ex-partner was responsible for the killing.

This figure converges with international norms. According to a number of studies conducted in the USA, between 40 and 50 per cent of female homicides are committed by men in the above three categories.

In the relevant cases, between two-thirds and three-quarters of the victims had previously been subjected to violence by their husband, ex-husband or partner.

Today the law deals with wife-killing as it would any other murder. But it wasn't always thus. On 26 July 1911, Alice Stone Blackwell wrote to the *New York Times* on the subject of wife-killers. She was exercised by the fact that in the allegedly civilised countries of Europe men who killed their wives got away with murder: "An acute observer has pointed out, as a peculiarity of the administration of justice in the United States, that here it is looked upon as just as bad for a man to kill his wife as to kill anybody else. In many foreign countries, this is not the case."

She cited a recent study in England of a number of cases in which women had been killed by their husbands. None of the husbands received more than a trifling punishment. Almost anything was accepted as a mitigating circumstance, such as that the man had been drinking, or his wife had given him "provocation" by failing to have his supper ready. "In one particularly bad case, the judge told the husband that he meant to make an example of him. Accordingly, he gave him three months in prison!" Blackwell wrote. "A prominent Englishwoman told me that if a workingman wanted to get rid of his wife all he had to do was to drink a few glasses of liquor and then kill her; he was almost sure to get off with a short imprisonment. If a woman of property was killed by her husband the courts took a more serious view of it; but the lives of poor women were cheap."

She went on to suggest that one of the reasons for the reintroduction of divorce in France a few years previously was that it had become almost impossible to convict in cases of wife murder. Juries tacitly assumed that if a man found his wife's conduct intolerable and had no other way to get rid of her, he was justified in killing her.

The letter highlighted society and the law's attitude to wife-killing at the time. It was murder, sure, but murder of a lesser moral standard.

In European terms, the general attitude towards this crime dated back to feudal times, when the law provided that a woman killing her husband should be put to death with torture, in the same manner as a subject who killed the King. On the other hand, a wife-killing husband could get off with a fine. The law was defended on the grounds that the relationship between husband and wife was like that between sovereign and subject.

We've come a long way. Today, generally in society, a man's killing of his wife is considered a cowardly attack by a physically stronger individual and regarded with the same, if not more, opprobrium as any other circumstance in which a man kills a woman.

Some might dispute that statement. A study in the Australian state of Victoria in 2007 found that those who killed within their families – generally wife-killers – received lesser sentences than those convicted of other categories of killing.

An analysis by the state's Sentencing Advisory Council concluded that people who killed strangers received on average an extra two years in prison. Penal reform campaigners in the state put the difference down to the fact that generally wife-killers have little or no prior record of serious convictions, which goes in their favour at sentencing.

The issue of provocation for killing within a marriage has also been transformed. Three of the men whose cases are dealt with in this book had alleged provocation in their trials. In 1970, it was introduced to the trial of Thomas Murray, and the result might shock some and would certainly have led to an outcry if it were to happen today. In the case of Henry Holmes in 1983, it was also central, but the apparent acceptance by the jury that he was provoked didn't cut much ice with the judge in sentencing. Provocation was introduced by Anton Mulder to his case, and this was one in which, had it occurred a century ago, he might well have pursued that line with profit.

But even if the crime is regarded today as seriously as other killings, that hasn't lessened the phenomenon. If anything, a more violent society has meant that some women who are in relationships in which drink and drugs feature are more likely than ever to be at the end of a fatal assault.

Why do these men kill? The question is the title of a book on the subject by American psychologist David Adams. He lists a number of different reasons, based on his research. Some are obvious, like jealous rage. In other instances, substance abuse was prominent. Academic Jacquelyn Campbell, who has done a lot of work in this area, studied 445 cases of intimate-partner homicide in the USA during the 1990s and found that the men involved in half were problem drinkers, and half used illegal drugs. There was a substantial overlap in the two categories.

David Adams also identifies the "materially motivated" killer. This is a husband or partner who kills not for profit but more out of fear of loss, particularly at a time when a union is breaking up.

The loss isn't just financial but may include status, or even having to move out of the family home.

Junctions of vulnerability to fatal attack have also been identified. A study in Dublin's Rotunda Hospital in 2003 found that one in eight women suffered physical violence during her pregnancy. Studies in the USA have also shown that this is a particularly vulnerable time. However, the point at which killing is far more likely to occur is during the break-up of a marriage or long-term relationship.

So what can be done to prevent or minimise this crime? Identifying risk is one of the major problems. Where there has been previous violence within a marriage, there is a possibility that risk can be identified. This would involve co-ordination between social services, the police, the courts and the deployment of resources to front-line agencies to train staff in identifying risk.

With cases that don't involve any documented, or even suspected, prior violence, it is difficult to see how risk can be identified or assessed. Some men have it in them to kill their wives, even if they have not previously been batterers. There are instances in which jealous rage inflames passion, and a swift act of violence occurs with fatal consequences. These instances are appalling for all involved, but they do happen.

There are also men who are capable of planning and executing the murder of their wives, over a long or short period, and identifying such individuals is nigh-on impossible. For example, nobody in Joe

O'Reilly's circle would have put him down as a killer. Nobody who knew Frank McCann would have imagined him capable of doing what he did.

This book was conceived following an approach from the publisher in the wake of the Joe O'Reilly trial in 2007, which I covered for the *Sunday Tribune*. There was major interest in the trial, and it brought to the fore the issue of men who kill their wives. Any number of cases that involved the trial of an accused husband might have featured in this book. I chose the nine stories that follow for various reasons. First, they represented a chronological spread between modern Ireland and what went before. Four occurred during the 2000s, and the other five between 1945 and 1992. In each case, the husband denied the charge, creating the requirement for a trial. In most of the cases, the man went to some lengths to maintain that he was not the culprit; the details around each one's conduct before and after the killing are fascinating in the study of how a killer behaves.

Another feature that unites these stories is that the men had no prior record of criminal behaviour outside the home that would have suggested they were of a violent disposition, with one exception.

The nine cases compiled were not selected because they were clear profiles of particular types of wife-killer. In most of the cases featured, it would have been difficult to predict that there was a real and present danger of a woman being killed by her husband.

For example, prior domestic violence was suspected in three of the stories featured and only confirmed in one. This is less than the 50 per cent figure identified in the US studies.

There are, however, features in these cases that resonate with research conducted in the area. Margaret Lehman in 1944, Mary Murray in 1969 and Anne Holmes in 1981 were attacked and killed during pregnancy. Gary McCrea, Anton Mulder and Brian Kearney killed their wives when their marriages were breaking up.

The reader will have no problem in spotting where jealousy featured in the various stories, but the traits of the 'materially motivated' killer can be seen in James Lehman, Henry Holmes, McCann, O'Reilly and Kearney. None of the cases featured here could be attributable to substance abuse.

Edward Hayes was found not to have been responsible for his actions, and therefore does not deserve to be categorised with the others in this book. His story was included because it was the first time that a guilty but insane plea was considered following the effective abolition of the death penalty in 1964.

There is one other point worth noting about recurring themes in these stories. In the earliest killing recorded here, there was an attempt to stage a suicide. The most recent murder, occurring some fifty-two years later, also involved a staged suicide. Irrespective of what inroads are made in identifying risk, some things will never change.

The stories in this book have been compiled mainly from the records of the criminal-justice system in which the cases were processed. That includes attendance at trials, transcripts from trials, court reports and garda statements.

I also interviewed a number of retired or serving gardaí who worked on the cases. Only one case, that of Frank and Esther McCann, includes an interview with a member of the deceased woman's family.

1. SECRETS AND LIES

The Case of Frank McCann

On the Saturday before the baby was born, Esther McCann and her sister-in-law Jeanette went from shop to shop, gathering the bits and bobs required for the visit to hospital. Esther was worried about Jeanette, whose baby had been due on 6 March, three days previously, and there was still no sign of anything happening.

That evening, when they got back to the house, Esther cried her eyes out. She didn't know why she was crying. She rang Dr Ormond to ask what they should do about the overdue pregnancy. He said they should go to the Coombe immediately. They set off for the maternity hospital, Jeanette, the prospective mother, calm and composed, Esther fretting enough for both of them.

The impending birth would have a major impact on

both women's lives. Jeanette had come to live with her brother, Frank McCann, and his wife Esther, when her pregnancy had become an issue with her mother in her own home. She wanted Frank and Esther to adopt the baby after his or her birth. The arrangement suited everyone, as Jeanette was unmarried and didn't feel ready for all that motherhood involved, while the McCanns were childless.

Jeanette was admitted at 8.30 p.m. that evening and brought off to be examined by the doctor. Esther hung around. At 11.30 p.m., one of the ward sisters came up to her. "It looks like nothing's going to happen for at least forty-eight hours," she told Esther. "You'd be as well off going home for the night." The sister told her that she would bring Jeanette up to St Brigid's Ward, where they would be able to keep an eye on her. Esther thanked her and returned home to Rathfarnham.

At 2.30 a.m., the call came through. Jeanette had gone into labour. Esther rushed back and was at Jeanette's side for the next three hours. The baby was born at 5.05 a.m. on Sunday 10 March 1991. She weighed five pounds two ounces and was to be called Jessica. Esther recorded the occasion later in a diary she began writing for the little girl.

You were cleaned up a bit, introduced to me and your mother and then very shortly after that brought to the care unit as you needed some special care because of your size.

The hospital kept you in the unit for two days doing all sorts of tests on you. Jeanette visited you there. All that Sunday I spent getting clothes for you and your mother and making sure everyone knew about your arrival.

Jeanette was moved to a semi-private ward in the hospital and Esther went about her preparations for bringing the new mother and baby home. Before Jeanette and Jessica were discharged from the hospital, Jeanette reaffirmed her wish that the baby would be adopted by her brother and Esther. Jeanette herself had been adopted into the McCann family as an infant, and she wanted her child to have a proper home. A real bond had formed between her and her sister-in-law who wanted the couple to give her baby the security of a loving family.

Esther and Frank visited the social worker attached to the hospital and explained the intention for the baby. On Tuesday they had another meeting; this time Jeanette attended too. Esther recorded the meeting in her diary for Jessica.

At the meeting on Tuesday Jeanette told us that on Thursday you were being discharged and that she wanted us to eventually adopt you.

We were thrilled and a little worried that maybe Jeanette had made her decision too quickly. She however felt it was the best

*possible arrangement for you and that she was
certain we would be good parents to you.*

Jessica was brought home on the Thursday. Soon
after, Jeanette moved out and resumed her pre-
pregnancy life. The McCanns entered family life with
their new baby. For Esther, it was the beginning of a
phase in her life for which she had longed. She wanted
to retain for posterity the joy she felt and committed
it to her diary.

*So here you are with us and we love you dearly.
I don't intend to give you a day-by-day account
of your life with us, but your early days have
been eventful. I will try to fill you in on all the
more important things that will happen to you
in your life and maybe we can keep a record for
you to read when you are older.*

Few who knew them would have put Esther O'Brien
and Frank McCann together. If opposites really do
attract, then this coupling was custom-made. Esther
was one of a family of four from Tramore in Co.
Waterford. Her father Thomas worked for CIE, but
he died young, leaving his widow, Brigid, to raise their
children through the teenage years.

On completing the Leaving Cert in 1973, Esther
went to University College Dublin to study psychology.
She moved in with her sister Marian, who had come up

to the city the previous year. The sisters had been close while growing up and remained so in adulthood. "We would have met or talked to each other practically every day," Marian Leonard remembers. "And this was in the days before mobile phones and the Internet made that kind of contact easy."

Esther took to life in the Big Smoke. Naturally outgoing and sociable, she quickly made friends. Her boyfriend journeyed from Tramore to Dublin every weekend to see her. Tragedy struck in 1978 when he was killed in a motorcycle accident travelling up to the city. Eventually, she was able to put the bereavement behind her and moved on.

Life in Dublin was opening up for her. In her second year at UCD she concluded that a psychology degree was not for her. Her interest was fast switching to the fledgling business of computers. "At that time the whole thing was about mainframe computers, which she was really into," Marian says. "She saw the benefit of email and the Internet long before most people. She would often have brought it up with me, but like most people, I hadn't copped on to it yet."

For three years she worked with the foot-care company Scholl, then moved to a position that involved training employees on word-processing and computers with Nexus office systems. She went on to work for accounting firm O'Hare Barry & Associates. When one of the partners, Bernard Somers, left, Esther went to work for him.

In the mid-eighties, Esther was in a relationship with a man called Paul, who wanted her to emigrate with him to Australia. After considering it, she declined – she did not want to be so far away from her family, especially her growing band of nieces and nephews. He left on his own. Soon after, Frank McCann, who had known both of them, began to show interest in her. Marian was surprised by her sister's choice of partner. "We just found him to be very conservative," Marian remembers. "He was a bit dull, but I would have said at the same time he was dependable and he had great friends. And if it was what Esther wanted, then that was good enough for me."

McCann was born in 1960, into a family of five from Dublin's southside. At the time of his birth, his parents, Frank and Joan, lived on Fernhill Road, but subsequently moved to Terenure. Frank was educated at Templeogue College. On leaving school, he followed his father into the Irish Distillers company as an apprentice cooper.

The trade, once popular but now disappeared, involved making staved conical vessels from timber, bound together with hoops, designed to hold beer. Frank was the last apprenticed cooper in the country. In an article in the *Irish Times* in 1985, he said he was the fourth generation of his family to go into coopering. "The craft of coopering was handed down generation to generation," he said. "It was a closed trade. To become a cooper you had to be the son or grandson of an operating cooper."

By then he was working for himself. In 1982 he had been made redundant by Distillers. He had got together with an older, more experienced cooper and set up a business, Irish Craft Coopers, based in the Greenhills industrial estate, in the west of the city. The business had mixed fortunes, as might be expected in a trade in steep decline, and eventually he bought his partner out for £9,000. Then, in 1989, a fire destroyed the premises. The blaze was suspicious. An investigation by gardaí suggested that the fire had had two sources and that inflammable liquid had been used. No charges were ever pressed. McCann sold his premises for £92,000. In 1991, he went into partnership with his brother to purchase a public house in Blessington, Co. Wicklow. They renamed it the Cooperage, in honour of the family trade.

To those who knew him, McCann cut a confident figure. A tall man, somewhat severe in appearance, he could be charming and articulate. He didn't drink or smoke and invested a great deal of his time in swimming, his main passion outside work. He swam at international level, and after retiring, he turned to coaching. He rose through the ranks in swimming administration to become president of the Leinster branch of the Irish Amateur Swimming Association.

McCann had known Esther when she was seeing Paul. They socialised in the same company around Dublin. Once Paul was out of the picture, McCann made his move. He was twenty-six, four years younger than Esther. "He was very old-fashioned," Marian

Leonard remembers. "He began wooing her with chocolates and flowers. He even brought flowers for me as her sister."

It didn't take Esther long to make up her mind that this relationship was going all the way. The couple bought a house on Butterfield Avenue in Rathfarnham. The location suited them both: it was close to where Frank had grown up and within easy reach of Marian and her young family in Firhouse.

Frank set about renovating the property, putting to use his considerable skills as a handyman, while Esther got stuck into making it a home. They were married on 22 May 1987. By then, Frank was already harbouring the secret that would propel him towards murder.

Some time in the previous year, McCann had impregnated a seventeen-year-old whom he was coaching at swimming. There is no evidence as to the extent of his relationship with the girl, but the encounter happened against a background that would not be exposed until some years later.

Two of McCann's contemporaries in swimming, George Gibney and Derry O'Rourke, were eventually unmasked as child sex abusers who preyed on young swimmers. No evidence emerged that McCann was involved to the same extent, but all the indications are that he was responsible for the teenager's pregnancy. Once the girl's predicament became known, her mother confronted McCann. The baby was born in August 1987, a few months after McCann's marriage to Esther.

A friend of the teenager's family, Father Michael Cleary, was deployed to broker a financial settlement between the parties. Ironically, Cleary harboured his own secret. A colourful and gregarious character, his parentage of two boys would not become public knowledge until after his death in 1994.

McCann agreed to settle the girl's hospital bills. An anonymous payment of between £500 and £600 was also made to the girl's father, believed to have come from McCann.

Meanwhile, back at Butterfield Avenue, Esther was blissfully unaware of her new husband's secret and his negotiations to keep it under wraps. Her focus was on making a home for the family she was going to have. "She really turned that place into a home," Marian says. "She was really into family. She would have loved to have about six kids."

Four years into the marriage, the McCanns had not yet produced a child. Esther had developed a common health problem, an overactive thyroid, which has implications for fertility. She cut back on her work commitments to ensure that the problem would be adequately dealt with. But by then a new addition was bound for the McCann household.

Thursday, 4 April 1991: A big day out for you.
Had your BCG in the clinic – Jeanette came too

– weighed again – nearly 8lbs and then to The Square to buy your car seat. Home for tea and then we went off to Gillian Walker's house to see about getting her pram for you.

The height of luxury – a Silver Cross – a lovely pram and lots of other goodies, including a buggy. Frank is to collect all tomorrow morning. Slept like a log from 9.30 p.m. (still in Gillian's) until 3.30 a.m. – good girl.

Esther threw herself into motherhood. Her sister Marian had already embarked on family life with her husband Billy, giving birth to two sons, Brian and James, and a daughter, also called Esther, after her adoring aunt, who was her godmother. The two sisters were in and out of each other's homes. Esther was particularly close to her nephew James, and all of Marian's family took to the new baby. "We adored Jessica," Marian says. "She was part of the family, one of us, no holds barred." Plans were set in motion for the official adoption of baby Jessica. Frank's family were informed. His mother, in particular, was happy that her daughter's child would have a stable home.

The new development in the family became known to a wider circle. One group who heard about it were those involved in swimming. The McCann family – Frank, some of his siblings and his mother – had a regular swimming evening on Fridays in the Terenure College pool.

Naturally, the family talked about the new addition, and, as is often the way, word rippled beyond their immediate circle. The mother of the seventeen-year-old who had given birth to Frank's child became aware of Frank and Esther's plan to adopt Jessica. On 16 April 1991, she phoned the Adoption Board to object formally to the adoption of Jessica by Frank McCann because of his conduct with her own daughter. Officials at the board recorded her complaint, but, at that point, the McCanns had not made an official application to adopt.

Wednesday, 17 April 1991: My suspicions are confirmed − you have chickenpox!!! Poor Jessica, very out of sorts and very spotty. Thanks are due to your cousin Esther who has just finished with the pox and there is a photo to prove it!!

On 20 May, just over two months after Jessica's birth, the McCanns lodged an application with the Adoption Board. Usually an adoption within a family is a matter of formality. Jeanette had nominated her brother and sister-in-law as the adoptive parents, which should have meant that the application would be dealt with speedily. However, the officials linked it to the complaint they had received the previous month.

The Adoption Board confronted McCann with the allegation. He denied it outright. Esther was unaware that a problem had arisen in the adoption process.

> *Wednesday, 17 July 1991: two-in-one injection in the Clinic. Frank in Brussels for six days with the Irish swimming team at Youth Olympics, back Monday next.*

The summer of 1991 darkened for Esther McCann's family. Her sixteen-year-old nephew James had developed health problems. Tests showed a possible tumour in his leg, which clouded Esther's blossoming joy.

> *Friday, 19 July 1991: 5 p.m. tests show a malignant tumour on his leg, to be treated in the Mater. Phoned Paddy McCann [Frank's uncle, a radiographer in the Mater hospital] and he will do all he can to help – nice man.*
>
> *Not a day to be forgotten for any of us, possibly the blackest day in a long time. Things will get better and James will be well again – after treatment.*

Summer turned into autumn without a result from the Adoption Board. As with much in their married life, Frank McCann was determined to take care of the details. All contact with the board was through him. He and Esther instructed a solicitor in an attempt to hasten the process.

Jeanette was growing impatient on behalf of her brother and sister-in-law. She began making independent enquiries of the board as to the delay. There was no response apart from the stock one that the process took time. Jeanette, too, was unaware of her brother's secret.

By the turn of the year, there was still nothing. While Esther was consumed by delight in her adoptive daughter, she was also desperately sad for her nephew to whom she was so close. It turned out that James had bone cancer. After treatment, he was in remission, but the dreaded prospect of secondaries now loomed. All of the family were becoming increasingly concerned at his condition.

"Since he had been a child, James always wanted to see his aunt Esther," Marian Leonard says. "They loved each other's company. On the night of James's eighteenth birthday the pair of them were up dancing together half the night." However, Esther's growing concern for her nephew was not shared by her husband. McCann, by then increasingly obsessed with the adoption process, didn't visit James on any of his several stays in hospital. He excused himself, citing pressure of work. He was attempting to grow the business at the Cooperage pub in Blessington, and swimming commitments kept him out of the house for extended periods. He had little time to show concern for Esther's ill nephew. "That hurt Esther," her sister remembers. "Not once did he go to visit James. He just didn't empathise with James's situation. He didn't know how to feel sympathy. He didn't have an emotional side to him. In that regard, he was the polar opposite of Esther."

Frank's emotional side was something that Esther worried about. His father had died two years previously, and, to Esther's mind, Frank had never really grieved for him. Esther wanted him to go for counselling but there was no question of that, as far as he was concerned.

Some time early in the summer of 1992, it became obvious to Frank McCann that the Adoption Board was going to reject his and Esther's application. The McCanns' solicitor received confirmation of this on 28 July, but all the indications are that Frank knew at least a month earlier. It can only be imagined how Frank McCann greeted that news. Naturally, he must have been devastated at what he might have seen as the termination of his and Esther's family plans but he would surely have known that there was no question of Jessica being taken from them. The child's birth mother wanted them to raise her. There was no suggestion that Jessica was regarded as at risk in the McCann household, even though he had fathered a child by a teenager. McCann would have known that Jessica would stay with him and Esther for the foreseeable future at least.

He must also have considered Esther's reaction. How could he keep from her the real reason for the board's refusal? And if, as was most likely, he had to divulge it, how would she react? Would he lose not just a new daughter but his wife as well? "He should have known that Esther would forgive him," Marian Leonard says. "If he knew her at all, he would have known that was her nature. And they wouldn't have lost Jessica. There was no question of that."

But McCann's character was such that he would have worried about the consequences outside his home. Among his own family, his siblings and mother, he was a dominant figure. From early on he had considered himself a leader, had demonstrated the qualities of leadership, in personal and professional settings, and enjoyed the status this gave him. The shame might drag him off his self-awarded pedestal.

He was now president of the Leinster branch of the Irish Amateur Swimming Association. If it was to emerge that he had had a sexual relationship with a teenage swimmer, he would be finished in the sport. His self-image as a confident, highly competent individual, and the opportunity his role in swimming afforded him to reinforce it, would be destroyed.

Then there was the pub. He was now on his third career, after working as a cooper, then running his own cooperage business. How would his current business suffer if his secret was uncovered? How would patrons regard him as he stood behind the bar, handing over pints? Most likely they would be contemptuous of an individual who had impregnated a vulnerable teenager.

Frank McCann had plenty to think about, within the limited parameters of his emotional intelligence and the confines of his self-image, as his past life returned to haunt him.

*

On 3 July 1992, McCann reported a gas leak at Butterfield Avenue. A Bord Gáis fitter was dispatched to the house but no leak was discovered. Two weeks later, on 16 July, McCann phoned Bord Gáis at 10.53 a.m. to report another suspected leak. A fitter was dispatched immediately and arrived at 11.10 a.m. He discovered a Class A leak, requiring immediate action, in a pipe leading into the house.

About a week later, Bord Gáis upgraded the gas meter in the house. One of the adaptations required in this process was the installation of two soldered joints close to the meter.

On 26 July, McCann reported another leak. Once more, Bord Gáis sent out a fitter, but this time no leak was discovered despite an extensive investigation. On the following day, 27 July, James Leonard was admitted to hospital for further tests. His mother Marian accompanied him to the Mater Private Hospital and made arrangements to stay overnight. Later, she would come to regard her absence from home that night as significant.

Meanwhile, Esther and Marian's other sister, Phyllis, a nun, was visiting from her base in England. That evening, she went to Butterfield Avenue to catch up with Esther. Frank was in and out of the house while she was there. Phyllis and Esther talked for a few hours. Phyllis noticed that her sister seemed drowsy. Eventually, she told Esther she was leaving because Esther was tired. Esther agreed and went up to bed, barely saying good night to her sister.

By that time McCann was in the house but had to return to the pub; he drove Phyllis back to where she was staying, then went on to Blessington.

Early the following morning, Esther woke with a blinding headache. She noticed a strong smell of cooking onions. It took her a few minutes to realise that gas was flooding through the house. She kept her head. She went into Jessica's room, picked up the infant and walked immediately to the front door. She didn't turn on any lights: she had had routine training on what to do in the event of a gas leak.

Once outside, she got into her car. She didn't turn on the engine but released the hand brake, allowing the car to reverse on to the road from the drive. When she was a safe distance from the house, she rang McCann at the pub on her mobile phone. He reported the leak at 7.55 a.m. on 28 July.

This time the Bord Gáis fitter found a major leak. The hallway and many rooms contained a colossal level of gas, enough to cause an explosion if a match was lit or a light switched on. Esther and Jessica had had a narrow escape.

The board undertook an investigation to determine how such a major leak could occur. The fitters found that the two joints that had been newly installed the previous week had parted completely. Soldered joints, such as they were, could only have been separated by the application of heat.

By now the leaks at Butterfield Avenue, combined with the two false alarms, were beginning to raise suspicions in Bord Gáis, but there was no evidence that anything untoward was afoot. The latest leak was far and away the most serious.

When Marian, still in hospital with her son, heard what had happened, she was shocked. She rang McCann. "We almost lost her, Frank," she told him. McCann brushed her off, said it wasn't as serious as it appeared. He lectured Esther to be more careful. "She was just glad he wasn't going to sue the gas company," Marian says. "He was into litigation and Esther didn't want to be dragged into that sort of thing there and then.

"Looking back, it was all strange. But at the time we were distracted by James and what he was going through. We probably weren't as alert as we should have been.

"We were all too busy trying to save James's life, while he [McCann] was trying to end Esther's."

Later that day, Frank McCann was contacted by his solicitor. The Adoption Board had been in touch with a ruling. The couple's application had been rejected. The board felt that all of those involved, Frank, Esther and Jeanette McCann, should be informed of the exact reasons why the application was denied. The solicitor was asked to respond in writing to the board within a month.

Esther, traumatised after her ordeal, had no idea of these communications. However, they appear to have lent added urgency to McCann's endeavours to ensure that his dirty linen would not be washed in public.

Two days later, Esther wrote her last entry in her electronic diary. The tone and content speak of the joy, confusion and despair that pervaded her life.

30 July: My darling daughter Jessica, you have grown and become a beautiful child. You have been walking now for a little over a week and have given up holding on to the walls in search of your one bit of independence. Cup of tea and up a daisy with constant talk of Daddy, oh Mammy and Mammy's baby. Lots of talk and every day brings new joys of every sort in sight, sound, speech and movement. Ten teeth to show for all the months of painful teething which gave you some problems with infections of all sorts.

Nana's little darling in everything you do, she never ceases to love looking at you and you can really amuse with your antics, including playing the piano with much style and seriousness. May Warner next door will have to take you for lessons soon. The hottest and driest summer in years. Your own darling James has had the most terrible news imaginable today and he doesn't even know it yet. Marian in pieces and I am not so good myself. Two tumours on [his] left lung to be operated on end of July – no end to this cruelty.

In August, Esther was feeling down. There was still no word on the adoption, and the prospects for James's recovery were bleak. Her self-confidence began to suffer. She went to see her doctor.

Early on 11 August, Esther awoke to the sound of the telephone ringing. She sat up to see, at the foot of her bed, an electric blanket on fire. She jumped out of bed and doused the flames. Then she answered the telephone. A garda from Blessington was enquiring as to Frank's whereabouts. The alarm in the Cooperage had gone off and was ringing madly.

Esther had presumed Frank was at the pub. It is unclear where he was at that point, or whether he had come home in the middle of the night and departed again. Even more bizarre was how the electric blanket had come to be at the bottom of Esther's bed, folded in four. The last time she had seen it, it had been on the back of a chair in the spare room.

The incident cast Esther into an even deeper gloom. She was now doubting herself and wondering whether her mind was playing tricks on her. Her doubts were fuelled when McCann told her she was imagining things.

Strange things seem to have been happening to Frank McCann at this time also. On 13 August, he reported to Rathfarnham garda station that he had received threatening phone calls to his home. The complaint was logged. Later that day, he walked into Blessington garda station and reported anonymous calls to his pub, which, he maintained, might have been construed as threatening.

Around the same time, another publican in Blessington, Tim Grace, of the West Wicklow House bar, answered the phone to an anonymous caller. The voice told him he'd better pay up or he'd be "burned out" of his business. Grace didn't pay too much attention to the call, but the next month it took on significance.

On 31 August, McCann would claim later, a slogan – "Burn You Bastard" – was painted on the rear wall of his premises. A few days later it was seen by a young barman working in the Cooperage.

On at least one occasion during that time, the gardaí called to Butterfield Avenue, following up on McCann's complaints. He ignored Esther's enquiry as to the nature of the call.

Towards the end of the month, Esther resolved to sort out the delays in the adoption process. She rang the Coombe Hospital and arranged for a meeting on 4 September to retrace the steps that had been taken from Jessica's birth to see if she could spot what might be causing the delay. She told Marian of her determination to get things moving. She had decided to take control of events.

Meanwhile, the family's solicitor had been on holiday through most of August, thus delaying his response to the Adoption Board. The deadline was now the following week.

The 3 September 1992 was a Thursday. Marian

Leonard was going down to her home place of Tramore with James to give him a few days near the sea in Waterford. Esther was in two minds whether or not to travel with her sister, but the appointment at the Coombe the following day meant she had to remain in Dublin. She had also arranged to give a word-processing class that evening in her home. She told Marian that she was going to have it out with Frank: things just weren't adding up where the adoption was concerned.

"I said goodbye to her and drove down to Tramore," Marian says. "I was hardly there an hour when she rang again. We were always in close contact, but with all the strange things going on at the time, that contact increased even more. Anyway, she was in good form when she rang."

In the early afternoon, down in Blessington, one of the barmen in the Cooperage went out of the back of the premises and saw, painted on the wall, "Burn You Bastard". Back in Butterfield Avenue, a fitter from the gas company called to the house once more. The gas installation was checked again for leaks. None were discovered.

Later that evening, at around 8.30 p.m., Esther began her word-processing lesson – she was teaching a young single parent, Helen Palmer. Jessica was tucked up in bed upstairs. McCann was down in Blessington.

At 10 p.m., Helen Palmer left the McCann household. McCann returned soon after, taking his customary hour's break from the pub. He would later say that when he arrived, he noticed a suspicious mark on the back door. He phoned the local gardaí and told them about it. He and Esther had a cup of tea and watched a film on the television.

Nobody knows whether, during this visit, he looked in on eighteen-month-old Jessica in her cot upstairs. He would say in a subsequent statement to gardaí that he took her out of her cot and played with her for a while, then tucked her back in and sent her off to sleep. Esther's family dispute that such a scenario is likely. McCann was not an affectionate father, and, having woken Jessica, it would have been no easy task to put her back down to sleep.

Maybe he did go in to see her, or even hold her, one last time. Maybe he did enter her bedroom and look at her to determine whether or not he had the resolve to go through with his plan. Nobody knows what his final words to his wife were either. There was no evidence that relations were particularly strained at the time by anything other than the delayed adoption.

Frank McCann might not have been a man of emotional depth, but the marriage was not violent or rancorous. There is nothing to suggest that Esther said or did anything in particular that night which prompted him to act immediately. All the evidence points to a plan hatched some months previously, which had undergone a few false starts but was now on the brink of fulfilment.

McCann returned to Blessington and the Cooperage, arriving some time before 11 p.m. At 12.30 a.m., he entered Peg Gething's chip shop in Blessington, where he remained for ten minutes while waiting for his order to be filled. At 1 a.m., the barman in the Cooperage left to go home. He reckoned McCann had about half an hour's work to do before he, too, went home. Around the same time, the chip-shop owner heard the Cooperage gate creak shut. She presumed that McCann was leaving the premises.

Around 1.45 a.m., a neighbour in Butterfield Avenue heard a loud bang, followed by another, then the sound of a car being driven away at speed. Some minutes later, a carload of people returning from a wedding in Co. Wicklow spotted flames leaping from the house in Butterfield Avenue. The emergency services were called. Neighbours gathered on the lawn outside the house, but by then there was no question of anybody attempting a rescue. The flames were too large, the heat too intense. Somebody fetched a ladder and it was raised to a first-floor window, but any attempt to scale it would have been perilous, and nobody appeared at the window.

At some stage during those minutes, Frank McCann came on the scene. He appeared to be distraught, even disbelieving. One neighbour, Marie Daly, recalled his demeanour: "He was visibly very upset and very distraught. He kept on saying, 'My wife and my baby are in there.'"

As the fire intensified, McCann made to go into the house, apparently unconcerned for his own safety in the interest of saving his loved ones. A number of the neighbours grabbed and restrained him. Soon after, McCann collapsed on the grass, seemingly overcome by the horror before him.

Eventually, the fire was brought under control. Esther's body was found on the landing. She could have tried to save herself by jumping out of the first-floor bedroom window. But she wasn't going to leave Jessica behind. By the time she got to the landing, she collapsed. She sustained extensive burns and died from inhalation of carbon monoxide. Jessica still had a soother in her mouth when her blackened body was taken from her cot.

Overall, the damage to the property wasn't extensive. Much within the walls, including valuables and the structure, was salvageable. Then there was the matter of McCann's chain of office, which he wore as president of the Leinster branch of the Irish Amateur Swimming Association. Earlier on the day of the fire, before she left for Tramore, Marian had noticed the chain on the hall table. Later it was recovered from the boot of McCann's car.

In a narrative where coincidences had long become jaded, it appears that McCann considered the chain to be of such value that he could not risk it being damaged in a fire designed to murder his wife and baby Jessica.

Immediately after the fire, Bord Gáis conducted an

examination. At 3.15 a.m., the fitter reported that there was no leak in the system at the house.

Around the same time, down in Tramore, Marian Leonard was woken by the sound of her mother-in-law crying. Marian's husband Billy had rung with the awful news. Marian has little memory of the following hours and days. She says she suspected McCann immediately. Through her grief, she couldn't help believing that her sister had been murdered. "I don't remember much of that day, or the ones that followed straight after. I've been told that I said, 'He did it.' I was supposed to have said it over and over again."

Just before 7.30 a.m., Detective Inspector Tony Sourke arrived in Tallaght garda station. He and Superintendent Pat King attended the scene in Rathfarnham. Already, there were suspicions about the fire. The intensity of the flames and the report that a neighbour had heard two bangs suggested there was more to it than a tragic accident. Suspicions were heightened when the initial examination of the scene uncovered evidence of an accelerant like petrol. A blowtorch and a gas container were recovered from the hallway of the house. As yet, there were no suspects. The gardaí began their enquiries.

A few hours later, the Cooperage barman opened the premises, unaware of what had happened during the night. Soon the phone was ringing. He answered. The caller asked whether McCann had got the bad news yet. The barman replaced the receiver. He felt that the caller had been attempting to disguise his voice.

The days following Esther's death were taken up with preparations for the funeral. Whatever suspicions Marian harboured she put away until Esther had been laid to rest. The O'Brien family wanted Esther to be buried in Tramore with her father. McCann had no objection. Her funeral mass took place in Mount Carmel Church, Firhouse, and the coffin containing the bodies of Esther and Jessica was received into the Holy Cross Church in the seaside town of Tramore, the same church where Esther had been baptised, had made her first communion and had been confirmed.

At the mass, McCann had to be helped up the aisle by Esther's sister, Phyllis. His grief appeared to be overwhelming, as might be expected of a bereaved husband. After the burial, he returned to Dublin. Later that evening, he hosted a sixtieth birthday party for his mother at the Cooperage. "We heard about it the next day," Marian says. "Friends who were embarrassed that they had been there after being invited came and told us. Somehow, I wasn't surprised. That was Frank. He was always doing the inappropriate thing. He was just incapable of emotion."

The investigation was moving apace. McCann wasn't available for interview until the evening of Saturday, 6 September. Two officers took a statement from him. At that stage, he was still being treated as a witness. He recounted how he had been at home earlier in the evening, then returned to the Cooperage. He worked the rest of the evening, bought some chips and eventually locked up around 1.30 a.m. As he was approaching home, he saw the flames and ran to join the neighbours on the front lawn.

He told the gardaí there had been a suspicious mark on the back door and sketched it. The obvious conclusion he wanted the officers to draw was that there had been a forced entry to the house.

Already, the investigation had been informed by officials from Bord Gáis about the series of leaks and false alarms. The information brought McCann into the orbit of suspicion, although he was still officially being treated as a witness at this point.

Then, early the following week, out of the blue, a motive was presented to the gardaí. An official from the Adoption Board contacted Tallaght garda station. He had seen a report in the newspaper that the fire was being treated as suspicious, which had alerted him to the McCann case. He outlined the background to the couple's application to adopt Jessica and the board's rejection. Tony Sourke and Pat King visited the Adoption Board for a full briefing. The news put a different complexion on the investigation.

Other strands were coming together too. Later in the week, Tim Grace, the proprietor of the West Wicklow bar, was drawn into the investigation. He had opened an accumulated bundle of post to find among it a warning message about his business. He brought this to the gardaí and told them about the previous month's threatening phone call to "pay up". McCann's complaints about threats in both Rathfarnham and Blessington took on greater significance.

Marian Leonard mentioned her suspicions to the gardaí. Apart from the strange events that had taken place, she wasn't completely surprised that on the two occasions when something serious happened – 28 July and then the fire – she had been safely out of the way. Esther and Marian had been practically inseparable since childhood. McCann, as far as Marian was concerned, wouldn't have moved against Esther unless he knew her sister was unlikely to be able to come to the rescue. Now she viewed the incident with the electric blanket in a new light. The gardaí agreed that it may indeed have been significant.

A picture was forming. The gas leaks and threats pointed to a degree of planning. The adoption decision offered a motive, but while everything could be put together logically, it didn't fit into any standard profile of a wife-killer.

Esther and Frank McCann had no money problems. The house was mortgaged, but not excessively so, and not to any extent that would render it a motive for McCann to kill Esther. The Cooperage was no gold mine, but neither was it in any financial difficulties. The marriage, to the extent that could be determined, wasn't rocky.

The only sore point appeared to be the adoption, yet even seasoned officers found it difficult to accept that this could motivate a man to kill his wife and niece. As they began to build up a profile of McCann, the gardaí lost their incredulity. The man in question was not your average anything.

With his home uninhabitable for the time being, McCann moved in with one of Esther's best friends, Emer Farrell. A few weeks later, on 18 September, he walked into her kitchen as he was opening a letter addressed to him. From the envelope he pulled a mass card purporting to have been sent to him by "Reverend Burn". On reading it, McCann collapsed in a heap. A doctor was called.

Three days later, Emer Farrell found an unad-dressed envelope lying in the hall under the letter flap. Inside, there was a card, wishing the recipient well in their new home. There was also a newspaper cutting with the words "lack of pigs" cut from a headline. It seemed as if somebody with a sadistic mind was attempting to get at McCann. Either that, or McCann was making a concerted effort for it to appear so.

On 24 September, the gardaí announced that they were now treating the fire as suspicious. By then, McCann must have been fully aware that he was the main suspect. He wasn't sitting on his hands. "He was here at our home all the time," Marian Leonard remembers. "He would be in and out every other day, asking all sorts of questions about the guards and what they thought. I think he probably went around to everybody who made a statement about the whole thing at some stage or another. He was showing an awful lot of interest in the investigation."

Marian Leonard was growing increasingly anxious about McCann's presence in her home. She remained firmly convinced that he had murdered her sister. And if this man – whom she had thought she knew and who had apparently loved Esther, despite his foibles – had murdered her, why would he stop there?

She began to panic when he appeared in the house. Her encounters with him took on an unreal quality. She and her family had to go along with his grief-stricken-husband act, while they suspected that his probing questions were related to his efforts to ensure he wouldn't be cornered.

Marian's family even avoided bringing up the embarrassing matter of the undertaker. After the funeral, the undertaker in Blessington had called Marian: he explained apologetically that McCann hadn't settled up, despite numerous reminders. In the end, Marian and her family paid to avoid a scene.

At the same time, the family was preoccupied with a more pressing matter: James's prognosis was bad. Marian wanted to spend as much time as possible with her son, yet the man whom she thought had murdered her sister wouldn't leave them alone.

The investigation was now advancing on all fronts. One question remained unanswered. How had the fire been started? A number of experiments were conducted using a gas cylinder and blowtorch, the two items retrieved from the house. More than two hundred people had been interviewed. All of the evidence was mounting towards a reasonable suspicion that Frank McCann had started the blaze.

The behaviour of the man himself fuelled suspicion. Aside from speaking to a number of those interviewed by the gardaí to find out what they said, at one point he invited one of the investigating officers, Sergeant Patsy Glennon, to his new home to discuss the case. Glennon met McCann, and the discussion developed over four hours. The garda recorded everything that was said in a detailed memorandum.

McCann was clearly a clever man. However, his attitude to the gardaí exposed his ignorance in the area of crime detection. One officer who worked on the case put it succinctly: "With a career criminal, they know that the gardaí have to prove certain things, that there are a number of fences that must be jumped before they are in the clear. Frank was different. He gave the impression that he was concerned with what the guards thought rather than what we could prove."

In late October, Marian Leonard decided to bring James to see her brother in Canada to allow James time to say goodbye and to get him away from McCann's intrusions. Her husband Billy and their other son Brian were going to Tramore, and Marian brought her daughter Esther to London to stay with her sister, Phyllis. "I just wouldn't have been happy being away if anybody else was left in the house in Dublin with him around, so I had to bring Esther over to my sister," she remembers.

On the night before they left, McCann called round. For Marian, his presence in their home was becoming unbearable. That evening she feared he might try to stop them leaving. She knew she was being irrational, but that didn't make the fear go away. "He was there and I was just afraid. My legs were weak. I couldn't stand up for fear of falling down. Eventually he left, and it was such a relief it was like a release."

Marian was in Canada only a few days when she received a phone call from Ireland. McCann had been arrested at his pub in Blessington.

On the morning of 4 November, the gardaí had conducted an experiment with the blowtorch and gas cylinder attempting to replicate the fire. It was the culmination of a number of experiments designed to clarify exactly how the fire was started. The experiment was deemed satisfactory, and a decision taken to arrest McCann.

Early in the afternoon, he was taken to Tallaght garda station. He showed no emotion when the detectives arrested him under Section 30 of the Offences Against the State Act, which would figure as an issue in the trial. Ordinarily, an arrest on suspicion of murder would be made under the Criminal Justice Act if the suspect or the killing wasn't associated with subversive activity or anything endangering state security.

At the time, the difference between arrest under the respective laws was that the suspect could be detained for a total of twelve hours under the Criminal Justice Act and forty-eight under Offences Against the State.

Two aspects of the case legitimised the decision to arrest McCann under the act, allowing for a longer detention period. The nature of the fire, including the report of two loud bangs, suggested that an incident had taken place that contravened the Explosives Act, which qualified as an offence against the state. The calls to the West Wicklow bar had included an alleged subversive element, with references to the IRA.

McCann was questioned for two days. He made a number of statements, including an admission that he had started the fire, which was rambling, even incoherent. He broached the problem with the Adoption Board, stating, "I was going to finish it all. I was going to clear up the whole mess, me, Esther and Jessica. I need to get away but I can't go from everything. I can't leave them. I can't leave without them."

The admission came towards the end of his detention period. While he was making his statement, the period expired. Frank went outside and returned of his own volition to complete the statement.

In delivering his version of events, he spoke in the present tense, rather as if he was talking about an out-of-body experience. He said he had had a can of petrol, and it fell over, and all he remembered was a lighted match and flames everywhere.

The detectives in attendance thought that, even in his admission, McCann was figuring out his next move. Even now that he was apparently cornered, he would make no full confession. The statement appeared calculated.

After McCann had completed his statement, he left the station. He booked himself into St John of God's psychiatric hospital, claiming he was suffering from a nervous breakdown.

The gardaí consulted with the Director of Public Prosecutions (DPP). A decision was taken to continue gathering evidence. The case was not yet of a standard that would point to a reasonably good chance of conviction. McCann wasn't regarded as a serious flight risk, so he was left at large.

Despite his alleged condition, McCann's charm remained intact. He met a woman in the hospital and began a relationship that continued after his release shortly before Christmas 1992. She lived in Stradbally, Co. Waterford, the next parish from Tramore, where Esther had spent her happy childhood. McCann moved there from Dublin. He saw no reason to maintain a low profile. Over the festive season, he attended the annual hunt ball in Stradbally, accompanied by his new partner.

By the following April, the investigation was complete, and the DPP was satisfied that McCann should be prosecuted. He was fitting out a new mobile home in Stradbally when detectives came for him on 22 April. He was arrested for the murder of Esther and Jessica McCann and detained in the garda station in Tramore, a few hundred yards from the quiet cul-de-sac where Esther had grown up. Later, he was charged at a special sitting of Waterford District Court.

Earlier that month, James Leonard, Esther's nephew, had lost his battle with cancer. He died on 5 April in his home with his family around him. In the hours before he died, he asked his uncle Pat if McCann was ever going to pay for what he had done to Esther and Jessica. To ease his nephew's mind, Pat told him that McCann had already been arrested.

McCann applied for bail to the High Court, but his application was rejected. At the hearing, evidence from the gardaí stated a belief that McCann now represented a flight risk. His new girlfriend had connections in Canada, and it was feared that he would not show up for his trial. Eventually, McCann went all the way to the Supreme Court in an effort to gain his freedom ahead of the trial, but to no avail.

The trial of Frank McCann for murdering his wife and niece began on 11 January 1994. The prosecution case was largely circumstantial, apart from the rambling admission McCann had made when arrested in November 1992. On 31 January, when the trial had progressed to the stage at which McCann's admission was to be given as evidence, McCann attempted to set fire to himself in his cell at Arbour Hill prison, using deodorant and a cigarette lighter. He was rushed to hospital and the jury discharged. It would be two and a half years before another trial began. Along the way, a number of tentative dates were set, but on each occasion, McCann's counsel requested a postponement on the basis of his health.

Eventually, the rescheduled trial began on 10 June 1996. Through the early weeks of the evidence, the judge and jury heard a reconstruction of the hot summer of 1992, when gas leaks appeared to be springing in the McCann household and anonymous threats were issued against McCann. His three brothers, two of whom had been present at his confession, were called to give evidence for the prosecution, who also mentioned McCann's motive in killing his wife as his shame over the Adoption Board's rejection. His alibi for the night of the fire was also examined, and appeared shaky.

In the middle of the trial, the jury was excused for three weeks of legal argument over whether McCann's confession should be deemed admissible. In the end, they heard it.

As the trial dragged on, other events may have been on McCann's mind while he sat in the court or back in his cell in Arbour Hill. The Olympic Games got under way in July, hosted in Atlanta. For the Irish swimming community, the Games were to be a seminal event. Michelle Smith won four gold medals, coming from nowhere to beat the cream of the USA and Australia, the principal swimming nations.

Had life gone differently for Frank McCann, he would in all likelihood have been attending the games as the president of the Irish Amateur Swimming Association. The four provinces rotated the presidency, and from his position as president of the Leinster branch, he would have been in line for elevation to the national office that summer. He would have been basking in the glow of an unlikely and thrilling triumph, instead of contemplating a future behind bars as his nature was dissected in open court. (Two years later, Smith was cast in a different light when she failed a random drugs sample and was exposed as a cheat.)

When it came to the defence case, McCann opted to give evidence in person. This is an unusual course for a defendant to take, particularly in a murder trial. The onus is on the prosecution to prove its case; the defendant doesn't have to prove anything. By giving evidence, and thus exposing himself to cross-examination, the defendant might leave himself open to compromise. It is rare that a defendant will take such a gamble, and experienced counsel usually advise against it.

On the afternoon of Thursday, 1 August, McCann was sworn in. He had barely begun his evidence when he suddenly began to tremble violently and appeared to be hyperventilating. Judge Paul Carney called an immediate recess and allowed McCann to receive medical attention. An hour later, he recalled the jury and advised them that he had been told that McCann was not fit to continue. The trial was adjourned.

From Marian Leonard's vantage point in the court, it appeared that McCann was pulling off another stunt. "He could switch that stuff on and off, he knew it all from his time in swimming," she says. "Frank would have dealt with young swimmers hyperventilating all the time and he knew how to start and stop it."

The trial resumed the following Tuesday. In the witness box, McCann made a number of allegations of mistreatment against the gardaí. He said he was threatened, shouted at, bumped into and made to stand by officers while he was questioned in November 1992. He said that when he was arrested in his pub a garda had shouted at him that he was a "murdering bastard", and that he was slapped around the face with photographs of the bodies of Esther and Jessica during interview. No third party witnessed these events. Neither had he complained about his treatment after his release.

He denied that he had murdered his wife and Jessica and claimed to have told Esther about the Adoption Board's rejection. He said he had never accepted paternity of the child born to the seventeen-year-old.

The defence called a forensic scientist, who told the court that he would have expected McCann to sustain injury if he had set fire to the house on Butterfield

Avenue. The scientist agreed with the prosecution that he had not visited the scene, had not been present when experiments were carried out and had not visited the Dublin Forensic Science Laboratory where the experiments were conducted.

McCann's senior counsel Barry White (who, a decade later, would preside as judge during the Joe O'Reilly murder trial) made a detailed closing speech on behalf of his client. He sifted through the prosecution case and suggested that the prosecution was attempting to throw dirt at McCann in revealing that he had hosted a birthday party for his mother on the night of Esther's funeral. People grieved in different ways, he pointed out. He said that McCann's November 1992 statement was "of no worth" and made in a surreal scene at Tallaght garda station. McCann, he said, had been almost forty-eight hours in garda custody when he had made it, and the statement itself didn't stand up to scrutiny. "I suggest he is reliving a nightmare which is not a reality," White told the jury.

The prosecution summing-up was straightforward: McCann had had the motive, the means and a history of unsuccessful attempts.

When the two sides had finished, Judge Carney addressed the jury for five hours in reviewing the evidence and outlining their duty. The six men and six women retired at 6.15 p.m. on 14 August to consider their verdict. At 8 p.m., Judge Carney told them to suspend their deliberations until the morning.

The next day, the jury continued working into the evening. At 6.15 p.m., the judge recalled them and told them they could now consider a majority verdict of 11–1 or 10–2, instead of a unanimous verdict. Half an hour later they were back with a unanimous decision. Frank McCann was guilty of the double murder.

Several members of Esther's family were crying, hugging each other and could be heard whispering, "Yes." On another bench in the courtroom, Jeanette McCann, who had given birth to Jessica, was also crying. McCann himself remained impassive as the judge imposed the mandatory life sentence.

The following April, McCann's appeal against the conviction was rejected in the Court of Criminal Appeal. In April 1998, Esther's mother, Brigid O'Brien, initiated a legal action to ensure that McCann didn't receive the proceeds from the sale of the house on Butterfield Avenue. Esther had bought the house with McCann, and her mother claimed entitlement to half its value under the Civil Liability Act. At the time, the action was unique and eventually succeeded. McCann only received half of the proceeds from the sale by auction of the house that Esther had tried so hard to turn into a home.

Brigid O'Brien died in 2003, never having fully reconciled herself with what had happened to her youngest daughter. "Mum, to the last, felt he should have told her he was sorry," Marian says. "There would have been times when she felt sorry for him."

For Marian Leonard, her family and siblings, closure is a relative concept. The spectre of McCann being set free haunts them. Like all victims, or relatives of victims, the onus is on them to keep themselves informed as to McCann's release. If a family contacts the Department of Justice, they will be notified. If not, they're on their own.

In 2006, Judge Paul Carney had to decide whether or not McCann's three years on remand between 1993 and 1996 should be taken into account in assessing the length of his life sentence. Marian, her daughter Esther and brother Pat provided the court with victim-impact statements, which had not been available to relatives at the time of the murder trial. McCann attended the hearing and was represented.

"When we saw him in the courtroom, he was still the same after ten years. No sign of emotion, just deadpan. It's a relief that he isn't out yet," Marian says. The hearing wasn't easy for the family, but they felt compelled to appear and put their statements on the record. Esther, who was only eight when her aunt was murdered, provided her own statement. "I saw him [McCann] looking at Esther as she was going up to the witness box," Marian says. "The judge knew what was going on too. He engaged Esther so McCann wouldn't come into her vision. It wasn't easy, any of it, but Esther wanted to do it."

The hearing was a formality. It would have taken extremely exceptional circumstances for the judge to rule that the three years on remand couldn't be taken into account. McCann, who has been a model prisoner and has studied for a postgraduate qualification in computer science while in prison, is due for a parole hearing in 2009. His chance of freedom is not high. One stipulation for parole is an acknowledgement of the crime and an expression of remorse. So far, McCann has steadfastly refused to show any remorse for what he did.

Marian Leonard is still nervous at the prospect of McCann being freed. She finds it difficult to believe that whatever it was in him that prompted him to murder the two people closest to him has gone. She prefers simply to remember her sister. "I like to think of Esther before she met McCann. For a lot of people she was a ray of sunshine in their lives, very loving, very kind. We grew up in a small town by the sea, where everything was local and friendly. She was just a very trusting person.

"When the problem with the adoption arose, all McCann would have had to do was tell her. She would have forgiven him. She didn't have a malicious bone in her body.

"We all took him in, made him one of the family. I knew what sugar he'd take in his tea, what vegetables he liked. I always made Pavlova for him because I knew how much he liked it. He was that close to all of us, and we didn't even know him. And for Esther that turned out to be the greatest tragedy of all.

"It's very sad that the person she decided to settle down with turned out to be like that."

Tony Sourke, who ran the investigation, experienced nothing else like it in a long career that ended with his retirement as a detective super-intendent in 2003: "The trauma involved in it was unbelievable. Everybody was a victim. There was innocent Esther and Jessica, and then the families left on both sides. What the McCann family themselves, Frank's siblings, were subjected to was equally appalling."

Esther and Jessica accounted for two of the state's forty-one victims of homicide in 1992.

2. GRIM DISCOVERY ON THE OLD BOG ROAD

The Case of Henry Holmes

They must have cut a strange sight entering the factory that evening. Garda Sergeant Chris O'Halloran was in full uniform, apart from his wellington boots. Father Denis O'Sullivan accompanied him. He wore an overcoat but was obviously a priest.

It was 29 December 1981, the clock inching towards 9 p.m. Nothing much was happening in Ballybrittas during this Christmas-holiday season, but the lights were on at the Semloh knitwear factory. Inside, the proprietor Henry Holmes was busy filling an order for John Connaire and his wife who had travelled by appointment to the Co. Laois town from East Galway.

On entering the factory, the garda could see Holmes, busy at work, while the couple waited.

He tried to attract Holmes's attention. In the end, Holmes, a thirty-seven-year-old man of small, compact build, spotted the pair and came over to them across the semi-lit factory floor. Something was up: a garda sergeant and a priest don't drop in for a quiet chat in the middle of the holiday season.

Holmes invited the two men to go with him to the factory canteen. "Don't fleece me while I'm away," he joked with the couple, as he left. The three men walked across the factory yard. In the canteen, O'Halloran told Holmes he had some bad news and suggested he sit down. Holmes declined. The garda's sombre tone told Holmes that he and the priest were there to convey news of the death of a loved one.

"Is it my father?" he asked. Henry Holmes's father was a seventy-five-year-old widower.

"No," O'Halloran said. "It's Anne."

Holmes lurched forward, about to collapse. The garda caught him and eased him down into a chair. Holmes began to cry. The garda and the priest stood above him until the sobbing eased. They told him that Anne had been found in her Datsun car, which had left the road at Coolnafearagh, the bog road that ran between Monasterevin and Portarlington. The sergeant asked Holmes whether he knew the area. Holmes said he didn't, even though it was only a few miles from his home.

"Would you like to see the body?" Sergeant O'Halloran asked gently. It had been removed to Portlaoise General Hospital. Holmes shook his head.

He couldn't stand the sight of blood. "The only hospital I can go into is a maternity hospital," he told the two men. Holmes was a father of three, and his wife Anne had been six months pregnant with their fourth child.

O'Halloran knew it mightn't be perfect timing, but he had to ask Holmes one or two questions. When had he last seen his wife? Holmes replied through his tears that it had been around five o'clock.

A lump hammer had been found in Anne's yellow Datsun. Would he be in a position to identify it? No problem, Holmes said. There was a pair of them in the house. He usually kept them in the racing car he owned. But O'Halloran would have to take it out of the Datsun if he wanted Holmes to identify it. He couldn't bear the sight of blood, he said again.

The priest arranged to bring him to the scene, to see exactly where Anne had drawn her last breath. As they were leaving the factory, John Connaire approached him. He put his arm round Holmes and murmured, "I'm sorry for your troubles."

Holmes looked at him. "Anne's in heaven, but what am I going to do?"

Father O'Sullivan accompanied Holmes to the scene of the crashed car. Afterwards, Holmes visited his mother-in-law, Kathleen Melia, to offer and seek comfort. "She's gone," he said to Kathleen, as he went to hug her. The tears began to flow again.

Later, he returned home to Ital House, the impressive

residence in Monasterevin, Co. Kildare, where he and Anne had been raising their family.

At around 10.30 p.m., Garda Pat Ryan called to the house. He and Holmes were friendly, both stalwarts of the local community. Ryan came in to commiserate. Holmes asked him to stay awhile. The garda listened as Holmes talked about Anne, their life together, their joy in rearing the kids, and their hopes for a fourth. The garda lent a sympathetic ear as his friend raked over the dreams that had been shattered that evening.

Garda Ryan stayed all night. At around 6.30 a.m., he suggested that a walk might do them both good. The two men left the house and stepped out into the cold December dawn. They walked up and down the road and round the block on the outskirts of the town. They returned to the house at 7.45 a.m., and Ryan left soon after.

In the nine hours that Henry Holmes and Pat Ryan talked, mainly about the recently deceased Anne, Holmes never once said when he had last seen his wife. Neither did he say where he had been in the hours before Anne's body was found, her head bloodied and bruised, behind the steering wheel of her car, in the ditch on the old bog road.

In the early 1980s, Monasterevin was little more than a hamlet. Forty miles south of Dublin on the main Cork road, it is a town with an inordinate number of bridges: the river Barrow and the Grand Canal both flow within its precincts. The town lies in flat country and boasts a number of Georgian residences.

Six years before Anne Holmes's death, Monasterevin briefly came to world prominence as the centre of a kidnapping siege. On 4 October 1975, Dutch industrialist Dr Tiede Herrema was kidnapped in Limerick. A ransom note was issued by Republican renegades Eddie Gallagher and Marion Coyle. Two weeks later, the couple and their victim holed up in a house in St Evin's Park in Monasterevin. Their presence became quickly known, and a siege ensued, the house surrounded by gardaí and military personnel. During the weeks that followed, the hitherto little-known town was at the centre of national news bulletins and hosted the international media corps. The siege ended peacefully on 8 November.

Henry Holmes had been born locally into a family of three, including two sisters. On completing his Leaving Certificate in the local Christian Brothers school, he went to work in Tyna Knitwear. Somebody in the factory spotted potential in the young, eager local lad, and he was quickly promoted. Later, he was appointed works engineer. The company sent him to Britain and what was then West Germany to gain experience and further his training.

He had barely started work at Tyna when he met Anne Melia, one evening during Lent when they came out of mass. Anne had also been born and reared in the town. From a family of four, she attended the local

Convent of Mercy until her Leaving Certificate, then also went to work for Tyna Knitwear, albeit briefly, until she found a position as a shop assistant in the town. The couple hit it off immediately. Anne was generally regarded as very attractive, while Henry was already displaying the attitude and confidence that would propel him to succeed in business. They were married on 3 August 1967, when both were still a few months shy of their twenty-third birthdays.

Their first child, Sharon, was born the following year. Russell Anthony arrived in 1970, and four years later Julia appeared. By then, Anne was eager to return to the workplace. As was common for the time, she had given up her job when she married. But now an opportunity presented itself for her to run her own outlet in the town's small shopping centre. With Henry's help, she opened Anne's Boutique and made the most of her husband's contacts and knowledge of the garment industry to generate business.

Around this time, Holmes began his own little venture on the side. He set up a small garment-making operation in a shed at the rear of his parents' house. Soon after he got it off the ground, his mother died.

The following year, Holmes was made redundant. The blow propelled him to redouble his efforts as an entrepreneur. He rented premises in the village of Ballybrittas, Co. Laois, a ten-minute drive from Monasterevin. The following year, he built new premises beside the existing ones with the help of the Industrial Development Agency. He called his company Semloh – 'Holmes' spelt backwards. Within a few years, he had established Semloh Export, to supply overseas markets, and by 1981, he was employing thirty people at the plant.

Away from work, Holmes had a penchant for fast cars, and the success of his business provided him with the money to indulge his passion. He raced as an amateur and even gained a position on the national go-karting team; one of his team mates was Rosemary Smith, who would go on to national prominence as a racing driver. He also bought a spacious detached home, Ital House, in the town. By 1981, Sharon was boarding at the Saletian Convent in Birr, while the two younger children were attending the local national school. Anne was pregnant with their fourth child, and it looked as if the Holmes family was set up for life.

All, however, was not that well. Anne had had a difficult first pregnancy, and since then had been prone to feeling down. Whether or not she suffered from clinical depression was never established, but she was prescribed Valium by her doctor. After her death, Holmes would claim that at one stage she was taking three tablets a day. He also said that when she attempted to give up the tablets, her moods suffered; at the time of her death she was drug-free. The extent to which she suffered mood swings would never become clear, but Holmes offered various interpretations of her problems at different times after her death.

Whatever about psychological concerns, both of

the Holmeses appear to have been religious. In the rural Ireland in which they grew up, observance was a way of life. However, by the early 1980s, the shackles of the past were loosening. Yet all the evidence is that both continued to be devoted to their Catholic faith. In late October 1981, Anne made a pilgrimage to Lourdes. Holmes did not accompany her.

Anne Holmes had her problems, but she also had plenty to live for: her personal and work lives held out the promise of fulfilment, all of which ended some time in the afternoon or evening of 29 December 1981. She was just thirty-seven when she died.

At 7.15 p.m. on that Tuesday, Trevor Shaw was driving from Portarlington to Monasterevin with his girlfriend and parents. At Coolnafearagh, he spotted what appeared to be a red light at the side of the road up ahead. As he advanced, he made out the tail-lights of a car, then the vehicle itself. He got out and ran down the side of the ditch to the driver's side. The front lights were on. The engine was running. There appeared to be practically no glass in the driver's window. And inside the vehicle, thrown from the driver's seat across the front passenger seat, lay a woman's body.

Shaw opened the door. In the half-light, he could see blood on the woman's hand. Strands of her hair appeared to be matted. Within minutes, he had been joined next to the car by Paul Twomey. He had been been travelling home to Offaly, in the opposite direction to Shaw, when he spotted the apparent accident.

Twomey had first-aid experience. He checked the woman for a pulse but found none. The men decided that Shaw would drive into Monasterevin to alert the gardaí.

Garda Pat Ryan's wife took the call in the station. At 7.35 p.m., Ryan arrived on the scene. He slipped down the incline and looked into the car. Almost immediately, he recognised the dead woman as Anne Holmes. Other than the window glass on the driver's side, Ryan also noticed a lump hammer on the floor at the passenger side. The only other detail to jump out at him was that Anne Holmes appeared to be missing a shoe, which, on first inspection, could be attributed to the impact of the crash. Ryan went back up on to the road and looked for the point at which the car might have left it. There were no obvious signs to suggest a sudden skid or impact with another vehicle.

Moments later, Sergeant Chris O'Halloran drove up. The two gardaí conferred and agreed that Ryan would accompany the body to Portlaoise General Hospital, while O'Halloran would take on the unenviable task of informing the dead woman's husband. He returned to Monasterevin garda station, where he met Father O'Sullivan. It was quickly established that Henry Holmes was most likely at his factory in Ballybrittas.

Already suspicion surrounded the apparent road-traffic accident. The broken window, the presence of a lump hammer that appeared to be bloodied, the engine that was still running prompted the gardaí to regard this as more than a tragic single-vehicle accident. There was also the problem of the missing shoe. Could Anne Holmes have set off in her car wearing only one?

At 8.30 p.m., the body arrived at Portlaoise General Hospital and was transferred to the mortuary.

Back at the scene of the accident, Dr Declan Gilsenan, a pathologist attached to the Eastern Health Board, surveyed the car and made for Portlaoise. At the hospital, he did a cursory examination of the body. Immediately he found a compound fracture, a severe injury that must have been inflicted with considerable force, on the right-hand side of Anne's head. He was mystified as to how such an injury could have been sustained in the accident. He returned to the scene to check whether he had missed something or whether any clue might suggest how the injury had occurred. He found nothing.

Back at Portlaoise, he examined the body further. There appeared to be superficial injuries around the neck. On completing his examination, he informed the gardaí that the injuries, in his opinion, had not resulted from a traffic accident. The deceased woman had been subjected to some form of an assault or violence, which had ultimately been responsible for her death. Word was passed up through the gardaí to the Criminal Investigation Bureau (CIB) in Dublin. A murder investigation was opened.

While this was taking place, Henry Holmes was at home in Ital House with Garda Pat Ryan, reminiscing about his wife, wondering how in God's name he was ever going to manage without her.

Over the next few days, the Holmeses' house was chock-a-block. Friends, neighbours, relatives filed through it. Some came and paid the briefest respects. Others lingered to remember Anne and offer comfort to the bereaved husband. Shock permeated the atmosphere. Holmes was in a daze, as might have been expected.

At some stage in the morning of 30 December, somebody from the gardaí informed Holmes that Anne had not died in a traffic accident but had either been murdered or committed suicide. The revelation appeared to throw him further into confusion. He later remembered saying he hoped for the children's sake that it wasn't suicide.

Soon after midday on 30 December, his sister Louise and her husband, Michael Mahon, showed up. Holmes brought them upstairs. He told them what the gardaí had said. He brought them into his son's room, wondering aloud whether Anne might have left a note.

As they were leaving the bedroom, one of the Mahons commented on a pile of dirty laundry lying near the door, then offered to bring it to their house, to get it out of the way, as Holmes's would be full of people in the coming days. While they were at it, they said, they might as well wash it. Henry would have enough on his hands.

Holmes thanked them but said there was no need for that, to just leave it in the utility room at their house and he would be over to collect it in a few days. The couple left with the laundry.

A few hours earlier, at Kildare garda station, an incident room had been set up to investigate the suspected murder of Anne Holmes. Two detectives from the CIB arrived from Dublin. Sergeant Tom Connolly was familiar with the area as he had previously been stationed locally and lived in Naas. He was a veteran of murder investigations, a cop of the old school, polite, dogged and determined.

Sergeant Gerry O'Carroll was another veteran of murder probes. Three years later, he would find himself at the centre of what became known as the Kerry Babies case, which led to a tribunal and a serious degree of controversy for the Garda Síochána.

The first move in the investigation was to conduct house-to-house enquiries in the area. A questionnaire was drawn up, and the door-knocking began. It was quickly concluded that Garda Pat Ryan's knowledge of and friendship with the Holmes family would be useful in furthering enquiries.

At 9 p.m. that evening, Ryan arrived at Ital House, from which he had departed just fourteen hours earlier after his all-night vigil with Holmes. He was invited in again. In the course of a brief conversation, he asked Holmes where he had been in the hours preceding the discovery of Anne's body.

Holmes said he had gone out jogging at around 5.15 p.m. He had taken a route that brought him through St Evin's Park and out past Tyna Knitwear. He said he had spotted a blue Cortina car outside the factory. He returned home and got into his own car without checking whether Anne was at home. He had driven to Ballybrittas, to meet the Connaires, as arranged with them, at 7 p.m. Ryan took note of Henry's account and left soon afterwards.

The following morning, Michael Mahon noticed something about the pile of clothes he had brought over from Holmes's house. Among the items there was a brown anorak. He picked it up and examined it. It bore several stains, which could only have been blood. He conferred with his wife, and they decided to call the gardaí. Michael asked to speak to Garda Pat Ryan.

Ryan arrived at the Mahon home soon after noon. Michael showed him the anorak. Ryan left with it and handed it over to a ballistics officer who had been deployed to the incident room in Kildare garda station.

At 2 p.m., Sergeants Gerry O'Carroll and Chris O'Halloran were at Ital House. They found Holmes in the middle of a meal. O'Halloran introduced him to O'Carroll, the detective from Dublin. Holmes began crying. The stress of bereavement was getting to him, and Anne's body was due to be removed that evening to the local St Peter and Paul Catholic Church.

O'Carroll put an arm around him and guided him over to the couch, where the two men sat down. O'Halloran joined them, and the officers told him they wanted to have a chat about the day Anne died and to take a formal statement from him.

They brought Holmes through his background, and how he and Anne had met. He detailed his business life. His family life, he told the police, was generally happy, although there were a few kinks that required ironing out. "My wife suffered from depression for seven years. She stopped taking tablets for it a year ago and seemed to be doing well without them. She had a difficult first three months of the pregnancy but did not go back on the tablets. She complained of varicose veins that made her feel down, but she still didn't go back on the tablets," he told O'Carroll.

The Christmas period had been normal, except that on St Stephen's Day an incident occurred involving Anne's uncle. The man had suicidal tendencies and was now in Carlow psychiatric hospital.

Then Henry Holmes retraced the day of his wife's death. He had left the house at 11 a.m. to go to the factory. He returned at noon. Anne was making dinner, and the children asked him to take them to their granny's. After dinner he dropped them up to the Melia home. He stayed a while talking to his mother-in-law, Kathleen. When he returned home, Anne was watching a movie on RTÉ, which featured Charlton Heston. He joined her to while away a holiday afternoon.

He had some work to do. He had intended to use the holiday season to lay a Marley floor in the hall. He left the film and got stuck in, cutting and measuring. At some stage, Anne's aunt called to use the phone. In the early 1980s, home telephones were common, but not every family had one. Holmes answered the door, and didn't let on that Anne was at home as Anne didn't want to be disturbed.

When the woman left, Holmes went into the TV room where his wife was still watching the movie. "I told Anne I was going for a walk. We had a conversation about a suit she was going to get dry-cleaned for me for New Year's Eve. She also said that I was always working at the factory.

"After leaving the house, I went up on to the main road . . . After I got home I got straight into my car, which is an Audi. My wife's yellow Datsun was not there. I can't remember if there were lights on in the house. I drove to Ballybrittas. I got there at 7.30 p.m. On arriving at the factory I met Mrs Connaire. Her husband had gone off to look for a phone because I was half an hour late. I went around Ballybrittas looking for Mr Connaire but I couldn't find him. When I got back, he was there at the factory. At nine o'clock, Sergeant O'Halloran and Father O'Sullivan came and told me the bad news."

His statement continued: "At that stage I believed my wife had died in a car accident. Later that night I remember hearing that she was either murdered or it was suicide. I remember saying that for the children's sake I hoped it was murder. I can't give any reason why she would be murdered. She didn't have any enemies. The only thing I can say is she never leaves home without her purse, and I couldn't find it. On returning to the house with Father O'Sullivan on Tuesday night I didn't notice anything disturbed in the house."

By the time the statement was finished, it was pushing 6 p.m. The gardaí asked Holmes if they could have permission to preserve the house in order to take fingerprints and examine it for any forensic clues. The implication – whether they conveyed it or not – was that they were looking for another suspect who might have left traces of his presence. Holmes agreed. He left the officers to prepare himself for that evening's removal of Anne's body to the church. Sergeant O'Halloran stayed to preserve the house and ready it for the forensic team.

Over the following hours, the manner of Anne Holmes's violent death began to crystallise. On examining the house, it became quickly apparent to the forensic team that the kitchen should be their main focus, and they employed powerful oblique lighting to seek out minute particles that might become clues. They found specks of blood behind the radiator in the room and more particles on the door jamb and its saddle. Many of the specks were consistent with being directional splashes from an already bleeding wound.

Within a few hours, the examination had yielded a pretty definitive result. A violent assault had occurred in the kitchen. But whose blood had been retrieved? In the days before DNA became a feature of investigations, this meant checking blood groups. If Anne Holmes's blood group matched that of the specks, the forensic evidence would take on greater significance.

Either way, although a statement had been taken from Henry Holmes just a few hours earlier, it was now time for another chat with him. The forensic results, coupled with the bloodstained anorak that the Mahons had handed over, pointed to some inescapable conclusions.

That evening, Anne Holmes's body was removed to the church in Monasterevin. Following prayers, the congregation drifted out. At around 8.30 p.m., Holmes was leaving the church grounds with a friend, Noel Kelly, when Garda Pat Ryan approached him. The three men sat into Kelly's car. The garda told Holmes that the detectives wanted another word with him.

"What do they want me for? I spoke to them earlier," Holmes said.

"I don't know," Ryan replied.

When they arrived at Kildare garda station, Ryan led Holmes to an interview room where they were joined by Sergeant Tom Connolly. Ryan left, and Sergeant Gerry O'Carroll joined his colleague at the table opposite Holmes. Connolly thanked him for coming and told him he was free to leave at any time. Then he cautioned Holmes and told him they believed he was responsible for his wife's death. Holmes denied it. He remained cool and composed.

O'Carroll told him about the blood on the anorak and the evidence retrieved from the kitchen at Ital House, which suggested an assault had taken place. Holmes admitted that he had given clothes to his sister and brother-in-law but denied he knew anything about blood. He said he had told the truth earlier in the day, when he had given his statement at the house. The interview continued in this vein. Connolly again asked him to come clean.

Holmes began to cry. "What about my children? What will become of my children? They're all I care about." The detectives didn't respond. "I'm here because of my temper," Holmes added. He sobbed some more. "What's the sentence for murder?" he asked.

"There is only one sentence for murder and that is life imprisonment," Connolly told him.

"What's the sentence for manslaughter?" he asked.

"That is entirely a matter for the court," Connolly replied.

Holmes asked whether the cops could give any indication as to what such a sentence might be. Connolly said that was not possible: it was up to the judge.

"I take full responsibility for what I did," Holmes said. "Can I talk to Pat Ryan?"

At this point, Connolly cautioned him again, and O'Carroll went to fetch Ryan to sit in on the interview.

When the men returned, Henry Holmes began to give a statement, which differed considerably from the one he had given earlier that day, in particular at the point at which Anne's aunt had come to the house.

"After she left, and when I was putting down the Marley, I made a mistake with cutting it a foot short on the part nearest the TV room. Anne came out and said, 'You made a bags of it, you can't do anything right.' She passed some remark about an incident in Ballybrittas a year ago that involved my family. It was opening up old wounds. She moved into the kitchen and we had further words. Anne slapped me on the face and it stung.

"When she hit me, I had the lump hammer in my hand [which he had been using to lay the Marley floor]. I swung and hit her with the hammer on the right side of the head.

"She turned and began walking away from me, and I hit her a few more times with the hammer. I can't say whether she was standing up or lying down when I hit her the second or third time.

"She did not have any weapon in her hand at the time she fell down and was beside the radiator. I said an act of contrition in her ear. Before I said that, I saw blood and fainted.

"I took her out to the car. I turned left and drove out the Portarlington road. I was in a panic. The car stopped on me as I had the choke out.

"I tried to get it going, but I couldn't. I saw a car coming from the Monasterevin direction. I jumped out of the car and turned the steering wheel to the right. I slapped the door shut. The car rolled down the incline. When the car went off the road I started to walk briskly back the road towards my house. The car that had been coming passed me when I had walked about ten yards."

Back at the house, he began the clean-up operation. "I changed my clothes and put them in the boys' room upstairs. I got a J-cloth and mopped up the blood. When I got back to the house I delayed there just about ten minutes and then drove to Ballybrittas.

"I am delighted now that I have told the truth. I was going to tell Pat Ryan on the night we went for a walk, and I was close to telling Gerry O'Carroll yesterday . . . may God forgive me for what I did."

The statement was read back to him before he signed it. One detail, vital in Holmes's mind, had been inadvertently left out. "You forgot to say that I said an act of contrition in her ear," he pointed out. The statement was adjusted accordingly, and he signed it.

The detectives wanted to clear up the loose ends. Where was Anne's other shoe? Holmes said it had fallen off her during or after the assault. It was back at the house, if the dog hadn't taken and eaten it. A garda was dispatched to Ital House and returned with the shoe, which Holmes identified.

He was asked whether he would submit to a blood test, which might eliminate him as the person whose bloodstains had been found in the kitchen. If Anne's blood group was different from his, this would indicate more definitively that it was her blood.

Holmes said he had no objection, but that it was unnecessary. He took full responsibility. The blood found was Anne's, he asserted.

By the time the details were cleared up, the clock had passed midnight. It was now New Year's Day 1982. For Holmes, what lay ahead was not renewal and rejuvenation but a long spell behind bars and disgrace. His business would suffer. His children would have to be reared without either parent, unless a judge found mitigating circumstances to merit a suspended or brief prison sentence.

The problems littering the vista of his new existence were far-reaching and daunting. But at least he had life, which was more than his wife did.

At a special court convened in Kildare garda station in the early hours of 1 January 1982, Henry Holmes was charged with the murder of his wife, Anne, on 29 December 1981. He was remanded in custody.

Detective Sergeant Joe Higgins was assigned to escort the prisoner to Mountjoy Prison in Dublin. On the way, Holmes told Higgins that he had been on his way to a doctor in Portarlington with his wife when the car stalled. He said that just a slap had started the whole thing.

He told the detective he was glad that he had got everything off his chest. And he complimented the gardaí who had interviewed him. They had been slick, professional and courteous. They had made an impossible situation possible.

Outside Mountjoy, Higgins pulled up. Holmes's friend Noel Kelly, and his brother-in-law Michael Mahon had followed them to Dublin, having been alerted to what had transpired. They asked the detective could they speak briefly to the prisoner. They pledged their support to him in looking after the children and attempting to maintain his business.

At 4.30 a.m., as New Year revellers straggled home along the North Circular Road, Henry Holmes was admitted to Mountjoy Prison. His wife, Anne, had become one of the state's thirty-five victims of homicide in 1981. Later that day, she was buried in Monasterevin, while her husband spent his first twenty-four hours behind bars. He didn't seek temporary release to attend the funeral.

At first glance, it may have looked like an open-and-shut case. A man kills his wife in a temper, after she had provoked him with a thoughtless remark and a stinging slap on the face. He had reacted instinctively and happened to have a weapon in his hand – for innocent purposes – with which he fatally assaulted her.

Panic had driven him to take the body from their home, perhaps, according to one version, going to seek out a doctor's assistance in Portarlington. That he initially attempted to cover it up was suspicious, but not definitively so. It was an instinctive reaction to committing a crime that was completely out of character. Then, having come clean, he was obviously filled with remorse. It looked as though a man had lost his temper with the wife who was belittling him.

Loose ends, however, continued to stick out from under the file. Why had Holmes not summoned medical help for his wife immediately after the assault, particularly if, as he claimed, he wasn't sure whether Anne was alive or dead? There was a telephone in the house with which he could have summoned a doctor or an ambulance.

He also appeared to have shown little concern for summoning spiritual help. The couple were religious. If he could see that Anne's life was hanging by a thread, or if he knew she had just died, the obvious thing would have been to call for a priest to administer the Last Rites. He would have known that Anne would want that more than anything at the end of her life.

There was another matter. In his confession, Henry claimed that the engine had cut out, which had prompted him to push the car off the road. Yet when the two motorists came upon it, the engine was still running. It was a small point but, in the context of a detailed confession, pretty significant.

A few more questions popped up in the first weeks of January 1982, as a number of people came forward with interesting observations about Henry Holmes.

*

In 1980, Ivan Poynton wanted a change. For years he had worked in the garment industry, and now he was going to try his hand at something else. An opportunity arose for him to get involved in the insurance business. Poynton grabbed it with both hands.

He secured a position with the Canadian company Sun Life, working out of his base in Tullamore, Co. Offaly. One of his first tasks was to drum up business, so naturally he attempted to exploit the contacts he had made during his time in clothing.

In January 1981, he contacted Henry Holmes. 'How're you fixed for insurance?' Holmes thought about it and decided he could do with more life cover. One small problem in the proposed deal was Holmes's involvement in motor-racing. A pastime that, for insurance purposes, might be classed dangerous required head office to approve the policy. In effect, this just meant more hassle for the agent and the prospective policy holder.

Poynton attempted to contact Holmes a number of times to finalise the arrangements, but Holmes, through pressure of work or lapsed interest, didn't return his calls. The policy lay dormant, and Poynton moved on.

Then, some ten months later, on Monday, 30 November, he received a note in the post from his old contact. Holmes indicated that his wife wanted life cover. Poynton contacted Holmes at his factory, and an appointment was arranged for 2 December at 7.30 p.m.

At the appointed hour, Anne Holmes opened her front door to Poynton, a man she had neither met nor heard of previously. He explained the purpose of his visit. Holmes was upstairs in the bath. Anne invited him in and asked him to wait in the sitting room.

Presently a freshly scrubbed Holmes came into the room. He told Poynton that he had intended their meeting to take place at his factory, rather than his home. Anne didn't join them for the conversation about a policy for life insurance that was to be taken out in her name.

Holmes explained that he was starting a new company to complement his existing ventures. It would manufacture children's clothes and would be in Anne's name. Then he said they would have to discuss details later. He and Anne were on their way out to dinner. An appointment was arranged at the factory on 7 December at 2 p.m.

Poynton arrived on the agreed date with various options in his briefcase. Holmes said he was looking at cover in the region of £150,000–£160,000. Poynton pointed out that the maximum cover that could be taken out without a financial report was £100,000. The report would take time. Holmes dismissed that option. He wanted to have the whole thing done and dusted by Christmas. "He said he wanted to get it cleared up as quickly as possible," Poynton recalled. "I told him that if she [Anne] wanted an endowment for that amount, it would cost £5,000 a year. He said that was too much and we settled on £123 per month premium, which would give an endowment after twenty years of £20,000."

In practical terms, the policy provided for a payout of £100,000 in the event of Anne's natural death. If she was to die by accidental means, the value of the payout would increase to £150,000.

Poynton went with Holmes to explain the policy to Anne. Her only concern was the medical examination she would be obliged to undergo to initiate the policy. By then, she was pregnant and nervous of anything that might impinge on her condition.

Poynton assured her that she could attend her own doctor for the medical, which seemed to allay her fears, and Holmes wrote out a cheque for the first premium payment. It was drawn on the Anne's Boutique account.

On 22 December, Poynton phoned Holmes at his factory to inform him that the policy had been officially approved. Holmes asked him for confirmation in writing.

The following day, he received written word of the approval. Within a week, Anne Holmes was dead.

In early January, Poynton contacted the gardaí with what he assumed was information they might consider relevant to their investigation into the death of his policy holder.

Outside his busy life, the latter months of 1981 had been providing Henry Holmes with other excitement. Anne Raleigh was twenty and had worked in Holmes's factory since she was sixteen. She was a native of

Portarlington, and her two sisters had also spent time on the factory floor. In early November 1981, while Anne Holmes was on her pilgrimage in Lourdes, Henry asked his employee out to dinner. During the evening, he unburdened himself of his woes.

His marriage had been unhappy for some time. Anne was going to leave him after she had given birth to the child she was expecting. She intended to emigrate to Australia. He was forced to seek affection outside the family home. He told his employee that she was the first woman with whom he had a relationship outside the marriage since his wedding fourteen years previously.

The pair saw a lot of each other in the run-up to Christmas. Henry would call for Anne Raleigh at her family home. Sometimes they went out to the Curragh, just to sit in the car and talk. On other occasions, the couple went back to the factory after everyone had gone home when it was empty and dark.

That Christmas, they exchanged gifts. He gave her a watch, and she presented him with a gold chain. Anne Raleigh was in love. There is no evidence to suggest that Anne Holmes was aware that her husband was having an affair.

On 31 December, Anne Raleigh went to the Holmeses' house to sympathise with Holmes on the death of his wife. This was hours before he would admit to gardaí his involvement in his wife's death. While she was there, he told her that his wife's purse had been missing since the evening her body was found.

A few days into the New Year, Anne Raleigh confided in her brother about the affair. He advised her to go to the gardaí, which she promptly did. "I am still in love with him but I would find it difficult to go out with him again," she told them.

Family obligations took Patrick Melia back to his home place of Monasterevin during the Christmas holiday season. On 28 December, he and his wife Rose drove down from Dublin to visit Rose's parents. As the afternoon wore on, Rose suggested they go over to see Patrick's sister, Anne Holmes. At 3 p.m., the Melias arrived at Ital House. Anne was in excellent form. She served tea and sandwiches as the couples caught up with each other. Patrick sensed that Holmes was being cool towards him but didn't think much of it.

In the course of exchanging presents, it emerged there had been a mix-up. Holmes had forgotten to buy a present for Patrick. He left without saying where he was going and reappeared some time later with a parcel. He had popped over to the factory to pick up a jumper for his brother-in-law.

Anne mentioned that if Patrick had known that Holmes was going to the factory, he could have gone along to see it. At around 5 p.m., Holmes suggested the two men travel over and leave the women to their talk. On the way back from Ballybrittas, Patrick noticed that Holmes had taken a different route from the direct one. They were going via the Portarlington–Monasterevin Road, along the old bog road, at a place Patrick knew as Coolnafearagh.

"He was driving slowly along the bog road," Patrick would tell the gardaí. "He appeared not to be noticing me at all. It was as if he was in a bit of a daze. I have gone to his factory a number of times but this was the first time that he travelled on the bog road."

It was in this area that Anne's car would be found just over twenty-four hours later.

Back at Ital House, Patrick noticed that Holmes now appeared on edge. "He didn't sit down with us when we got back. He told Anne that her car was low on petrol. She said there was enough in it but he said he'd fill it up. He left without saying goodbye to us."

The Melias left Anne at around 6.30 p.m. They were going to the Melia parents' house, and Anne asked them to stay there until she called over a few hours later. Patrick and Rose Melia waited at his parents' house until 9 p.m., but Anne didn't appear. They returned to Dublin that evening. Twenty-four hours later Patrick heard that his sister was dead.

The three statements added another dimension to the garda investigation. Now, there appeared to be motive, both in terms of Henry Holmes's romantic entanglement and the insurance policy. Patrick Melia's recollection of the night prior to Anne's death also suggested planning.

The post-mortem report of state pathologist John Harbison threw further light on the case. He found that the victim had suffered several injuries to the right-hand side of her head. By his estimate, she had sustained around ten blows to this area. His opinion was that she died from haemorrhaging as a consequence of a depressed fracture of the skull, due to multiple injuries. He also found that she had sustained several bruises to her neck. Even if Henry Holmes had hit his wife a greater number of times than he had remembered, the neck injuries didn't fit into his description of the attack. One possible explanation was that at some point he had attempted to strangle her. Either way, the cause of death was attributable entirely to the head injuries.

There was one final strand of evidence to come to garda attention. On 6 January, the local public-service vehicle inspector, John Daly, examined Anne Holmes's yellow Datsun. He noticed some superficial damage, a slight dent on the left front of the vehicle, and a leaking radiator. He also discovered something amiss with the accelerator pedal: "When the pedal was depressed and pressure released, the pedal did not return in the usual manner," he reported. "I found the spring [which is designed to be] attached to the pedal, which returns the pedal when pressure is released, was disconnected. With this out of place, it meant that the pedal remained in whatever position it had been put into. The accelerator-release spring is made from strong steel and clips into a tiny hole in the bracket. It would take substantial pressure to open . . . I am satisfied it would not open under normal pressure."

The evidence again called into question Holmes's assertion that he had got out of the car and pushed it off the road in a panic response to the approach of a car from the other direction. It would not have been possible to drive the car to Coolnafearagh bog unless the accelerator-release spring was intact. Yet, by the time the vehicle was recovered by the gardaí, it was detached. The only obvious conclusion is that somebody took off the spring out there on the bog road, on that chilly December night, as Anne Holmes's body lay in the car.

Henry Holmes was granted bail in the second week of January 1982. His release required his own surety of £5,000 and an independent surety of the same amount. He was free to raise his children alone and go to work, albeit in the suspended reality of conditional freedom, pending a trial.

In the interim, he tried to carry on as usual. His business suffered, although how much of the downturn was due to prevailing economic conditions is unclear – all over the country, people were being laid off during the early 1980s.

Fourteen months later, on 10 March 1983, Holmes went on trial at the Central Criminal Court in the Four Courts. He pleaded guilty to manslaughter but not guilty to murder.

Opening the trial for the prosecution, senior counsel Patrick Geraghty told the jury that they would have to take into account that Anne Holmes was six months pregnant and not at her most attractive. They would also have to consider that the court only had the accused's word that a row had prompted him to hit her. "He struck her about ten times," Geraghty told the eleven men and one woman. "Two of the blows were particularly heavy ones about the ear. There were also signs that constriction and bruising around the neck had been carried out, suggesting an attempt at manual strangulation."

On the second day of the trial, Anne Raleigh gave evidence. She told of her affair with Henry Holmes, which had begun in the months before Anne Holmes's death. She said that they had met around twice weekly. Holmes had told her that he had been unhappy for the last six years of his marriage and that his wife was going to leave him once the baby was born. Then, a week before Christmas, they found themselves in the storeroom of the factory one evening when everybody had gone home.

Geraghty asked her: "What happened in the storeroom?"

"Do I have to answer that?" she replied.

"I'm afraid you do."

"We got carried away. We were both lonely. We went further than we should have," she said.

Garda witnesses and the insurance man Poynton gave evidence. Professor John Harbison was called to present the pathology evidence. His report included the detail that among Anne Holmes's injuries was a black eye, which could have been caused by a punch.

On the third day, the extended members of Henry and Anne's family were called. A notable feature of the trial was the somewhat differing views the respective families held of the Holmeses' marriage.

Kathleen Melia told of the night of Anne's death. Holmes had called to her home and broke down as he told her of her daughter's death. Asked about his temper, she replied: "I knew he had a bad temper. He'd knock the kids on the head and face. He'd hit them for not doing their homework. He'd use his fist. That was the only violence I saw." She said that she visited Anne and Henry practically every day and she considered that she had had a good relationship with her son-in-law prior to the killing. Under cross-examination, she agreed with Holmes's counsel, Seamus Sorahan, that she never saw Holmes strike his wife, that he was a good father and husband and that he had set Anne up in business.

Holmes's sister Louise Mahon was called, and she told the court that for some time before Anne's death she had noticed a deterioration in the marriage.

On the fourth day of the trial, Holmes took the stand. The court was full to overflowing. He was calm and composed as his counsel brought him through the events of the fateful day. He described the moment when, he said, Anne had hit him. "It was a stinging blow. It stung me. The surge came through me. I could not believe it. She had never raised a hand to me before.

"The first thing I remember is Anne lying on the ground. I saw the blood and passed out. When I picked myself up I said, 'My God, what have I done?' I started to sweat. I spoke to Anne and I said an act of contrition in her ear.

"I think I was still talking to Anne, trying to get her to talk back, when I thought about going out for a doctor, or to a hospital. I grabbed my coat and put it over her."

He told the court that at Coolnafearagh, the engine cut out, and he could not restart it. This prompted him in a panic to push it off the road.

Asked about extra-marital affairs, he admitted that Anne Raleigh had not been his first, as he had told her, but the third in which he had engaged during the eighteen months before Christmas 1981.

Then the counsel brought him through the strains in his marriage. He said Anne complained a lot: she complained about her car; she complained about the house; she wanted a fitted kitchen, which cost £5,000, but she complained while the work was being done, so he sent her on a two-week holiday.

Anne had suffered post-natal depression after her first pregnancy, he told the court, and had been prescribed Valium. At one stage, she was taking three tablets a day. "There was never anything she asked for that I did not get," he testified. "In that respect, I was a good husband. I was always trying to help her out with the problem of the tablets. At times it appeared hopeless, but other times it would improve."

Any time he did anything wrong, Anne referred to his five foot four inches height. She was taller than him with high heels on. She was always complaining about what other people had in terms of material possessions.

Throughout his first day in the witness stand, Holmes answered the questions concisely. The court adjourned at four o'clock.

The following day, he resumed. Sorohan brought him back to the night in question. Why hadn't he contacted somebody after the attack? Why had he abandoned Anne in the car?

"I had this awful feeling. I didn't know what to do. I just didn't know how to handle the whole situation," he said. He described how he had returned home, got into his own car and driven to the factory, where the Connaires were waiting for him. He now had to face his customers, having killed his wife within the past two hours. Before he'd left for the factory, he'd popped one of Anne's Valium tablets.

"When I met them [the Connaires], my stomach was turning inside me. I didn't know what I was going to do, or how I was going to tell someone what had happened." The guilt began to eat away at him, but he couldn't bring himself to confess. "I didn't tell them [the gardaí] because I wanted to attend the funeral," he said. Asked once more about the state of the marriage, he said there had been several rows between him and Anne of a greater magnitude than the one on the day of her death.

Finally, his counsel asked him how he felt about the tragedy. After a day and a half in the witness box, Holmes's composure cracked, and he broke down. "I'm exceptionally sorry and ashamed," he said. "I'm sorry for the shame it brought on the children and the family and I'm sorry for what I did to Anne. And I'm terribly sorry for the sorrow I've caused her mother and her family. Words just can't express it."

At that, his lawyer resumed his seat, and Geraghty, for the prosecution, stood up to begin his cross-examination.

In response to questions about his marriage, Holmes said that Anne was the dominant partner. Moving on to the day of her death, he denied that when he put her body into the car after the attack he had been preoccupied with escaping rather than getting help. He also denied that he was faking an accident by pushing the car off the road.

"When I saw the car coming and mine would not start, I panicked and I leaped out and slammed the door and pushed it," he said.

"Weren't you trying to save your own skin?" Geraghty asked.

"Yes."

Geraghty explored the significance of Holmes's affair. "When you were having the row with your wife, were you making a mental comparison with the young lady you had been taking out?"

"No."

Then he was asked if he had thought of the insurance policy during the row.

"No, not at all," Holmes replied.

The cross-examination ended without the telling revelation or dramatic flourish that informs Hollywood court dramas. Later that day, the evidence was completed.

Geraghty gave his closing speech first, urging the jury to put aside their emotion and consider whether a woman had been murdered, as defined by the law. "In some senses, it is a rather horrifying and tragic case, and the ripples have spread beyond this courtroom to others, notably the children," he said. "Your sympathy may be with them but your duty is a wider issue."

Summing up for his client, Sorohan appealed to the jury to deliberate closely on the evidence they had heard from Holmes. Nobody who had heard the opening address by the prosecution could think anything other than that his client was a "low wretch". But his few hours in the witness box had been the "most vital period of the whole case".

"Did he strike you as a man whom you must inevitably and reasonably come to the conclusion was telling lies? Did he make himself out to be a saint? Did he try and convince you that it was not his fault at all?" He urged them to find the defendant not guilty of murder.

Charging the jury, Judge Gannon laid out their duty. He said they had to determine whether or not this was a case of murder. The absence of intent to kill or cause serious injury would leave the killing defined as manslaughter. He said a difficulty had been raised in the case in terms of provocation. And the way it had been raised might seem to imply that Holmes had had to prove that he was provoked, but that was not so.

On completing his charge, he sent the jury out. After two hours, they returned with a query for the judge. He answered them, but it was unclear whether this helped in their deliberations. While they were out, Holmes remained in the courtroom, occasionally reading a newspaper, now and again lowering his head into his hands. He was flanked by two prison officers, in the event of the judge ordering that Holmes be taken into custody.

Two hours later, the jury returned again. They were unable to reach a verdict. Holmes showed no emotion. The judge discharged the jury, thanking them for their service through the six-day trial. Sorohan got to his feet and requested bail for his client.

"There are matters in his factory which urgently require his attention if he can give them his personal on-the-spot attention," the lawyer told the judge. Geraghty hopped up to say he had no objection, but the judge appeared unimpressed by the request.

He said he could not see fit to grant bail, as Holmes had pleaded guilty to manslaughter and couldn't be treated as an innocent person. He remanded the prisoner in custody for a week.

Emerging from the Four Courts, Holmes was bent low, as if to protect himself from onslaught by the outside world. His face was hidden behind a newspaper. The Melia family walked out afterwards. One was asked for a comment and replied that all it meant was that everybody would have to go through the whole ordeal again.

They didn't have long to wait. Holmes's second trial began just four weeks later, on Tuesday, 12 April. Judge Gannon was replaced as presiding judge by Ronan Keane. The evidence differed, albeit only in nuance, from that heard at the first trial.

Again, the couple's respective families had different views on the state of the marriage. Kathleen Melia told the court she had never heard her daughter nagging the accused.

Sorohan's cross-examination sought to unite rather than divide. "I am instructed by the accused that he regards you as the best mother-in-law in the world . . . that he loves you."

"He must not have loved my daughter," the witness replied. "I know one thing. She was a good wife and mother. She never deserved the brutal death she got."

Kathleen Melia's daughter and Anne's sister, Kathleen Carroll, painted a benign picture of the couple's relationship. Often she said, when she arrived at the house, Henry and Anne were "cuddled up on the sofa, like they were on their honeymoon". She knew her sister was on tablets, but she didn't suffer from depression as far as Kathleen Carroll knew.

By contrast, Holmes's sister, Louise Mahon, told the court that she had noticed a change in the marriage over the last three years. Anne had become more possessive and jealous and complained whenever Henry had to drive girls home after they had been working overtime. She said she had heard Anne "nagging" her brother several times.

Holmes's own evidence was again central and was given to a packed courtroom. He said there had been constant rows, and that Anne gave the orders. "She would wait until nobody was around," he said. "She kept harping on." His affair with Anne Raleigh had been initiated out of "loneliness".

The Valium didn't help Anne's stability, particularly when she had come off it. "That made her very, very aggressive," he said. "That coupled with the fact that there was a personal family argument going on made Anne aggressive."

Then he was asked about his assault on his wife. This time, his story was different, delving into more detail. After she had become angry with him, the heat had been cranked up with cruel words. "She said I was no good, how could I be? 'Your mother was a bastard,'" Holmes told a silent court.

"You were reluctant to bring this out at the first trial?" his counsel suggested.

"That is true. I retaliated with a remark about her father."

The respective closing speeches followed a similar pattern to those of the first trial. The prosecuting counsel, however, raised one other matter this time around for the jury to consider. "Did things happen as he said they did, or did he magnify the unpleasantness in their marriage?" he asked.

Judge Keane laid out the framework in which the eleven men and one woman had to consider the evidence. Provocation was the issue on which the accused said the charge should be reduced to manslaughter. Two conditions had to be satisfied before circumstances of provocation could lead to a reduced charge.

First, the jury must be satisfied that the accused had been provoked to such an extent that, having regard to his temperament, character and circumstances, he had lost control at the time of the wrongful act.

Second, the act or words of provocation when related to the accused must bear a reasonable relationship to the amount of force used.

The jury had to determine whether these two essential conditions had been fulfilled.

He pointed out that Anne Raleigh's evidence showed her relationship with Holmes had progressed beyond a mere flirtation, beyond an innocent friendship. The jury might think the evidence indicated that this relationship was still in progress around Christmas 1981.

They should also consider how much weight should be attached to the fact that, a relatively short time prior to his wife's death, Holmes had taken out an insurance policy on her life.

The jury was out for ten hours. Eventually, they returned a verdict that Holmes was not guilty of murder. Seated between two prison officers, the defendant showed no emotion. Judge Keane put back sentencing for two days.

The following day, Thursday, 21 April, Holmes was visited in Mountjoy Prison by Brian McCaffrey, the clinical director of psychiatry with the Eastern Health Board. McCaffrey would tell the sentencing hearing that he had gone in to see Holmes without advance notice.

"I went on the attack from the beginning. It could be called an interrogation rather than an interview. That is not my normal style." He gained the impression that, from a fairly early stage in the marriage, Holmes's wife was constantly nagging. She did not support him emotionally and showed no interest in his business. The psychiatrist said that, while it was not confirmed, it was his impression that Anne Holmes had suffered from a psychiatric illness.

The interview in the prison lasted an hour and twenty minutes. Holmes told the psychiatrist: "I miss Anne a lot. I get masses said for her every month. I still talk to her. I keep saying, 'Anne, forgive me for what I have done.'"

At the sentencing hearing, the judge didn't spare Holmes. "The jury's verdict was merciful," he told the defendant. "And on the evidence they would have been entirely within their rights to find you guilty, but I accept the verdict as I am bound to do."

The matter that weighed heaviest in Holmes's favour was his three children. "I'm deeply conscious that I am adding to their tragedy by the imposition of a severe custodial sentence," the judge said. "I am depriving them of both parents. They have already lost a loving mother, but the facts of the case demand a severe custodial sentence."

Henry Holmes was sentenced to ten years in prison.

Outside the court, *Irish Press* reporter Tom Reddy asked Anne's father John Melia to comment on the sentence. "For the death she got, it was nothing," he said. "I am terribly disappointed. I thought he would get at least twenty years. The three children are better off without him."

Henry Holmes served his full sentence with one-third remission. On his release, he moved back to the Kildare area. Soon after he rejoined society, tragedy struck his family again. His son, Russell Anthony, who had been eleven when his mother died, was killed in a road-traffic accident.

Holmes remarried and now lives in Co. Laois.

3. A SUICIDE THAT WASN'T

The Case of Brian Kearney

Brian Kearney sat at the end of the bench, his body turned towards the judge, away from the public, away from his wife's family. If he looked to his left, his eyes would have fallen on the McLaughlins, occupying their own bench, a few metres from where he sat. The parents, five sisters and brother of his wife, Siobhan, were predominantly dressed in black. All of the female members of the family were blonde. They presented a striking image.

It was Wednesday, 13 February 2008, the scheduled first day of his trial for murdering his wife, and Kearney sat alone. Occasionally, he dipped into a leather satchel and extracted a sheet of paper. Once or twice, he looked around to take in the rest of the room. His eyes didn't linger when they swung across his wife's family.

The bench he sat on was to the side of the main body of Court Three of the Round Hall courts in the Four Courts. The bench ran at right angles to the rest of the seats in the room, apart from the jury box, which was on a raised platform opposite Kearney.

Strictly speaking, the defendant can sit anywhere he or she wants to in a courtroom. The dock has long been abolished. Defence barristers will encourage him or her to make themselves known, so that the jury can put a face to the person on trial. Now and again, a close relative or friend will move up and sit next to the defendant. The bench on which Kearney was seated was just a few feet from where his counsel and solicitor sat, allowing for easy communication – through whispers or notes – if required. The other end of the bench is typically occupied by prison officers or reporters.

Further back, on that morning, there was standing room only. The McLaughlins sat directly behind the lawyers. All of the public-gallery seats downstairs were taken by witnesses, extended family and the media. The gallery upstairs was full. Entry into the court would require co-operation with those standing inside to allow the door swing open. The trial had struck a chord in the public imagination. The circumstances, the prominence of the victim's family, the fact that the couple were comfortable middle-class businesspeople, all added to the interest.

Before the proceedings could get under way, the presiding judge, Barry White, revealed that a jury member had declared an interest. He had worked for a company that checked the house alarm at Carnroe, the house in Goatstown, south Co. Dublin where Siobhan Kearney had been found dead nearly two years previously.

After some legal discussion, the judge decided to swear in a new jury and put the trial back to the following Monday. Everybody trooped out, with another five-day wait ahead for the families of the victim and the accused.

When the trial finally started the following Monday, Kearney was no longer sitting alone. Beside him were his two brothers, Niall and Patrick, his daughter from a previous relationship, twenty-two-year-old Aoife, and his sister Lauri.

That afternoon, the Kearneys were joined on the bench by their parents, Bernard and Maeve. Over the course of the thirteen-day trial, uncles, aunts and family friends slipped on to the bench. On a few occasions, a new arrival hugged the defendant before the day's proceedings began.

Brian and his brothers were dressed in dark suits, as befitting any middle-class family assembled for an official engagement. The women were also appropriately attired. A jury member looking across the room might see a family taking a pew at mass or one of the ritual celebrations that punctuate family life. A jury member, a few feet away, looking at the bench full of McLaughlins, would see a family dressed as if for a funeral.

Above all, a jury member would have seen families once united by marriage but now divided over whether or not Brian had murdered Siobhan. The jury could consider nothing but the evidence, although there is no legislating for the subconscious. The choreography in the trial of Brian Kearney was like nothing ever seen before in the Central Criminal Court.

Niamh McLaughlin was late. Usually, she arrived at her sister's house some time before 9 a.m. That morning she had slept it out and was running at least half an hour behind schedule. She pulled into the driveway of Carnroe, the large four-bedroom home on the Knocknashee estate in Goatstown. It was a Tuesday morning, the last day in February 2006.

Niamh McLaughlin followed this routine every weekday. She drove to Siobhan's where she left her car. From there, she either walked or Siobhan dropped her up to the Dundrum Luas station, where she caught a tram into Harcourt Street in the city centre, near her place of work, Ernst & Young, accountants. The arrangement allowed Siobhan to have use of Niamh's car during the day.

Niamh had a key to let herself into Carnroe. On that morning she did so and, on entering, called her sister's name. There was no response. She checked the kitchen, and the sitting room. Almost straight away, she encountered Daniel, Siobhan's three-year-old son.

He appeared to be wandering around the house unattended. Niamh found this strange. She comforted the child and went in search of his mother.

Upstairs, she tried the door to Siobhan's bedroom. It was locked. Again, she called Siobhan's name. No response. She looked through the keyhole into the room. There was a clear view through it, with no key in the lock. She could see that the bedclothes were ruffled. She could also see across the floor and the blinds on the windows. There was no sign of Siobhan.

Niamh McLaughlin's sense of foreboding was growing by the minute. She rang her parents at their home in Dalkey, a few miles away.

Within a half-hour, Owen and Deirdre McLaughlin arrived at the house. Niamh and Daniel were downstairs in the kitchen. Owen McLaughlin made his way up to Siobhan's bedroom. Deirdre McLaughlin attempted to keep her grandson comforted.

Suddenly, they heard banging from upstairs. Owen McLaughlin was trying to break down the door into his daughter's bedroom. After a few attempts, he succeeded. Inside, he was confronted with a sight no parent should have to witness. His thirty-eight-year-old daughter was lying on the floor on the right-hand side of the bed. She was dressed in red pyjama bottoms and a white top. There appeared to be some kind of wire or flex thrown loosely across her body. On the bedroom floor there was a scattering of family photographs.

Owen McLaughlin put a hand on his daughter's arm and her leg. Both limbs were so cold that he knew straight away she was dead. He left the room in a hurry and made his way downstairs in something approaching a state of hysteria. "Siobhan is dead," he shouted.

He came into the room and picked up the phone to ring the emergency services. The trauma of what he had seen became too much for him when he tried to relate to the operator what he had found. His wife took the phone from him and explained the situation.

Then she picked up Niamh's mobile and rang Siobhan's husband, Brian Kearney. "Something terrible has happened," she told him. "Get back here now."

Kearney responded, "Oh, Jesus," and the call ended. Deirdre McLaughlin didn't feel able to tell her son-in-law over the phone what had been discovered in his home. The room in which she stood with her husband, daughter and grandson was enveloped in the horror of a new, brutal reality. Daniel was crying, and Owen was extremely upset.

In the following minutes, before the arrival of the emergency services, Deirdre McLaughlin ventured upstairs. The discovery of her daughter's body in a locked bedroom pointed towards suicide. She found that difficult to fathom. She entered the bedroom and noted how untidy it appeared, the ruffled bed, the photographs on the floor. This wasn't her Siobhan: Siobhan was an organised woman. And if she was going to end her life, she would have left some explanation, some solace for her family, which had always been a tightly knit unit.

There was no note that Deirdre could see, no envelope left in a prominent position on the vanity unit or the bed. She lifted the pillows to check underneath. Nothing. Whatever about the apparent circumstances of her daughter dying behind a locked door, Deirdre McLaughlin simply couldn't believe that she wouldn't have left a note.

Within minutes, the emergency services were on the scene. The initial assumption was that Siobhan had committed suicide. The ambulance personnel, practised in these matters, scoured the bedroom for some kind of medication that she might have taken. They couldn't find anything. As they attended to the body, the two crew members noticed the purple flex. There were knots in it and a loop, which might have been used as a noose. There was also a red mark around Siobhan's neck, which suggested that a ligature had been applied.

Detective Sergeant Michael Gibbons was one of the first gardaí on the scene. When he entered Siobhan's bedroom, he noted the damaged door and the photographs. A key lay a foot or so from the doorway. The duvet on the bed was bundled up. He put a blanket over the body and stood for a quiet moment to say a prayer.

While his initial conversation with the ambulance crew had suggested that this might have been suicide,

Gibbons couldn't ignore the suspicions that were surfacing in his mind. Something was amiss.

Downstairs, Brian Kearney pulled up to his home in his company van. In the half-hour or so since he had received Deirdre McLaughlin's call, he had not rung back to find out more. He got out and approached the door, where he was met by his father-in-law. "Siobhan is dead," Owen McLaughlin told him.

Kearney looked shocked. "Oh, my God," he said. He put his hands on his head and turned his back to McLaughlin, as if he couldn't face the horror that had been visited on his home.

By now other members of the McLaughlin family had arrived. Two more of Siobhan's sisters, Brighid and Aisling, had come to the house together. Their shock was such that they had lost their way driving to Goatstown from Shankill, seven miles away. Somebody contacted Kearney's parents who lived on nearby Drumartin Road. His two brothers, Niall and Patrick, and his sister, Lauri, were on their way.

Kearney met Deirdre McLaughlin as he was going in. "We were going to be together for ever," he told his mother-in-law.

Shock manifests itself in different ways. Brian Kearney appeared to be hyperventilating. Brighid McLaughlin came into the room where Kearney had eased himself into a seat. She said hello. The two had never been close, although she and Siobhan had been.

"Poor you, Brighid, and all that happened to you and Michael," Kearney said. Brighid's husband had drowned in an accident three years previously. There was some suggestion that his death had been suicide, although the official verdict recorded was one of accidental death. It appeared to Brighid that Kearney was implying she had lost a second person close to her through suicide.

Kearney's own family began to arrive. Lauri massaged his shoulders in an attempt to ease the hyperventilation.

Daniel had been dispatched to his grandparents' house in Drumartin Road. Somebody asked Kearney what should be sent up to keep the little boy occupied. Aisling McLaughlin, who was standing nearby, observed his response. He stopped hyperventilating, issued specific instructions about what toys were to be packed and appeared to resume his breathing difficulty.

Meanwhile, up in the bedroom, the gardaí were growing increasingly suspicious about the cause of death. Gibbons had been joined by Detective Inspector Martin Cummins. They conferred. "Having made certain observations and heard certain things, I decided that the situation was a lot more sinister," Cummins would tell the court two years later.

The bedroom was cleared and declared a crime scene. The two gardaí had a word with Owen McLaughlin. Then they went downstairs and spoke briefly to Brian Kearney, where he sat, as his sister continued to massage his shoulders.

Lauri told the gardaí that her brother needed a doctor. Gibbons said one was on the way.

Garda Charlie McConalogue was also on the scene that morning. He was there in a personal capacity. McConalogue had gone out with Siobhan many years previously and was a long-standing family friend to the McLaughlins. Brighid had rung him and asked him to come out. At a time of great confusion, with gardaí swarming through the house, it couldn't do any harm to have a personal friend from the force at their side.

The two detectives brought McConalogue upstairs. From the doorway to the bedroom, he identified Siobhan Kearney. They brought him down the corridor to another, smaller room, where he sat on a single bed and told them what he knew of the McLaughlins.

Then McConalogue went back downstairs. He met Brian Kearney and commiserated with him. The two men had met a few times previously. In 2002, after her wedding, Siobhan had invited McConalogue to her new home for lunch to see the wedding photographs. McConalogue told Kearney that the detectives would want to speak with him in a few minutes.

Kearney looked at him. "Charlie, Charlie, will I be able to go through with it?" he asked.

"They only want to speak to you," McConalogue replied.

Kearney asked him whether the detectives would want his clothes. McConalogue was taken aback by this but didn't let on. "You'll have to ask them about that," he said.

McConalogue went into the kitchen. "There was great devastation in that room," he later testified. The atmosphere in the room weighed heavy with grief, but there was also anger. At one stage, one of Kearney's brothers came in from the front room to fill a kettle. Aisling McLaughlin told him to get out. Her mother intervened, but there was no escaping the heightened tension. As far as some of the McLaughlins were concerned, regardless of whether or not Siobhan had committed suicide, Brian Kearney was behind her death.

Upstairs, Gibbons and Cummins sat the bereaved husband on the bed in the back room they had commandeered. They asked him when he had last seen Siobhan. He told them it had been on the previous evening when she returned home after visiting a friend. She had arrived back at around 8.30 p.m. or so with Daniel. They had spoken briefly. He had got the child ready for bed, and Siobhan had gone up to the attic room to answer some emails on the family computer. He and Daniel had slept in one room – he had fallen asleep reading his son a story. Siobhan had had the master bedroom.

Kearney told the cops that Siobhan had wanted a divorce, but there was no animosity between them. That morning, he had got up around 7 a.m. and gone downstairs with Daniel. They had had breakfast, and he had put on a DVD to keep the little boy occupied. He went upstairs and washed his teeth. He tried the door to the master bedroom but it was locked. He shouted through the door that he was off to work and that Daniel was downstairs. He had left around 7.40 a.m., arriving in Kelleher's, the electrical wholesalers in the nearby Sandymount industrial estate, at 7.50 a.m. The first intimation he had had that something was wrong was the call from his mother-in-law.

Gibbons and Cummins listened and took notes. Kearney asked whether they would want his clothes. Cummins said that would be a good idea. Kearney suggested alternative garments he might wear, which were stored in another room. He specified a pair of jeans and a top. The request for specific replacement clothes raised a smidgen of suspicion with the guards. They told him to hang on to the clothes he was wearing. "We'll get them off you later," Cummins said.

Back downstairs, the McLaughlin family were leaving. They walked the short distance to the Goat public house, accompanied by Charlie McConalogue. Therein they waited for word that they could go back to the house for the removal of Siobhan's body.

Within hours, the state pathologist Marie Cassidy was on the scene. She was brought to the bedroom and began her examination. From early on, it was apparent to her that the dead woman had died due to neck compression. There was a red mark running around her neck, with the skin above the line discoloured compared with the pale skin below. A number of pinpoint haemorrhages on the face and in the eyes were also consistent with death due to asphyxiation.

The question was whether Siobhan's death had been self-inflicted or not.

Cassidy noted that the purple flex was not wrapped around the victim's neck in a noose. She was assured that neither the gardaí nor the ambulance crew had disturbed it. Even if the flex had broken during hanging, it would still have been around the neck, and the end would still be attached to the suspension point from which the hanging had been executed. Again, there was no evidence of this.

Closer examination found three fractures to the victim's Adam's apple and deep bruising to the neck. Both of these factors were more usually found after manual strangulation.

Cassidy told the gardaí of her findings, with the proviso that she would require to make an even closer examination to reach a definitive conclusion. The results confirmed the gardaí's growing suspicion that all was not as it seemed, or had been set up to seem, in the bedroom.

It was pushing on for 7 p.m. before McConalogue received a call from Gibbons that the body was being taken to the morgue. The family and a few friends made the journey back to the house. A coffin lay on two chairs in the living room. Deirdre McLaughlin led her family in a decade of the rosary for the repose of the soul of the woman they intended to bury under her maiden name, Siobhan McLaughlin. No member of the Kearney family was present when Siobhan departed from her home for the last time; Kearney had gone to his parents' house to take care of his son.

At the end of a long day, Detectives Cummins and Gibbons called to Brian Kearney's parents' home on Drumartin Road. His mother answered the door. She told them that her son was in bed. They asked could they retrieve the clothes he had been wearing that morning, as they had arranged with him earlier.

Maeve Kearney told the two officers that she had washed the clothes because they were soiled and sweaty. She brought the gardaí out to the garage where the clothes were hanging on a line. There was a black T-shirt, a black polo neck, black trousers, blue socks and a navy jumper, cleansed of everyday grime and, from a garda point of view, any forensic evidence that might have been of interest to them.

Brian Kearney wore his wedding band in court. The ring was clearly visible whenever he placed his hands on the bench in front of him. Two years after the death of his wife, he felt compelled to remember her with the ring she had given him on their wedding day.

In the weeks before her death, Siobhan had stopped wearing hers. Carol Summers, a friend of Siobhan's, told the court of meeting her for dinner in a city-centre restaurant in late February 2006. Siobhan hadn't been wearing her wedding and engagement rings, Summers said. She had detected that her friend was experiencing serious marital difficulties.

For the most part, Kearney showed no emotion during the trial. Sometimes, when he arrived early, he would chat with family, or a friend. In these unguarded moments he felt free to laugh or smile in the course of a conversation. Once the McLaughlin family arrived, he would stiffen noticeably.

During the earlier part of the trial, his two brothers sat closest to him. Both took notes, his youngest brother Patrick often writing copiously in a hard-covered notebook. Occasionally, one or other would dip into a bag at their feet and extract some official-looking document, most likely witness statements.

Kearney was represented by a leading lawyer, Patrick Gageby. His family gave the impression that they believed wholly in his innocence. His brothers took notes to ensure that the family would be clued into every detail of the case.

As the trial wore on, either Kearney's daughter, twenty-two-year-old Aoife, or his sister Lauri sat next to him. Each morning he was photographed arriving at the Four Courts with Aoife. In court, she often held his arm. During one of the legal arguments that require the jury to absent themselves, Lauri massaged Kearney's shoulders, just as she had after the discovery of his dead wife.

The McLaughlin family remained dignified throughout the trial. At times when the evidence was particularly sensitive someone would bow their head for a private moment. At other times, they might throw a glance at Kearney, the contempt barely concealed.

The treatment of the victims of crime has improved significantly in the last decade. The McLaughlins sat directly behind the two main gardaí in the case, Cummins and Gibbons, who often turned to confer with them or to explain a point. The prosecuting lawyers, Denis Vaughan Buckley and Dominic McGinn, also made themselves available to queries from the family.

A victim-support counsellor was close by the family every day. She made sure they had drinking water and routinely gave one or more of them a reassuring pat on the back. Yet despite the support, the stress of their pursuit of justice for their sister and daughter could be seen on their faces as the days wore on.

The hardest part must have been the pathology evidence on the fifth day of the trial. Professor Cassidy ran through the injuries on the dead woman's body, then held up a close-up photograph of the deceased's face. The image was visible to the McLaughlins, three rows back from the front. One by one, their heads dropped as they were confronted with the images it threw up of Siobhan's final moments.

They had met in an electrical factory, Yamaguchi, based in the west Dublin suburb of Mulhuddart. Brian was thirty-one, Siobhan ten years younger. He was employed there as an electrician, the trade into which he had followed his father. Siobhan was working in the canteen, pursuing a career in catering. "I thought she was older, she was so in control of the place," Kearney would reflect nearly twenty years later. "I asked her out a few times. Eventually she said yes."

Kearney was the eldest of a family of four. His parents, Bernard and Maeve, had settled in the Dundrum area soon after marrying in 1955. He was born two years later; a sister and two brothers followed over the following decade. His father had started his own electrical-contracting business, and as it became successful he had invested in property around the southside of the city.

Siobhan was one of a family of eight, seven girls and a boy. She grew up in Dalkey, a few miles from Dundrum. After leaving school, she studied to be a chef, completing her training in the Shelbourne Hotel. One of the couple's first dates was to the "afters" of the wedding of Siobhan's sister, Aisling, in 1989. This was the first occasion on which many of the McLaughlin family met Kearney. Over the following twenty years, through the ups and downs of his relationship with Siobhan, he never grew close to her siblings, most of whom remained in the south Dublin area and in close contact with Siobhan.

As their relationship blossomed, the couple decided to move in together. Siobhan was living in an apartment and Kearney in a house in Ballinteer. He was also raising his three-year-old daughter, Aoife. Siobhan gave up her apartment and moved in with them.

In 1995, the couple got engaged. In the same year, the engagement was broken off. There was much speculation as to the cause of the about turn. Some of Siobhan's family would later claim that Kearney was insisting on a pre-nuptial agreement, which Siobhan found distasteful.

Siobhan moved out and rented an apartment in Clontarf, on the far side of the Liffey. She threw herself into her work. By then, she had her own catering company and had acquired a contract as the main supplier to one of the city's major construction firms. Along the way, she also bought a house in Shankill. Eventually, though, the stress of self-employment in what is a cut-throat business had its repercussions, and in 1999 Siobhan checked herself into St John of God's psychiatric hospital for two weeks.

Although they had broken off their engagement, the couple still saw each other. Siobhan sometimes accompanied Kearney and Aoife on his boat on the Shannon. The prospect of reconciliation was always in the air.

In 2001, Siobhan became pregnant but miscarried. Later that year, she was pregnant again, and the couple decided to marry. The wedding took place in January 2002, and Daniel was born in July.

The couple honeymooned in Granada, in Spain, and on returning home stopped off at a boat show in London where they formed a plan to buy a boat in Spain with a view to spending a lot more time in the sun, work permitting. Later that year, they went back to Spain to check out their options. In Majorca, they visited the Hotel Salvia, and Siobhan promptly fell in love with the place. They decided to exploit it as a business opportunity. Siobhan intended to give up her business anyway, so why not run the hotel during the summer months? Her background in catering made her an ideal manager. And Kearney could commute between Dublin and Spain. Eventually, perhaps, they could move permanently to Majorca.

The hotel opened in March 2003. The couple had raised the €2.2 million they needed to buy it with a mortgage and the proceeds from the sale of Siobhan's house in Shankill.

Coming from a family background in business, Kearney had an eye for opportunity. He had bought a new house, Carnoe, in Dundrum, a few years before they married. The site on which Carnoe was built was large enough to accommodate another house. The property market was booming. You simply couldn't go wrong. He applied for planning permission, which was eventually granted. The house was completed in mid-2005.

By then, however, Siobhan wanted out of the marriage. There was no pressing matter prompting her actions, no violence that might necessitate a barring order, nothing in the line of an emergency. It's impossible to speculate on the exact reasons why, but it was clear that, for Siobhan, the marriage was over. The hotel was put up for sale. Her sister Brighid recommended a family-law solicitor, Hugh Hannigan. Siobhan made contact with him on 28 September but didn't follow through on an initial consultation for two months. On 7 December, Hannigan received a letter from her, including a request to send correspondence to her sister's address in Shankill rather than the Kearney family home in Goatstown. After that, there was no further contact until late January, when Siobhan attended a meeting with Hannigan, accompanied by Brighid and Aisling. Earlier that month, she and Kearney had holidayed in Austria. Whether or not the holiday prompted Siobhan to accelerate her divorce plan is unknown.

The process gathered pace. Hannigan sent a series of letters to Kearney outlining Siobhan's wish that the break-up be amicable, in the interests of three-year-old Daniel.

One of Siobhan's concerns was Kearney's plan to rent out the new house. She wanted to move into it, on a temporary basis at least, in order to accommodate an orderly break-up and make sure that Daniel was in close contact with both his parents through a stressful time.

The hotel was another pressing matter. There had been no takers for the business in the four months it had languished on the market. Kearney thought that Siobhan should go back to Majorca and continue to run it as a going concern. He needed the cash that would generate.

But Siobhan had had enough of the place. If her mind was fixed on bringing her marriage to an end that February, it was also occupied with Daniel's future. She got word that he had been accepted at the nearby

Our Lady's Grove primary school. To be on the safe side, she also had his name down for St Killian's on the Roebuck Road.

On the night of 26 February, she stayed with her sister Brighid in Shankill. Daniel was at home with his father. The following morning, she met Kearney at Kelleher's in the industrial estate, where he handed over Daniel. Later that morning, she rang for a hair appointment at Gerard Paul, just up the road from her home. She had been going there for eight years. She was told that Alice, who usually did her hair, wasn't in, but she would be back tomorrow. That was fine by Siobhan. She confirmed the appointment for 12.30 p.m. on Tuesday.

Some time after noon, she rang the Citizens Advice Bureau (CAB) in Sandyford. She wanted advice on legal separation. The secretary gave her an appointment for 9 March. She asked for an earlier appointment but was told they were all booked up. She could try the CAB office in Dun Laoghaire.

In the afternoon, Siobhan got ready to go into the city to meet a friend. At some stage before she left, she received a call from another friend, Carol Summers, with whom she had been out to dinner the previous week. Carol was calling from her home in Scotland to say she was coming over for the rugby international between Ireland and Scotland on 10 March. They arranged to meet on the Saturday of that weekend.

It was fast approaching 5 p.m. when Siobhan arrived, with Daniel in his buggy, in Bewley's of

Grafton Street to meet Anne Clohessy. The two friends talked for more than an hour, then walked across town to Anne's apartment in Wolfe Tone Street. Anne's partner, Julian Lawlor, was also home that evening. The couple had been to London and had brought back some toys for Daniel. Julian and he played on the floor, while the women talked and cooked.

Around 8.30 p.m., Siobhan said she and Daniel should go home, and Anne drove them out to Goatstown. When she dropped them off outside Carnroe, she noticed that Kearney's company van was in the driveway.

Later on that evening, Siobhan logged into cyberspace. Her brother Owen was living in Italy with his partner, Alessandra Benedetti, and two children. Alessandra had sent Siobhan some translations she had needed doing for the hotel. At some time after 11 p.m., Siobhan logged on to reply. "Hi there Ali," her email began. "How are Tom and Kevin? We are so thrilled you guys are coming over in April – can't wait to get my mitts on them." She went on to write that Daniel was "all action – I can't keep up with him, he is just mad out – wild, wild, wild. He loves Madonna and wants to listen to her CDs all day and then watch John Wayne movies. He's gun mad, football mad, can't sit down for one second. I lost three pounds last week. I hate to think about the time he is due to go to school. Say a prayer for me. Talk soon. Big love and kisses to all the famiglia. Love. Siobhan."

Siobhan logged off soon after and went down from

the attic to her bedroom. She may have slept soundly after a busy day. She may have tossed and turned, preoccupied by the travails of a disintegrating marriage. There is no precise time for her death, but the best estimate is some time after 6 a.m. and before her sister arrived at the house around 9.30 a.m.

In the court, the reading of Siobhan Kearney's last email was difficult for those closest to her. Aisling and Brighid were sobbing. A few metres away, sitting next to the defendant, Aoife Kearney also shed tears. Siobhan had been in her life since she was just three. Even over the years that Siobhan and Kearney had spent apart, Siobhan had kept in regular contact with Aoife and her father. Now he was on trial for killing her. As her last communication was read out, everyone was transported back two years, to an attic in south Co. Dublin, where a young woman at a keyboard articulated the joy she felt in motherhood.

Earlier in the trial, the white door that divided the master bedroom from the en-suite at Carnroe was displayed in court for the jury's benefit. It was from this door that any alleged suicide by hanging, was deemed to have taken place.

Throughout the trial, Kearney faced the front of the court. He turned into the room only when he spoke to his daughter or sister beside him. On some of those occasions, he took the opportunity to glance round the packed court, including the McLaughlins.

Frequently, he tapped the fingers of his right hand on the wooden surface in front of him.

The trial was interrupted in the second week by a juror's bereavement. It was, however, becoming obvious that it would take considerably longer than the estimated six weeks. However, the case of the People versus Brian Kearney was not as complicated as originally feared: most of the prosecution evidence went unchallenged. Most of the facts were agreed.

The day after the discovery of Siobhan Kearney's body, her husband gave a statement at his parents' house to Detective Sergeant Michael Gibbons. He recalled his seventeen-year on-off relationship with his wife, then fleshed out the details he had given when interviewed at Carnroe the previous day. On the Monday night he had come home and had a shower. After Siobhan and Daniel had arrived back, Siobhan had asked him to put Daniel to bed because he was over-excited. Kearney had slept with the child, taking him to the toilet at 2 a.m. when he woke.

He repeated the events of the morning, himself and Daniel downstairs, a DVD on for Daniel, shouting goodbye to Siobhan from outside the locked door.

The detective sergeant had taken down his statement and left. By then the gardaí were of the opinion that they were dealing with a murder, and there was only one suspect in their sights.

At 7.10 a.m. the next day, there was a knock on the door of the Kearney parents' house in Drumartin Road. Detective Sergeant Gibbons told Brian Kearney he was being arrested in connection with the death of his wife. The suspect was brought to Dundrum garda station. At around 8.45 a.m., Gibbons and a colleague began an interview. They informed Kearney that his wife hadn't died by suicide.

"I find that hard to believe," he replied.

"Somebody strangled her. Do you accept that?"

"If you say so."

"She is dead. She didn't kill herself, she was strangled," he was told.

"I didn't kill her. We didn't fight. We didn't have rows."

"Why did you kill Siobhan?"

"I didn't kill Siobhan."

The interview progressed along those lines for some minutes. The gardaí asked Kearney about the proposal to rent out the adjoining house. "Did she object to the property being let?"

"Yes, and I said no problem, and I was reasonably happy with it other than it would be claustrophobic."

The gardaí pursued this line.

"You had a good few rows over what was going to happen to the house?"

"No. There were bigger rows over the fireplace."

By 9.30 a.m., Kearney's solicitor had arrived at the station, and soon after that the interview ended. He was released later that day. Little of substance had emerged from the interview, apart from one crucial admission.

Early on, it was put to Kearney that when Siobhan had died there had been nobody in the house apart from himself and three-year-old Daniel.

"Correct," he replied, which implied an admission that no other party was in the frame for Siobhan's violent death. Either she had committed suicide, or Kearney had killed her. And over the months that followed, the theory that she had taken her own life crumbled in the light of the scientific facts.

The house alarm was examined. It had been activated on the Monday evening after 11 p.m., and was deactivated at 7.40 a.m., roughly the same time that Kearney maintained he had left the house. There were no signs of a break-in, according to a detailed check of all the downstairs windows and external doors. The possibility that any third party could have been involved was growing increasingly remote.

Incidental evidence was also collated by the gardaí. A search of Siobhan's bedroom revealed a €500 note, tucked safely away at the bottom of a chest of drawers. A further search of the house uncovered Siobhan's passport and a diary hidden behind the hotpress upstairs.

Motive was another matter. In cases of spousal homicide, motive is often tied up with jealousy. Research has shown that women who have been attacked or killed were most vulnerable at a time when the relationship was breaking up. While the Kearneys' marriage was coming to an end, neither appeared to have been involved with anybody else.

This pointed to the next most likely motive: money.

Here, it is not the profit from a killing that is the prime motivator but rather the fear of material loss that might result from the ending of a marriage or relationship.

The gardaí retained accountant Toni Massey to examine the family's finances. On paper, Brian Kearney was a wealthy man. A liquidation of the couple's assets could have yielded a sum of €5.1 million, €4.6 million net of tax. He had a 25 per cent stake in a family business, Associated Electrics. He was also a 20 per cent stakeholder in another family firm, which rented out properties on the southside of Dublin. But he owed a mortgage of €844,000 on the family home, and monthly repayments of €10,000 on the couple's hotel in Majorca. Although it had been for sale since the previous September, there had been no bid by the time Siobhan died.

Massey told the Central Criminal Court that the couple were heavily in debt. "They needed to sell an asset to reduce the €850,000 borrowed on the family home," she testified. "If they did that, they would be OK."

Kearney's solution would have been for the family to move into the new house and sell their existing home, thereby avoiding capital gains tax. But if Siobhan had moved into the new house during a separation, that avenue of relief would have been clogged up. Kearney's comfortable lifestyle and prospects of greater wealth later on were in clear danger if the break-up went ahead. The gardaí were satisfied that they had established a motive.

In the year after Siobhan's death, the case was kept in the public arena. The McLaughlin family were well known in the media, mainly through Brighid's former job as a high-profile journalist with the *Sunday Independent*. The search for Siobhan's killer was a regular source of stories. Her death had occurred at a time when there were a number of unresolved cases of women dying violently in their homes. In death, Siobhan Kearney became an iconic victim, somebody whose youth and photogenic qualities symbolised for the media the violent and random nature of crime. That nobody was charged with her murder for a prolonged period left the case wide open to comment and fed into the notion that violent crime was now going unresolved by the law.

Brian Kearney moved out of his home and into the new house next door, which he called Salvia, after the hotel in Spain. He gave Carnroe the new name Thornberry and rented it out.

On 10 December 2006, the McLaughlin family held the first of several vigils outside the house where Siobhan had died. Kearney, who was living next door, didn't attend.

At 6.50 a.m. on Wednesday, 30 May 2007 – fifteen months after his wife's death – Brian Kearney was arrested at his new home and charged with her murder. Some of the McLaughlin family, including the parents, attended the brief court hearing in Dun

Laoghaire where he was remanded in custody to Cloverhill Prison. A week later he was granted bail.

The trial came down to a single question: did Siobhan Kearney commit suicide? Of course it was possible that she was alive when her husband left at around 7.40 a.m. that morning. It was possible, too, that somebody had come into the house during the next two hours without forcing entry. It was even possible that this person had gone upstairs and gained entry to Siobhan's locked bedroom, strangled her and left, locking the door again on his way out. Anything was possible. Realistically, either she had died by her own hand or at the hand of her husband.

The pathology evidence, including the three fractures to Siobhan's Adam's apple, pointed towards manual strangulation, although the finding wasn't conclusive. One scenario Cassidy put before the court was that the killer had used his hands until Siobhan lost consciousness. Then he had finished off with the flex.

Dr Neal Murphy had performed a series of experiments to determine whether or not Siobhan could have hanged herself with the flex as had initially seemed the case. If she had done so, the most likely scenario was high-level suspension. This would have involved Siobhan hanging herself over the door that led from the bedroom into the en-suite. This would have required her to make a noose, throw the other end of the flex over the door and attach it to the handle on the far side. She would then have had to effect the hanging by raising herself up onto the noose.

It would have been possible to do this by standing on a stool or other small object and kicking it away. No such object was found anywhere near the body. The length of the flex was also a problem: it fell short of the handle on the other side of the door by five centimetres.

There was no break in the noose that would have resulted in her falling to where she was found. The far end was not attached to the door handle. And when Murphy had experimented using a weight equivalent to Siobhan's, the flex had snapped after five seconds. The whole scenario as presented to the court was highly unlikely, veering towards impossible.

Low-level suspension, from a door handle or a handle on the vanity unit, was also unlikely. The break on the flex would have been different, and again there should have been a noose round Siobhan's neck when she was found.

In Kearney's favour, the Hoover found in the bedroom and the Hoover flex were tested for his DNA but found negative. Another, unidentified, male's DNA was found on the Hoover.

At the conclusion of the state's case, Kearney's lawyer, Patrick Gageby, applied to the judge to have the jury discharged. The state hadn't proved its case, he said. They had nothing but circumstantial evidence and therefore should have established every separate leg of the case in evidence. It was also pointed out to Judge White that Professor Cassidy had left open the possibility that

Siobhan was alive when Kearney had left the house that morning. The judge dismissed the application.

Summing up for the prosecution, Dominic McGinn made reference to the charged atmosphere in the court. "This can't be easy on Brian Kearney or his family. But this isn't about which family do you prefer . . . do you feel more sympathy for one family or the other." He ran through every strand of the evidence, then put forward his theory on Siobhan's death.

"Brian Kearney must have gone in that morning and something caused him to put his hands around her neck and begin to strangle her.

"It's impossible to know for how long the manual strangulation went on, but at some stage he grabbed the flex and put a knot through the flex to strangle her. After killing her he attempted to make it look like suicide . . . but the second knot never reached the handle of the door.

"Once the flex broke, he abandoned further attempts – he knew Niamh McLaughlin was going to arrive shortly. He locked the door and threw the key underneath.

"The scientific evidence contradicts any other reasonable conclusion."

Gageby put forward a different take on the evidence. He told the jury to beware of science, citing the Birmingham Six and the Guildford Four cases in which the science had been shown to be flawed. Also, if Kearney had staged a suicide, "Why isn't he spinning a story about suicide in the days after?" he asked.

He also cautioned them to consider very carefully the evidence that his client's DNA was not found on the Hoover while that of another man had been.

The next day, Tuesday 4 March, Judge Barry White summed up, signalling his awareness that there had been huge interest in this particular trial. "Ladies and gentlemen, the law treats everybody as equal. The law is the same whether you are rich or poor." After 4 p.m. the jury retired. Nobody realistically expected a verdict that evening, and so it turned out. They reconvened the following morning at 10.30 a.m.

At 3.20 p.m., Judge White recalled them and told them he would now accept a majority verdict. Minutes later, Brian Kearney was seen walking around the Four Courts car park with his brother, Niall. He walked over and back from the exit a couple of times. He may well have guessed that his life was about to change for ever. Either he would be able to put the death of his wife behind him, or he would be imprisoned on a life sentence. If the latter were to be imposed, that walk would represent the last time for many years to come that he would be free to do something as innocuous as stroll around a car park. It must have been a sobering thought for a man of fifty-one.

At 3.45 p.m., the jury foreman knocked on the door. They had a verdict. Within minutes the court was packed. Judge White entered and said he would appreciate it if there were no emotional or triumphant outbursts when the verdict had been read. Aoife Kearney clung to her father's arm. The McLaughlins clasped hands.

The court registrar read out the 11–1 majority verdict: "Guilty." Immediately, Aoife Kearney was sobbing into her father's shoulder. He remained impassive. The McLaughlins appeared to sag with the relief that justice, as they saw it, had been done. Lauri Kearney, just down the bench from her brother, threw herself into a relative's arms, her whole body racked with sobs.

Judge White handed down the mandatory sentence. As Kearney stood, his daughter clung to his arm. The judge refused a request for a victim-impact statement to be read out in court by Deirdre McLaughlin. He said there was no legislative provision for such a statement.

Afterwards, before the prison officers came for him, Brian Kearney took off his wedding band and handed it to his daughter. He hugged her, his brothers, sister and other relatives before he left.

Outside, the McLaughlins were heading towards the public entrance of the Four Courts when a prison van entered the car park. Somebody said it would be taking Kearney away. The family and their friends waited beside the van as it was brought up to a door.

Within minutes, Kearney was whisked outside and into the van, a brown overnight bag thrown in after him. As the van pulled out, there was a muted round of applause.

At the entrance, the family had to be brought back inside the gates as the media hordes threatened to overwhelm them. Then Aisling McLaughlin stepped forward and, in a clear, strong voice, read a prepared statement.

"The faith and trust that we have had in our criminal justice system has not been misplaced, and we have not been let down. Today Siobhan has got justice, we have got justice, and Siobhan's murderer has got justice, and for that, we are most thankful.

"Since that day, Tuesday, 28 February 2006, our lives have been utterly destroyed by this brutal and pointless act of savagery, from which they cannot, nor ever will, be the same. As a very close family we are haunted by the fact that we were not able to help Siobhan that morning – that she was alone in the last and the worst minutes of her life – unaware that the place she felt safest in was, in fact, the most treacherous. We agree with Pavel Kalite's sister that people who do these things cease to be human."[1]

"We are so blessed to have known and to have someone as special as Seanie in our lives, but we miss her every hour of the day, and the unbearable longing to see her, to hold her and to protect her never leaves you, even though you know it's too late.

"But Siobhan has been with us every day since that day, she has never moved, and she continues to live in each one of us – she is strong and she has given us extraordinary strength to keep going. Siobhan needs peace now, to sleep peacefully, knowing that everything that can be done has been done.

---

[1] Pavel Kalite was a Polish man who had been murdered in a random attack in Dublin the previous week

"We would like to thank all the gardaí who worked on this case, and particularly Detective Inspector Martin Cummins and Detective Sergeant Michael Gibbons for their dedication to Siobhan and their unwavering commitment to bringing the person responsible for her murder to face justice. It means so much to us that when Michael Gibbons arrived at the scene he said a prayer over Siobhan.

"We thank the office of the DPP, Mr Denis Vaughan Buckley, Mr Dominic McGinn, Sandra Manthe and Aisling Kelly; we thank the ambulance and fire crews who arrived that morning to try and help Siobhan, and we thank Father Ivan Tonge.

"Finally, we can only say thank you to all our friends and to the many, many people we have met during this time, for their great kindness, support and love."

A few minutes later, the family filed out the gate and made their way home to attempt to effect some degree of closure. The Kearney family left quietly by another exit.

In 2006, there were sixty recorded murders committed in the state with another six violent killings classified as manslaughter.

4. LOOSE TONGUES

The Case of Thomas Murray

Christmas Eve, 1969. In the remand wing of Limerick Prison, two inmates get talking. Andrew Murphy is awaiting trial on a charge of larceny of jewellery worth £6,000. He is harbouring a secret that won't go beyond his lips. The loot is hidden, and nobody else will be getting their hands on it.

His confidant is Thomas Murray, a twenty-eight-year-old from Tipperary. He has his own secret. He is charged with the murder of his wife, but he claims to know nothing about it. Now he wants to unburden himself of a few things that are bothering him and a few others on which he needs information.

The two men huddle close against the cold. Murphy is all ears. Thomas Murray begins to talk, relating the events of 12 September 1969, the evening wife's life came to a violent end. Mary Murray had

138

been found strangled and battered to death at her home in Cork city. Murray told the gardaí he had nothing to do with it. He had returned from a walk to find that his bride of five months had been viciously assaulted by an intruder. Her life was ebbing away when he got to the house so he had run to get help from a neighbour.

The cops didn't believe him, and, after a number of interviews, he was charged. He made one incriminating statement, which would ultimately be disputed. If he had a role in his wife's death, its exact nature remained unclear at the time he was charged. Still, the gardaí felt there was enough evidence for a successful prosecution.

Anyway, on Christmas Eve of 1969, Murray's tongue loosened. He and Murphy hadn't known each other before circumstances had thrust them together under the one roof in the big house. Men do strange things when they find themselves together in prison. For those who are unaccustomed to periodic or lengthy stretches behind bars, for those who didn't grow into adulthood knowing the inside of penal institutions, it is easy to believe that an elevated kinship exists between inmates. Maybe that was what prompted Murray to tell Murphy how he had killed his wife and how he intended to beat the rap.

He began by telling the robber (Murphy would later be sentenced to three years on the larceny charge) that the gardaí wanted to take a blood sample from him. His wife had been pregnant at the time of her death. One avenue of investigation on which the gardaí were embarking was that Murray wasn't the father of the child. As a novice in dealing with the forces of law and order, Murray was looking for some advice. Would he be forced to give a blood sample, and what might it prove?

"I told him that in English law such a test could not prove that he was the father of a child, but it could help to prove that he was not," Murphy later recalled.

Then, in hushed tones, the killer told him what had happened on the night his wife died.

He had been in a very bad mood on the day in question. Mary had come home, and they had had an argument about the amount of food in the house. It had been her last day at work: she had given up because of her pregnancy. After the row, Murray went into another room and settled down with a book he was reading about a man who had committed a murder.

Later, the row resumed. At some stage, Mary told Murray that he wasn't the father of the child she was carrying. The tension increased. Mary told him she wanted to return £25 to her mother in repayment of a loan. Murray turned to her and said: "Why don't you keep it for the kid? I'm not buying anything for it if it's not mine."

Then he made a dive for his wife. He grabbed her around the neck and squeezed. "He showed me how he did it," Murphy said. Mary Murray lost consciousness.

At some stage, Murray went out to his car and returned with a tyre lever, which he left in the kitchen.

"When she seemed to be coming through, he ran into the kitchen and picked up the tyre lever and gave her a few whacks of it across the head," Murphy said. "He said he left her lying on the floor; the place was all blood. He took his trousers and shirt off and washed the tyre lever and his hands in the bathroom. He put some clean clothes on and put the bloodied clothes and the tyre lever in a carrier bag. The time was somewhere around 8.45 p.m."

Murray took the bag out to his car, drove up the Old Youghal Road and turned off into a side road. He hid the carrier bag underneath some rubbish on the verge but retrieved the tyre lever and brought it back to the car. He drove on, until he arrived at what he considered an appropriate spot. The city of Cork was now fading in the car's rear-view mirror. He took the tyre lever from the car and buried it in a field adjacent to the road so that, he told Murphy, "It would be like a needle in a haystack."

He drove home and switched on the TV, which would serve as an alibi. He would be able to tell the gardaí what he had been watching. *The Saint* was on.

He left the house again at 9.27 p.m., to go for the walk in order to bolster his alibi. He saluted a man he knew. He stopped to talk to three young girls, so he would be remembered. He returned home at 9.55 p.m. He unlocked the back door, to make it look as if there had been a break-in or an attempted robbery. Then he knelt down beside his wife and picked her up, ensuring that he got blood on his clean clothes, authenticating his story that he had arrived home to find her the victim of an assault. Then he ran from the house, screaming, as if he had just made the most horrendous discovery.

In the course of their conversation, with the background noise of steel on steel echoing through the corridors of the prison, Murray brought up the case of an American criminal, Caryl Chessman. Murphy hadn't heard of Chessman, but he had been a cause célèbre around the world. Murray had read all about Chessman.

Throughout the 1950s, Chessman had been on Death Row for kidnapping two women. He wrote three books during his time in jail, and his case had been taken up by prison reformers and show-business types around the world. At one point, a city council in Mexico had requested that he be granted a reprieve.

Chessman was represented by a famous US lawyer, George T. Davis, who was vehemently opposed to the death penalty. Davis pioneered the concept of using hypnosis in the criminal-justice system as a defence. The idea was to subject a defendant to hypnosis to show that he was telling the truth when he denied being responsible for the crime of which he was accused.

The idea had a mixed reception. It was predicated on the notion that hypnosis was a form of truth serum, which it is not. Hypnosis allows access to the subconscious mind, which can allow a subject to recall events that their conscious mind may have forgotten, or blocked out.

However, the subconscious is also the seat of personal values. If a person is inclined to lie when he or she is conscious, then they will probably do so when they are under hypnosis.

Having read about Chessman, and his lawyer's methods, Murray was well up on this stuff. As a result, he told Murphy, he had offered to undergo hypnosis in the days after his wife's death. This would stand in his favour in any trial. The result would enable his lawyer to point out that he mustn't be guilty because he didn't reveal anything incriminating while under hypnosis. (What Murray may not have told Murphy is that after numerous appeals, and despite a repeal of the law that had condemned him to death, Caryl Chessman went to the gas chamber on 2 May 1960.)

Murray said he was confident of beating the rap, but he peppered Murphy with questions that suggested he wasn't as confident as he appeared. "Would I have got away with it if I said it happened under a blackout?" Murray asked Murphy.

"Why don't you make it manslaughter?" Murphy asked.

"I can't. It's neither up nor down. I had a motive," Murray replied.

The motive was Mary's pregnancy. Murray said he wasn't the father of the child. "That's what I'm trying to tell you. She was eight months pregnant when I killed her," he said. When the couple had married the previous April, Murray was under the impression that Mary was six weeks pregnant, which would tally with the only time the couple had had intercourse prior to the wedding. As it turned out, he knew now, she had been three months pregnant at the time.

He told his confidant that he had not known what kind of woman his wife was before he married her, and if he had, he would never have got involved.

"Why wasn't the child saved by Caesarean section?" Murphy asked.

"I'm glad it wasn't," Murray replied. "The child could have had different blood to mine, and the guards would then have a motive." Ultimately, Murray felt he wouldn't be convicted. He had told the gardaí that the child was his, no question about it. And, crucially, the murder weapon had never been found.

If the worst came to the worst at the trial, he might say he had done it during a blackout.

And if he was convicted, he was going to sort one man out when he was released. At Mary's funeral, her brother had come up to him and said, "Have you got a solicitor yet?" That man, Murray told his fellow inmate, would be the first to get it with the tyre lever on the head when he got out.

At the end of the conversation, Murphy went back to his cell. He was disturbed by what he had heard. He was no angel, but there was a world of difference between robbing jewellery and battering a woman to death.

Over the next few days, he had trouble sleeping. He went to a doctor but the medical help he received did little to ease his conscience. He went to a priest, and told him the outline of what he had heard, without revealing the specific details. The priest told him that the matter was obviously on his conscience, and if he didn't do something to relieve it, there it would remain for the rest of his life.

Fortified with this evaluation of his dilemma, Andrew Murphy requested to speak to a garda in order to relate what he knew about the forthcoming trial of Thomas Murray for the murder of his wife Mary.

On the evening of 12 September 1969, Gerard Daly was working on his garden. Daly and his wife Joan lived on Mayfield Road, on the northside of Cork city. He was employed as a director with Jeremiah O'Connor and Sons, a well-known undertaking firm based in Coberg Street. Mayfield Road was then at the outskirts of the city, consisting mainly of a ribbon of bungalows. The Dalys were one of the few families in the area with a phone. Gerard Daly required one so that he could respond to a call from work at any time of the day or night.

Taking advantage of the stretch in the evenings, Daly was in the garden well past 9.30 p.m. Suddenly he heard shouts and screams. He figured they came from next door, but then they stopped. They had been a man's screams, he thought. He went back to work.

A few minutes later, he heard more roaring, this time apparently from the front of his own home. He went to the door, opened it and saw Thomas Murray in an agitated state.

He had known Murray by sight for the last few months since Murray and his wife had moved into Annaville, the bungalow next door. He had never seen Murray as he looked now. There was blood on Murray's hands and face, and his shirt was blotched with it. He grabbed Daly's arms, in the manner of a man who is pleading for something.

At that point, Daly's wife Joan joined them. Through his incoherence, she made out that he was saying something was wrong with his wife, Mary.

Joan Daly had seen little of the Murrays since they had moved in next door. She knew their names. They appeared to be a happy couple. Mary was pregnant, and Joan had assumed they were excited to be embarking on family life.

She followed Murray and her husband across to the house next door. The two men walked in first. When Joan Daly went into the dining room, she saw the body on the floor. The television was on. Immediately, she hurried home, picked up her telephone and rang the gardaí and the local priest, Father Gerard Kelleher.

Over in the Murrays' house, Gerard Daly was taking in the scene before him. Voices droned from the TV. One of the chairs in the room was upturned. By then, Murray had gone to his wife's prostrate body.

"Why did it have to happen to you, Mary?" Murray said. "You were so good . . . Why did I leave you? . . . Mary, attacked."

Daly went over to him and half carried him to one of the chairs. Then he knelt by the body. He checked for a pulse and thought he felt one. He bent down near the woman's ear and began praying: "Oh, my God, I am heartily sorry for having offended Thee, and I detest my sins, above every other evil, because they displease Thee . . ." He whispered the full act of contrition into her ear.

Garda Francis O'Callaghan arrived a few minutes later. As he entered the house, Murray and Daly were coming out of the living room. Daly had a word with the garda, then directed Murray into another room. It was bare. Daly went out, got a chair and brought it back to Murray. The bereaved husband sat into it, sobbing.

In the living room, Garda O'Callaghan surveyed the crime scene. The woman's body was lying near one wall. An orange glow emanated from the fireplace. It was obvious that nobody had tended it for some time.

The woman's head was close to the skirting board, resting in a pool of blood. Her right hand was outstretched towards the fireplace, and her left hand was across her forehead. The TV, he noticed, was switched on at a low volume.

O'Callaghan went into the kitchen. There was no light on in this room, but he observed that the back door leading from it was slightly ajar. Then he went to the room where Daly was comforting Murray. He noticed that the latter had blood on his clothes and face, and that his hair was tossed. He looked like a man in profound shock. The garda located a bottle of brandy and a glass and brought it to Murray.

"His hands were constantly moving, and his whole body was twitching as if he was in a shocked state of nerves," the garda would later say. He offered Murray the drink but quickly realised the man wasn't even able to take the glass. He held it to Murray's lips. After sipping, Murray had one question to ask. "Is Mary all right? She's giving up her job tomorrow."

Soon after, Father Gerard Kelleher arrived. He attended to Mary Murray's spiritual needs, then talked privately with Thomas. In the subsequent murder trial, Father Kelleher would claim privilege on his conversation with Murray that night.

At 10.45 p.m., Dr Patrick Hennessy attended the scene. He concluded that the twenty-two-year-old woman was dead as a result of head injuries. The body was still warm, but the presence of a fire in the room might have contributed to keeping it so longer than would be normal after death. In the doctor's opinion, Mary Murray had died within the previous two hours.

Superintendent Thomas Kenny of MacCurtain Street garda station had a chat with Murray at 11.10 p.m. "What happened?" the garda wanted to know.

Murray told him he had been out for a walk for

about half an hour or forty minutes. *The Saint* had been on the TV when he was going out. He had walked down as far as the Cotton Ball, a well-known pub in Mayfield, intending to go in for a drink, but then changed his mind and kept walking. When he arrived home, he went into the dining room where he found his wife lying on the floor. The light was switched off, but he could see her body by the light of the TV screen. Before he left on the walk, his wife had been sitting in front of the TV and the light was on. When he returned, he knelt down beside her and lifted her up. He began shouting and ran from the house.

"Do you know who might have killed your wife?" the superintendent asked him.

"I have no idea at all," Murray replied. "We had no enemies."

By then, just over an hour after the discovery of the body, the gardaí knew enough to launch a murder inquiry.

Thomas Murray was from Templederry, a hamlet some ten miles from Nenagh in Co. Tipperary. After leaving school, he spent two years studying agriculture at Belcamp College in Dublin. From there, he returned home to a position as a bartender in a pub in the Glen of Aherlow, in the same area of Tipperary.

The bartending didn't pay much, so after a spell he went to work on the family farm. In 1965, armed with £250 from his father, he emigrated to New Zealand.

At the time, Australia and New Zealand were offering attractive incentives to entice Europeans to go Down Under to boost the two countries' emerging economies.

Once there, he attempted to settle into a new life, but the pull of home was strong. Another nagging feature of life in New Zealand was the prospect of being conscripted to serve in Vietnam. That was enough to send Thomas Murray home in September 1967 after eighteen months in New Zealand.

Once back in Tipperary, he didn't return to the family farm. He worked initially for a seed manufacturing firm in Waterford, before finding a position as a gardening supervisor at Gouldings, an agriculture-supply firm in Cork.

Mary Walsh was six years younger than Thomas Murray. She was a native of Borrisleigh, a small town around eight miles from Thurles. On leaving school, she had worked as a barmaid. She spent one season in the then fashionable holiday camp Butlins, in Mosney, Co. Meath, before returning home. When Thomas came back from New Zealand, Mary was working at a public house in Nenagh.

The couple had known each other for a number of years before Thomas emigrated. It is unclear exactly when they started seeing each other seriously. In August 1968, an incident occurred that suggested Thomas was serious about their relationship. At some point in that month, Mary was "missing" for a few days, during which it turned out she had been to Dublin. Thomas was under the impression that she was away seeing another man. Mary would later tell friends that when they were reunited, Thomas grabbed her by the cheeks and told her that if she ever went away again he would kill her.

The couple were married on 29 April 1969. Sexual mores at the time in Ireland determined that sex before marriage was not widespread and most certainly was not publicly acknowledged. After Mary's death, Thomas would say that he and Mary had only had intercourse once before their wedding.

By Friday, 12 September, the day she died, Mary Murray was eight months pregnant, indicating that conception occurred some three months before she was married. This was at least six weeks before Thomas's estimate of their only pre-marital sexual encounter. Whether Thomas only became aware of this discrepancy on the final night of his wife's life became an issue in the murder investigation.

Once married, the couple continued to live locally, until Thomas acquired his position with Gouldings in Cork. They moved down there in June. They took the bungalow in Mayfield, but the weekly rent proved to be a drain on their finances. At the beginning of August, Mary began working as cashier in the Grand Canyon amusement arcade on Grand Parade, in the centre of the city. Thomas earned between £25 and £30 a week, while Mary took home six.

Like most of the population, the couple struggled to make ends meet. They weren't well off, but they appeared to be relatively happy, setting out on a new life together, with the first addition to their family on the way. That scenario, whether it was real or illusory, came to a violent end on the evening of 12 September. The post-mortem on Mary Murray's body would confirm that she was carrying a female infant, weighing four and a half pounds; it was only a month short of reaching full term.

Ninety minutes after the discovery of the body, Thomas Murray was interviewed in MacCurtain Street garda station. He returned the following morning and made a formal statement. For the most part, the detail was consistent with his version of events the previous evening.

At 11.30 a.m., he identified his wife's body. Three hours later, his brother James came and collected him from the garda station and brought him back home to Templederry, to await the funeral.

On the Saturday, detectives from the murder squad were dispatched from Dublin. As in most domestic cases, the husband or partner was immediately under the spotlight. Murray's alibi was curious. The walk he described included a number of different encounters with people or sightings of others. The descriptions he gave were vivid. Experienced gardaí knew that if somebody was asked about a journey or walk they had undertaken, there were various things they might remember. Murray seemed to remember an awful lot, far more than might be expected of somebody out for an evening stroll. It was nearly as if he had been specifically looking at people and things so that he would remember them for later reference.

However, the gardaí still had to consider all possibilities.

A questionnaire was prepared for delivery to all homes in the Mayfield area. Local intelligence from officers on the beat and members of the public was broken down and analysed. Over the past weeks there had been occasional reports of what were then referred to as "Peeping Toms" in the area. These men got their kicks from looking through the windows of private homes in the hope of seeing women in a state of undress. While this activity was distasteful, the gardaí made it known that the culprits were not considered dangerous.

There had been a report on the Friday evening of another incident, a mile or so away from the Murray home. A young woman had been the victim of an assault and attempted rape. Enquiries were made as to whether it might be linked to the murder of Mary Murray but within the first forty-eight hours of the investigation, this was discounted.

Officially, the gardaí were giving little away about whom they were putting in the frame. "We have no suspect at present," Superintendent Kenny told the *Cork Examiner*, "and we are keeping an open mind on the situation."

Locating the murder weapon was the most urgent task. The hedges that bordered Annaville were searched, as were the gardens of houses up and down Mayfield Road. A building site just off the road attracted attention: steel reinforcing rods were brought into consideration. Despite the gardaí's best efforts, though, no weapon was located in the immediate aftermath of the killing.

On the Sunday, as the gardaí combed through the area, priests in the two Mayfield churches urged mass-goers to give them every possible assistance. The death of a young woman, albeit only a recent addition to the community, had sent shockwaves across the north of the city.

On Sunday evening, Mary Murray's body was taken from the city morgue and brought to Borrisleigh church for removal. Thomas Murray was in the church, as were a number of plain-clothes detectives. The shared feeling of bereavement that permeates the burial ritual also had to accommodate a degree of tension. Mary Murray was dead, and as her family and friends gathered to say farewell, there was no escaping the heightened suspicions.

The Requiem Mass on the Tuesday was packed. Thomas Murray noticed the tension that seemed to be directed at him. At one stage during the morning, Mary's father approached him: "Tom," he said, "you know you did it. Why don't you give yourself up?"

Thomas didn't respond.

In the course of another encounter, Mary's brother asked him sharply, "Have you got a solicitor yet?"

Following the burial, Thomas didn't attend at the

Walsh family home but instead invited some work colleagues who had travelled to the funeral back to his own parents' home for a meal. While they were there, local garda Hubert Finnerty called. Finnerty was a friend of the family. He told Murray that the detectives in Cork would appreciate it if he would go down to sort out a few details about his statement. Murray agreed and travelled to Cork with Finnerty and some of his work colleagues who were returning home.

At around 7.30 p.m. that evening he gave another statement to the gardaí at MacCurtain Street. The gist of the information was the same as he had provided in his statement of two days previously. Murray emphasised to the gardaí that he wanted to find out the truth of how Mary had died. To this end, he suggested that he see a hypnotist in case he had blacked out due to shock. Hypnosis might enable him to remember events exactly as they had occurred.

The request was unusual. It was passed up the line to Superintendent Kenny. As the clock ticked into a new day, he came in to see Murray and asked him if he wanted to see a hypnotist.

"I will go to anyone you select," Murray said. "But I want a qualified man, I don't want to go to a quack."

Superintendent Kenny asked him how he thought his wife had been killed.

"I could have come in and found her with a man and I . . ." The sentence trailed off as Murray was racked with sobs. The decision was taken to accompany him to Dublin to see a hypnotist.

Murray's family was contacted, and his brother James agreed to go with him. One of the gardaí present, Inspector Daniel Murphy, was assigned to travel with them. After a few hours' sleep, the party set off for Dublin on the morning of 16 September.

At St Luke's Hospital in Dublin, Murray was met by Dr Jack Gibson, a surgeon who also practised hypnosis. In the presence of James Murray and Inspector Murphy, he set to work on his patient.

Within minutes, Murray went into a deep trance. The doctor began asking him questions about the night of Mary's death. Murray appeared to be having very clear visual hallucinations of his wife. He described himself kissing her before he went out for his walk. She had not wanted to go out because of her advanced pregnancy. He described his journey down to the Cotton Ball. He looked in through the window but couldn't see anybody he knew. He stood outside for a while, listening to the music wafting out from the pub.

He began walking home. At this stage, Dr Gibson pierced Murray's right hand with a pin and pushed it through to the other side. The exercise was to determine whether Murray was really in a trance. There was no reaction from the patient, indicating that he was under deep hypnosis.

Murray then described arriving home and seeing Mary, battered and bleeding. A chair in the room was upturned. At this point of the hypnosis, he became very agitated.

The doctor moved on to another topic. Did he think anybody had had an affair with his wife since they had begun going out together?

Murray mentioned a man named Murphy in Dublin. He became agitated again. Dr Gibson asked him would he kill this man. No, Murray replied, he certainly wouldn't go that far. Soon after, the doctor eased his patient back to full consciousness.

"My impression was, whether or not he killed his wife, that he did not know anything about it. He appeared to have no recollection of any kind of having done anything to her," Dr Gibson would later report. The issue of whether or not a patient could limit what he might reveal under hypnosis was eventually explored in court.

The exercise completed, Inspector Murphy brought the two brothers for a few drinks in a city pub. Soon after, the party left Dublin and returned south. The garda dropped the Murrays at Templederry and carried on back to Cork. From the investigation point of view, the excursion to the hypnotist had done little to move things forward. By that stage, there was no other suspect. The gardaí were back to the painstaking business of gathering evidence.

The following day, accompanied by Garda Finnerty, Murray travelled over to Borrisleigh, to the home of Mary's parents. He was brought in and addressed the bereaved couple in a sombre tone. "I came down to tell you, if you did not already know, I didn't kill Mary, but we had our rows." The Walshes nodded in acknowledgement and added that they were hoping and praying all the time that he had not done it.

For the following two weeks, Murray stayed at home in Templederry. Practically every day, Garda Finnerty called to see him. They talked about Mary's death in some detail. In Cork, the investigating officers combed through the evidence, particularly attempting to piece together the threads of Murray's alibi.

On 1 October, Garda Finnerty came calling again to the Murray household in Templederry. The lads in Cork would like another word with him. The two men drove down to the city.

At MacCurtain Street, Murray was informed that there were discrepancies between his evidence and that of other witnesses. In particular, the times he had given for his walk – which formed the basis of his alibi – differed from those supplied by witnesses he had encountered on the way. They wanted another statement.

He agreed to give it. At first, he maintained the narrative of his previous statement. It was pointed out to him again that there were discrepancies. The clock was pushing towards midnight. Murray, sitting in the interview room, went silent. He began rubbing his hands as he looked down at the floor. He raised his head and addressed the officers. "I done it," he said. "I done it."

The next statement was entirely confessional in tone. He had come home that evening as described.

"Mary asked me what would I say if she told me the baby she was expecting was not mine," he said. "I thought she was joking. Then she told me that the baby wasn't mine. She said it a couple of times."

Lost in a blind panic, he hit her on the head. He didn't remember much of the detail after that. He had no memory of getting the jack from the car. (Later, he would claim the murder weapon was a tyre lever.) There was, however, no departing from the main thrust of his confession. He had killed his wife that night after she had told him she was carrying somebody else's child.

When he was done confessing, he said he was glad it was over. He turned to Garda Finnerty, the local man from home, whom he could trust. "I can't believe it. I was going to say it to you today. I needed something to convince me. I couldn't and wouldn't believe it. I am glad it is over."

At 1 a.m. on 2 October 1969, Murray was charged with the murder of his wife on the previous 12 September. When asked if he had anything to say, he replied, "No." He was remanded in custody.

The case against Thomas Murray appeared to be strong rather than watertight. He had confessed, albeit not in great detail. He certainly had a motive. His behaviour after the killing might sway a jury to opt for a murder verdict rather than manslaughter.

Then, on Christmas Eve, Murray opened up to his

fellow inmate, Andrew Murphy. Murphy's statement brought the case on further but also threw up a few anomalies. To the gardaí, Murray had suggested he had used a jack from the car as the murder weapon. In talking to Murphy, he had said the weapon was a tyre lever, which he had buried in an unknown location. The details of the row, how it started and how it had advanced, were also different. Still, in the round, his prison confession added further ballast to the prosecution case.

In March of the following year, the guards had another break. A second prisoner came forward with details of a conversation with Murray. Patrick McLaurence was serving two years for safebreaking when Murray had told him about the murder in similar detail to what he had said to Andrew Murphy. McLaurence took notes of the conversation immediately afterwards and contacted the gardaí. The case was now a lot stronger than it had been on the night Murray was charged.

The murder trial opened in the Central Criminal Court on Monday, 4 May 1970, before Mr Justice Kenny. Murray pleaded not guilty before the court. The case for the prosecution was outlined by W. R. Ellis. He brought the jury through the events of 12 September, how the accused had reacted and the subsequent statements he had made to the gardaí. This included the incriminating statement of 1 October.

He also referred to the conversations Murray had had with the two inmates in Limerick Prison.

The evidence began in the afternoon with the first witness, Joan Daly, who told of Murray knocking at her door on the evening in question.

Then Father Gerard Kelleher was called. When he took the stand, he told the judge he wished to claim privilege over his evidence. After a short consultation between the judge and the lawyers, the priest was told his evidence would not be required.

On day two, the garda evidence dominated the proceedings. Superintendent Kenny was the main witness. He was brought through his various encounters with the accused from 12 September right up until the crucial 1 October interview. At that point, Murray's barrister rose to his feet and asked that the jury be retired so that he could make a submission. His problem was with the admissibility of the statement taken on 1 October.

The judge told the jury to go home. They came back the following day and were sent out again. The court sat late on that Wednesday. Legal argument in the absence of the jury continued into the Thursday. Later that day, the jury was recalled.

Justice Kenny told them he had to discharge them from their duty. "It is not desirable that I should say anything about why," he told them. They were free to go, but Murray wasn't. He was remanded in custody until a new trial could be fixed.

The whole argument centred on whether or not

that statement was admissible and whether the manner in which it had been taken breached Murray's constitutional rights. After he had heard all submissions from both sides, Justice Kenny ruled that the statement was inadmissible on the basis that it breached Murray's constitutional rights due to the manner in which he had been detained that evening. The problem was that in opening the case, the prosecuting counsel, Ellis, had made reference to the statement. Therefore, the jury had heard the bones of a piece of evidence that the judge had now ruled was not to be put before them.

The ruling considerably weakened the case against Murray. Now all the prosecution had was a largely circumstantial case, coupled with the admissions he had made to the two prisoners.

The second trial got under way the following month, on 8 June before Justice O'Keeffe. This one went the distance. The most interesting evidence came from the defence. Opening the defence case, David Goldberg told the jury that the state had based its case on the timing Murray had given for his walk. This, he said, was entirely irrelevant because the actual time of Mary Murray's death could not be precisely determined. "Did it matter what time he left the house unless they knew the time of his wife's death?"

Then he turned to the incriminating statements to the two inmates. Murray admitted talking to one of them but completely denied ever saying that he had killed his wife.

"Is it not a very strange thing for these two men, without any prior arrangement with one another, to go off and write down everything they said Murray had told them?" the counsel asked the jury. There was only one conclusion they could come to: "That this is one of the greatest conspiracies and untruthful pieces of evidence ever produced in court by two men who would go to any lengths to get remission of their sentences."

Murray took the stand in his own defence. He outlined the details as he had done in his earlier statements to the gardaí. He had gone out. He had returned to a scene of horror. "I then saw my wife lying in a pool of blood with her head over against the wall. To the best of my knowledge, I picked her up and asked what had happened to her. She did not answer and she made some kind of sound like a gurgle."

The next thing he remembered was being outside with Mr Daly, the neighbour who brought him back to his own house. The police and a priest had then arrived.

The hypnotist, Dr Gibson, was also called for the defence. He told of the exercise in which he had taken part and his conclusion that Murray knew nothing of the killing.

Cross-examined by Seamus Egan SC, the doctor agreed that the general perception was that hypnosis was some form of a truth test, but this was not necessarily the case.

In response to a question from the judge, Gibson

said that he could not completely rule out that a person having decided to undergo a test could also have made up his mind what he was going to say under hypnosis.

The jury retired to consider a verdict at 3.50 p.m. on 15 June, the sixth day of the trial. At 9.05 p.m., they returned. The foreman informed the judge they had not reached a verdict and there was really no hope of doing so. There was no visible reaction from Murray in the dock.

Justice O'Keeffe discharged the jury and put the trial down for a new date. He remanded Murray in custody until the following day, when a bail application could be made. The application was successful, and Murray was released to await the third trial.

It was five months later that Murray was back in court, before Justice Sean Butler this time. The trial's pattern followed that of the second. Apart from the circumstantial evidence, the case was largely built around the prison confessions.

Andrew Murphy and Patrick McLaurence gave evidence of the incriminating conversations they had had with the defendant. Murray said again that he had never spoken to McLaurence. He had had a conversation with Murphy, but all he had revealed was that the gardaí suspected he was not the father of the unborn child.

The defence also called Patrick Treacy, who had met Murphy and McLaurence while on remand in

Limerick Prison the previous February. Treacy told the court that the two men had told him they had made up the statements they gave to the gardaí about conversations with Murray. They did this, Treacy alleged, so that they might get a reduction in their own sentences.

Cross-examined by Egan for the prosecution, Treacy said he had been horrified by what he had heard, but "People inside will do anything to get out," he said. He had received no inducement to give evidence.

Charging the jury, Justice Butler told them that the prosecution's case must satisfy them that Murray had murdered his wife and that it hadn't been manslaughter. A killing might be considered manslaughter if the perpetrator had suffered a sufficient degree of provocation, he told them: "If you come to the conclusion that Murray killed his wife, I do not think you can rule out the possibility of his having learned for the first time of his wife's unchastity during an argument and that he then lost control of himself.

"If Murray killed his wife in these circumstances, he was still guilty of a crime, the crime of manslaughter."

The jury retired late in the afternoon of 27 November. They returned after two hours. Thomas Murray was declared not guilty of murder but guilty of manslaughter. Justice Butler told the members of the jury that it was a verdict he endorsed. Then he turned to Murray to address the sentencing issue.

The accused, he said, had been in custody for almost nine months since being first charged in October of the previous year. Therefore, he would impose a prison sentence rather than penal servitude. This allowed for the time already spent in custody to be taken into account.

But he would also have to take into consideration that this young woman's life had been cut off just a month before she was due to give birth to her first child and that after committing the crime the accused had acted with a great deal of callousness and self-possession in the extent to which he had covered his tracks. Were it not for the fact that he had spoken to prisoners in Limerick Prison, he might have succeeded in getting away with it.

The judge said he must take the view most favourable to Murray that it was on this occasion that he had first learned that the child his wife was expecting was not his.

He then sentenced Murray to two years' imprisonment.

By today's standards, the outcome of the trial might appear perplexing. The verdict of manslaughter was returned, which implied that the jury believed he was responsible for Mary's death. In this, it is safe to assume they set great store in the evidence of the prisoners to whom Murray had confessed.

That version of events had Murray effectively assaulting Mary twice. After he had wrung her neck, he told Andrew Murphy, he had finished her off with the tyre lever when she appeared to be coming to. Any action by him at the height of rage was now exacerbated by a calculated intent to kill her. He was lucky that the jury opted for manslaughter rather than murder. They must have been impressed by the tenor of his own evidence.

The issue of provocation was mentioned by the judge. Here, it was accepted that Murray wasn't the father of the child and had only heard about it for the first time on the evening of the killing. Again, it is difficult to see why the judge placed such significance on provocation if Murray had effectively assaulted his wife twice.

The sentence handed down would be considered bizarre today, and outrageous in some quarters. Murray hadn't confessed to the court. He hadn't shown any remorse. He had pleaded not guilty. And the nature of the killing, as told to the prisoners, was surely an exacerbating factor of the crime. Yet, he got two years. The first question that might be asked is, how long would he have got if he had pleaded guilty to manslaughter? Judges are obliged to take into account a guilty plea, so presumably he would have been sentenced to even less, possibly as little as a year.

In the Ireland of 1970, there was no outrage. There were no groups representing the victims of crime, violence or sexual assault to voice their opinions. Even if there had been, the mores of the time didn't accommodate the questioning of authority.

The identity of the father of Mary Murray's unborn child was never resolved beyond doubt. There was some evidence that she had had a relationship with a man in Dublin for up to a year prior to her marriage. However, it was never fully established whether or not he was the father. All the court had to go on was the version of events as told by Murray to two prisoners, which coincided with the post-mortem results that the pregnancy was a month short of full term.

After serving his sentence, Murray emigrated to the UK. He has lived there ever since, only sporadically returning home to Tipperary for events like family funerals, according to local sources.

5. THE TELEPHONE TRAIL

The Case of Joe O'Reilly

On the day in question, Joe O'Reilly rose just after 5 a.m. His mood was not good. As he regularly did now, he had slept in a different bedroom from his wife, Rachel. The previous evening, he and Rachel had rowed. She suspected he was having an affair. He denied it, but for him the row may have been the last straw. At some time later that evening, or perhaps in the course of a restless night's sleep, he resolved that on the following day, Monday, 4 October 2004, his marriage would end.

It was still dark when he left the house at 5.25 a.m. He drove south towards the city, through the dark-ened roads of north Co. Dublin, then joined the M50, which rings the greater city area. He left the motorway at the Finglas exit, en route to Tesco

Clearwater; he wanted to fill his car with the cheaper petrol that was available there.

He arrived at the pump at 5.40 a.m. and filled the tank of his Fiat Marea estate with €49 worth of petrol.

At 5.45 a.m., he was still in the Finglas area when Nikki Pelley rang. Frequently, he called to Pelley's house on the way to work. The lovers spoke for twenty-seven minutes. Pelley says she recalls little of the conversation. In all likelihood, O'Reilly was letting off steam about Rachel and the row that had taken place the previous evening.

By the time the call was terminated, O'Reilly was close to the Citywest Business Park, off the Naas Road. He drove into the car park of the Jackie Skelly Fitness Club. Dawn was struggling to break. He spotted Derek Quearney's Citroën Xsara. He got out of his car and walked over to Quearney's through the sharp morning chill. The two men had become friends after Quearney had joined Viacom, the outdoor advertising company where Joe was employed, around two years previously. They talked for a few minutes, waiting for the fitness club to open.

Once inside, the men decided to forgo a workout. Instead, they made do with a sauna.

From there, it was a short drive to Viacom. O'Reilly entered the office soon after 7.30 a.m. For the best part of half an hour, he got on with his work. That morning, he was due to travel to the Broadstone bus garage in Phibsboro: Viacom was involved in applying advertisement posters to the Dublin bus fleet. One of O'Reilly's functions was to oversee the work.

At 8.04 a.m., he emailed a friend, Kieron Gallagher, about a lunch date they had arranged for that day.

Hiya,
I will be out and about most of the morning, and in poor phone coverage areas, so unless I hear otherwise from you, lunch at 2pm, usual place? Got the 40 quid off my brother at the weekend! Later.
Joe

When he sent the email, he knew he wouldn't be keeping the appointment, but cancelling it might leave a trail for the cops. There was perfect mobile-phone coverage around Broadstone bus garage, but he didn't want anybody calling him.

Eight minutes later, O'Reilly left the Viacom building. He spoke with Quearney on the way out. They arranged to meet at the garage. Quearney said he would follow in his own car.

When O'Reilly left his office, it was as Joe Citizen, a man who had grasped the opportunities presented in life and made the most of them. He was no angel, but who was? He was a highly regarded employee and got on well enough with those who reported to him. His personal life was messy. An early marriage was in the process of dissolving, and his and Rachel's two children ensured that the divorce would be complicated and painful. He had found new love, and the prospect of a new life, with Nikki Pelley. Until that October morning, as he drove out of the Bluebell industrial estate, Fate had been a friend, albeit a temperamental one.

By the time he returned to the office, about four hours later, his own life and many others would have changed irrevocably.

A few minutes after he had left Viacom, Pelley phoned again. As they spoke, he made steady progress through the Monday-morning traffic, heading north, retracing the route he had taken to work that morning.

By the time the call terminated, twenty-five minutes later, he had negotiated the worst of the traffic and was close to joining the M1, which swept into north Co. Dublin. He was within twenty minutes of arriving home.

Looking in from the outside, the O'Reillys had a good life. Thirty-two-year-old Joe and thirty-year-old Rachel were already on their second home. The previous year they had moved from the north Dublin suburb of Whitehall to the country. Their new home was a comfortable bungalow, Lambay View, situated in Baldarragh, outside the village of The Naul. The move was designed to give the two boys, Luke and Adam, a better, safer upbringing. The mortgage of €230,000 was well within the couple's financial capability.

Rachel worked only one day a week in a solicitor's

office in Donnybrook. She supplemented her income as an agent for the cosmetics company Avon. She was also involved in selling Tupperware. On the day of her death, there was €840 in cash in her home, the proceeds of some of her work. The schedule she had established allowed her to devote plenty of time to her children.

Most of their financial health could be attributed to O'Reilly's position as a manager in Viacom. He had worked his way up through the ranks in a number of different companies, and now he oversaw a staff of twenty-six. In many ways, the O'Reillys had been beneficiaries of the opportunities on offer for a considerable slice of the population in Ireland today. Neither had attained much educationally beyond second level. Neither had qualifications in one of the traditional professions or trades. Before the boom in the 1990s, when opportunities were limited, they might have been candidates for emigration or confined to a lower socio-economic bracket.

By 2004, hard work and aptitude were enough to provide them with the wherewithal to realise their dreams of middle-class comfort and a bright start for their children. They had a good life, healthy kids, a lovely home in the country and no money worries.

Eight minutes after Nikki Pelley and O'Reilly terminated their call, Pelley sent him a text message. By then he was on the M1. He was well on his way home, where he knew Rachel would be returning after dropping Adam at a local crèche. The previous Saturday, she had sustained a minor injury while playing hockey. O'Reilly had advised her not to go to the gym that morning in case she aggravated the injury. He knew she wasn't expecting him until some time that evening. He was armed with the element of surprise.

Rachel O'Reilly's mother, Teresa Lowe, had been seventeen and single when she had given birth to a baby girl on 10 October 1973. The baby was named Teresa and put up for adoption. Within weeks, she had been adopted by Jim and Rose Callaly, who renamed her Rachel. The couple would eventually adopt five children and raise them in their home in Whitehall in the north of the city.

Teresa Lowe married soon after giving up her daughter for adoption. She found the maternal instinct difficult to ignore. She discussed the matter with her husband, and they decided to attempt to get her daughter back. She was told by the adoption agency that the baby had already been adopted. There would be some dispute later as to whether this was in fact so at the time.

In any event, Rachel grew up a Callaly. All the indications were that she had a very happy childhood, as one of two girls in a tight-knit family. Jim worked as a plumber and went on to establish his own contracting business. Rose worked in the home. Rachel attended the local school where she is remembered as a bubbly, friendly girl.

One of her schoolfriends at St Mary's in Glasnevin was Jackie Connor. The friendship deepened as they became adults: Jackie was Rachel's bridesmaid and godmother to her elder son, Luke. "She was outgoing, caring, sporting and self-sufficient," Connor would later testify. "We were friends since we were fourteen."

After she left school, Rachel worked in different jobs. She moved into a flat in nearby Fairview. When she was seventeen, she looked up her birth-mother. By then, Teresa Lowe had three other children. Mother and daughter established ongoing contact. Rachel was introduced to Teresa's family and got on particularly well with her son, Thomas.

Soon after leaving school, she began working part-time in Arnott's department store in the city centre. Joe O'Reilly also worked there. Rachel was just eighteen when the couple began dating.

Joe O'Reilly grew up in Kilbarrack, a few miles from Rachel's home in Whitehall. He has a brother, Derek, and two sisters, Ann and Martina.

When O'Reilly was nineteen, his parents' marriage ended, and his father moved to Wales. A few years later, his mother, also Ann, moved out to Dunleer in Co. Louth, where his sister Ann lives.

Joe and Rachel's friendship developed, and they moved in together. By 1997, they were committed to marrying. The forthcoming nuptials were to prove troubling for Rachel. Having re-established relations with her birth-mother, and formed a friendship with her half-siblings, she wanted to invite them to her wedding. The idea didn't sit well with some of the Callaly family. The stand-off caused tension, and relations between Rachel and her birth-family cooled to the point at which contact became sporadic.

The newly married couple bought a house in Whitehall, and Luke was born in 1999, Adam two years later. After Luke's birth, Rachel gave up full-time work but still did one day a week in the solicitor's office where she had been employed. In May 2003, the O'Reillys moved to Baldarragh, outside The Naul. The progress of family life was going according to plan.

Rachel had re-established contact with the Lowes after O'Reilly had bumped into Teresa's other daughter in a gym. Second time around, Rachel made a serious effort to get to know the Lowe family. By the time of her death, Thomas was a frequent visitor to Baldarragh.

After O'Reilly left Arnott's, his career took off. He moved to software firm Oracle, where he was appointed a team leader, the first step on the management ladder. He is remembered by one former work colleague as "a bit of an oddball, but on the whole, fairly sound". Another source recalls that he used to come to work nearly every day in the same clothes: "He was always wearing a pair of slip-on shoes, tracksuit bottoms and one of those patterned jumpers you get for Christmas."

He was regarded as an excellent worker, who was entirely focused on the job at hand.

Murder victim Esther McCann, who died alongside Jessica, the baby she hoped to adopt, when her husband Frank set their home ablaze in 1992.

Below: Frank McCann is escorted from court having received the mandatory life sentence.

Henry Holmes, *right*, who pleaded guilty to the manslaughter of his wife Anne. Holmes received a ten-year prison sentence after the jury found him not guilty of murder in 1983.

Siobhan Kearney who was murdered by her husband Brian in February 2006. Kearney unsuccessfully attempted to stage the murder to look like suicide.

Brian Kearney alongside his daughter Aoife, arriving in court during the trial, February 2008.

The McLaughlin family stand together determined to see justice for their loved one Siobhan, on the first day of the trial. Parents Owen and Deirdre (third and fourth from left) and siblings (from left) Owen, Ann-Marie, Deirdre, Brighid, Niamh and Aisling.

The McLaughlin family embrace outside the court after the verdict is delivered.

Gardaí outside the Murray home a few hours after Thomas Murray attacked his wife, Mary, September 1969.

Photo credit: *The Irish Examiner*

Left: Rachel O'Reilly who was murdered by her husband, Joe, in October 2004.

Below: Rachel and Joe O'Reilly.

Photo credit: Mark Condron, *Sunday Tribune*

Joe O'Reilly arriving at court with his mother Ann, during his trial at the Central Criminal Court in Dublin.

Photo credit: Mark Condron, *Sunday Tribune*

Relief for the Callaly family after Joe O'Reilly is found guilty of murder. From left, Rachel's sister, Ann, and her parents, Jim and Rose.

The stairwell at 11 Leinster Road, Rathmines, leading to the rooms rented by James Lehman and his wife Margaret. *Inset*: The room where Margaret died having been poisoned by her husband. She was in the late stages of pregnancy.

Gary McCrea, having been found guilty of the murder of his wife Dolores (inset) in November 2005. He murdered his wife in January 2004 and then attempted to burn her body.

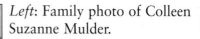

Left: Family photo of Colleen Suzanne Mulder.

Below: Anton Mulder after his murder conviction was set aside and a new trial ordered, May 2007.

Happy with the verdict of the retrial: Clinton Mulder, son of Colleen Mulder, speaking to the media on leaving court. He is accompanied by his girlfriend and Ann Czerepowicz, sister of Colleen, far right.

Another source said he was fine unless you fell out with him: "Then he'd try to get at you without confronting you. If he knew he could intimidate you, he'd dominate you," he said. "But even though he's a big man physically, if you stood up to him, he'd back off."

The picture painted of O'Reilly is borne out by the experience of Wesley Kearns, an employee who worked under him at Viacom. O'Reilly fired him for transgressions he considered serious, although Kearns disputed that. On the day of the sacking, Kearns lost his temper. He picked up a fire extinguisher and went for O'Reilly. Kearns was a shortish man of medium build. O'Reilly towered over him at six foot three with the build of a second-row rugby forward. Yet, when O'Reilly saw the smaller man come for him, he fled into his office and locked the door. Kearns had to be restrained before O'Reilly agreed to come out.

From Oracle, O'Reilly moved to Microsoft. "He was a bit smarmy, but fine as long as you got on with him," said one former colleague there. He didn't drink, which may have helped him focus on his career. At one stage, he supplemented his earnings by working in a video shop in Inchicore in the evenings.

O'Reilly got on well with the Callalys. Rachel's youngest brother Anthony was a frequent visitor to Lambay View, often staying overnight. "I was extremely close to Rachel, Joe and the kids. Me and Joe used to go to the flicks together," Anthony would say later. "I have a lot of good memories from that house."

At home in Baldarragh, Rachel got involved in community activity. There was local opposition to the erection of a mobile-telephone mast in nearby Murphy's Quarry. Rachel went on the then Dublin radio station Newstalk 106FM, to argue the case for residents. In a bitterly ironic twist, the mast would prove vital in fingering her killer.

Rachel was particularly sporty and played hockey regularly with the Botanic Club in Glasnevin, near where she grew up. The couple both got involved in softball when O'Reilly was working in Oracle. From there, they joined another team, the Renegades. In 2003, Rachel was voted player of the year. At the end of the season, the team was invited to the O'Reilly home for a party. At least a dozen members attended, and tents were pitched in the back garden. Everybody stayed the night, partying into the small hours.

On the fateful morning, as he neared Baldarragh, the good times from the past were most likely far from Joe O'Reilly's mind. He replied to Nikki Pelley's text at 8.48 a.m. Eight minutes later, his colleague Derek Quearney attempted to ring him but the call was aborted. He was now only a few miles from the family home.

Beneath the surface of the good life, dark currents swirled through the O'Reillys' marriage. When O'Reilly met Nikki Pelley in January 2004, he had told her that he and Rachel had been sleeping in separate bedrooms for eighteen months. That might have been a gross exaggeration, but there were problems. At softball games, the couple's unhappiness manifested itself in public rows. "They were often at it," one former Renegades member recalled. "Particularly Joe, starting off these screaming matches. It got to be a bit much for the whole team."

At some point, the couple was spoken to about the rows, and things cooled down. But at one get-together there was another flare-up, over which of them would play in a forthcoming tournament and who would mind the children.

By then, O'Reilly was seeking companionship outside the marriage. "I never would have put him down as a womaniser," a former work colleague from the mid-nineties said. "One of the lads at work was playing around, and Joe used to let on he was too, and went on about all the things he did with women. But you could see through it. I was very surprised to learn about the affair."

In 2003, he had an affair with a sportswoman but that fizzled out after a few months. Then he met Nikki Pelley. Their affair grew into a relationship, and by the summer of 2004 he was seeing her at least twice a week, Tuesdays and Saturday evenings. All the indications are that by October Rachel was suspicious. He spent less and less time at home. There were a lot of overnight bus inspections around the country. And when he was around they often slept in separate rooms.

Exactly how much she knew, whether it was intuition or he had admitted it to her, has never been established. Her best friend Jackie was asked about the relationship in court. "Rachel said she wasn't happy," Jackie testified. "Joe was working a lot, she was on her own a lot of the time. Family life was suffering."

Text correspondence and Pelley's evidence indicate that she and O'Reilly had had plans for the future. In a text on 16 July that year he had written, "Hey, I want only to be your husband, I know my place." The following morning at 8.29 a.m.: "Good morning beautiful. I'm completely crazy about you and can't wait to see you again."

On 15 September, just three weeks before Rachel's violent death: "Ditto, my beautiful bride to be." He introduced his sons to Pelley. They had gone to the zoo on occasions, appearing as a family unit, while Rachel played her Saturday hockey.

Whatever about his marital infidelity, he appears to have been a good parent. "I would categorise Joe as a very caring father," a softball team mate, John Austin, later told the Central Criminal Court. He also testified that O'Reilly spoke of leaving the marriage to rent a flat in nearby Balbriggan in order to be close to the children. Pelley told the court of how they had talked of a possible future with the kids.

The text traffic between Nikki Pelley and O'Reilly gives a clear indication that he saw his future away from the marriage. These things happen – but in a deteriorating marriage, particularly one that involves children, animosity often surfaces.

An exchange of emails on 9 June 2004 between O'Reilly and his sister Ann illustrates O'Reilly's growing animosity towards Rachel. The day before, the O'Reillys had visited a social worker following an apparent anonymous complaint about Rachel's mothering skills. It emerges in the emails that the complainant had been O'Reilly's mother; they also show that O'Reilly's sister was certainly buying his portrayal of life in Lambay View.

> *From: Ann O'Reilly*
> *To: Joe O'Reilly*
> *10.16 a.m. 9 June 2004*
> *Hiya,*
> *I'm just asking how you got on yesterday. How are you?*
> *Wanted to leave you alone yesterday to get your head together, but trust me, I held back on calling or mailing you. Let me know how things are and if you need anything.*
> *Concerned banana*

> *From Joe O'Reilly*
> *To: Ann O'Reilly*
> *10.41 a.m.*
> *In a nutshell, it was a big steaming pile of shite. They told us both that shouting at the kids was okay, 'sure we all do it'.*

Hitting kids is okay in the eyes of the law, as again 'we all do it'. They never come out and visit homes of kids reported as being abused unless the allegation is of a sexual nature or after several cases of non-accidental hospitalisations.

Could it have gone any worse??? Yes!!!

Rachel is a 'good mother' because she admits to having problems dealing with the kids and confessed to shouting at them on a daily basis. There is some Mickey Mouse course run once a year, to help parents cope with 'difficult kids' and 'parenting difficulties', and Rachel has volunteered to go on one. She was also playing the 'Home Help' card but didn't get anywhere.

The best I got was a commitment to getting the district nurse pay a visit, as Adam is due his developmental check-up. Should have got it last year, but in the words of his mother: 'you know yourself, what with the house move and so on, it's easy to forget these things'.

Anyway, I gave them the go ahead to drop out whenever they want to see the kids. Hopefully, the DN [district nurse] will see her at her 'best' or else the state of the house that lazy cunt leaves it in, etc...

Positives? Very few. At least it's on record that I don't need to attend the course, I've no issues in dealing with the kids and the complaint had nothing to do with me.

To answer your question as to how I am. Well, to be honest, I wasn't expecting much as you were no doubt aware, so I wasn't too shocked with the apathy displayed by our wonderful child protection people.

That said I think matters may get worse as she told me in the carpark that 'I knew you were overreacting going on to me about shouting at the kids. Did you hear them? Everybody does it and I am a good mother.'

Instead of give her a slap on the wrist, it appears that they've forgiven her and patted her on the back for a job well done.

Did you get to talk to Derek [their brother] by the way? Had to physically restrain him on Saturday night, not good. He's too much of a hot-head, but that said, you really couldn't blame him.

Adam was 'reefed' up by the arm and dragged to bed and she nearly tore Luke's ears off putting his pj top on over his head. As usual I had a right go at her, but as usual, by that stage the damage is already done.

Shouldn't really complain though, she is a 'wonderful mother' in the eyes of the state.

Joe

PS Interesting choice of terminology used by the social worker. Everything was Rachel is the main care giver and I was the secondary care giver.

I'm already Mr Weekend custody in the eyes of the state. Doesn't bode too well does it? Oh, nearly forgot, the case is now closed to their satisfaction.

From Ann O'Reilly
To: Joe O'Reilly
11.01 a.m.
Well, at least you get the DN coming out on unexpected visits, that can't be too bad really.

Dan was talking to her yesterday and she told him that she now counts to ten and examines the situation with the kids, so let's hope something good, even if it's a little, will come out of this.

So you're going out for a meal on Friday night with her. Should be good fun, all nice and romantic (not). Try again to talk to her about her lack of motherly instincts. Have you told her she's none? Does she admit to it?

Try a bit harder to talk to her about it. Tell her everything, be open and honest. I know I'd keep on trying constantly. I wouldn't give her ears a break from the subject. Otherwise she's just going to keep on living in cloud cuckoo land.

Did Derek say anything to Rachel about her manhandling Adam and Luke?

Ma was very worried about it yesterday. If you get a minute could you ring her, put her mind at rest? I went straight into Ma's yesterday to see what the story was and she was saying that Rachel came in and was all over Adam and just blanked Luke *(fooking bitch).*

That hurt Ma, she wanted so much to say something but didn't. Anyway, Rachel stayed for chips, eggs and bread and was very calm and happy so Ma was left thinking.

Call her. She's our mammy and does really worry about us.

Don't let on that I told you. You know what she's like!

So do I still have to be on my best around Rachel keeping my mouth shut? If I see her hit or manhandle the kids can I speak up?

From: Joe O'Reilly
To: Ann O'Reilly
3.42 p.m.
Hiya,

So she now counts to ten, eh? Believe that and you're not my sister!!!

Where the hell did you hear I was going out for a night with that cunt??? A meal? I'd rather choke. Absolutely no way, never, not happening.

To quote your good self Ann, never look back, only look forward, eh? Just to drill the point home, Me + Rachel + Marriage = over!!!

I keep telling her, straight as you like, exactly

what I think of her mothering instincts. Yes. In fact, to be even a little fair, I'm very aware that I'm over critical at times, although I don't feel guilty about it to be honest, as she repulses me.

Derek didn't say anything, I wouldn't let him. Bad enough I have to bite my tongue and restrain myself, don't need him losing it. Not for her sake, but the kids wouldn't like to see their mother abused by their uncle Derek, and I don't want his halo around them diminished in any way.

(You're getting competition Ann!!)

That's where you need to be careful. When Ma reported the incident that brought about yesterday's farce, it very nearly came out as to who did the reporting!!!

You are prime suspect number one, you know it. By all means, drag her fat ass outside and kick it into the middle of next week, but not in front of the boys, and don't leave any marks that can and will be used against you in a court of law.

As I've said repeatedly, there is no talking to her. She doesn't listen. Mind you there's a lot of that about. I told you and I told Ma that this would amount to nothing, and you both knew better than me and went through the usual series of questions.

I'm not having a go Ann, but it really wound me up last time, as I go through every angle I can with the boys before I make a move. Yesterday proved yet again the injustices that exist in this country.

As a mother, you can shout and scream and smack almost as much as you want to, once you admit to having a bit of a problem and then volunteer to a lip service parents' course.

Maybe now you will both listen to what I have to say and not go about with your heads in the sand.

Being a father in this country, no matter how good, will land you with weekend visitations and not much else. You know of one case where full custody was given, that's great, and good for him. I know of dozens where it went the other way.

Yesterday was my first personal indication of how much I will lose if I don't try different angles. After all I'm only a secondary care giver.

I do appreciate your support; and I know the boys mean the world to you, they are my life and I am nothing without them.

Adam was the one singled out as the child whom the concerns were about. More bad news for Luke as proved yesterday, in your own words and observations.

Ann, there is only so much crap the kid can deal with and patients [sic] are running on empty. You saw first hand the number she did on him before. I'd rather die than see him go through that again. He won't go through that again, end of story.

Be as good as you can around Rachel for now, but tell me everything you see, do not hold back.

If you see her being excessive, then step in. I want to know as much as possible, and I can't be there all the time. Ann, you're my sister, my blood, she's not. What you tell me will not be questioned. You have carte blanche visitation rights to my house, and to my kids. In fact, the more you're around, the better. Same with Dan, but I don't want him knowing too much.

I plan on calling Ma later tonight. I know she's worried, but I couldn't call last night, as I didn't know if she had a visitor and her family. The 'World's Greatest Mum' is out tonight, getting laid with a bit of luck, so I'll have time to talk to Ma properly when the boys are asleep.

I'll be home in Ma's on Friday with the boys, so I'll see you then?

Thanks for the concern, sorry for the long email!!!

Joe

From: Ann O'Reilly
To: Joe O'Reilly
4 p.m.
Your meal is probably a surprise. Well of course it is.

She got Dan to book it last night for ye then you are staying in Ma's but she asked me last week if she ever wanted to venture up to Dunleer and eat out could she stay with me???

So she knows the marriage is over then and it's a divorce. What does she say to that? Maybe that's why she's taking you out on Friday. Say nothing.

I do get it now. Your fooked as a father in this dump. Ask her to move abroad. I really dunno how you're going to get out of this one.

So when are you filling for legal separation then?

If you want I can kidnap you and kids on Friday night before she has chance to get hold of you. We could go on a trip in my car??

Or you could just go with her and ignore her the whole night or stare at sexy ladies.

The correspondence has to be seen in context. There is nothing to suggest that Rachel was the type of mother portrayed by her husband and his sister. By June 2004, O'Reilly was deeply involved with Nikki Pelley and wanted out of his marriage. He also wanted custody of his two children. Painting his wife as an unfit mother might pay dividends if the matter ever came to court.

Painting himself as the model parent, up against a family-law system weighed heavily towards mothers, creates the impression that he is the real victim of what is unfolding. His sister, for one, seems to have bought the portrayal.

Early on in the correspondence, O'Reilly referred to the meeting with the social worker: "Interesting choice of terminology used by the social worker. Everything was Rachel was the main care giver and I was the secondary care giver. I'm already Mr Weekend custody in the eyes of the state. It doesn't bode well, does it?"

The observation fitted neatly into the case O'Reilly was making for himself but conveniently ignored the reality of his family life. He worked long hours, and when he wasn't away working, he was away having an affair. He saw precious little of his children during the week. He stayed with Pelley most Saturday nights. How could Rachel not have been the primary caregiver?

The correspondence referred to a get-together by the O'Reilly siblings the previous weekend at which O'Reilly, his brother and sister were apparently disturbed by Rachel's parenting skills: "Adam was 'reefed' up by the arm and dragged to bed and she nearly tore Luke's ears of putting his PJ top on over his head. As usual, I had a right go at her, but as usual, by that stage the damage is already done."

Later in the emails, he makes a reference to the future, which was telling: "It really wound me up last time as I go through every angle I can with the boys before I make a move. Yesterday proved yet again the injustices that exist in this country."

Rachel's crime as a mother was to shout at her children. Is that unusual for a parent of two small children? Her son was discommoded as she pulled his pyjama top over his head. She grabbed one of the boys roughly. There are few parents who couldn't identify with that behaviour in moments of frustration. However, it's difficult to envisage how this amounts to such bad parenting that it requires the attention of a social worker. Unless O'Reilly had another agenda in propagating the notion of Rachel as a bad mother. He certainly wanted his own family to go along with it "Maybe now, you'll both [his sister and mother] listen to what I have to say and not go about with your heads in the sand."

Earlier in the emails, he tells Ann what had happened after the previous day's appointment: "She told me in the carpark that 'I knew you were over reacting going on to me about shouting at the kids. Did you hear them? Everybody does it and I am a good mother.'"

Rachel felt compelled to reassure herself that she was a good mother, because her husband was trying to convince her otherwise. She knew her marriage was under pressure and, feeling vulnerable, may have been short with the kids at times, as any parent would. If there was any abuse going on, there is evidence to suggest it was emotional abuse, perpetrated on her.

His real agenda was obvious elsewhere in the correspondence: "By all means drag her fat ass outside and kick it into the middle of next week, but not in front of the boys, and don't leave any marks that can and will be used against you in a court of law" and "the state of the house that that lazy cunt leaves it in".

If O'Reilly's purpose was to portray his wife as merely a bad mother, the mask began to slip. She "repulsed" him, he had said. He wanted rid of her but was afraid he might not get custody of the boys. Other "angles" would have to be explored.

On the evening of the killing, O'Reilly told gardaí of the meeting with the social worker. He said he had supported Rachel through the process, following the anonymous complaint about her. He didn't tell them that the complainant was his own mother.

His portrayal of himself as a loyal husband was at odds with the emails and with Pelley's evidence. When asked in court how he referred to his wife after marital rows, Pelley replied: "Wasp. Or cunt. It wasn't a term he used often."

Through the summer of 2004, Rachel was largely unaware of what her husband was doing behind her back, either his affair with Pelley or his concentrated efforts to portray her as a terrible mother. She wanted her marriage to work.

Summer turned to autumn, but things didn't appear to be improving. If anything, O'Reilly was spending more time outside the home, leaving Rachel to ponder on how the family could be saved.

On Sunday, 3 October, the day before Rachel's death, all appeared relatively well in the O'Reilly family. Rachel was a bit sore from the minor leg injury she had sustained at hockey the previous afternoon. The four of them went out for the day to Liffey Valley shopping centre. Afterwards, they called on Thomas Lowe at his home in Walkinstown and stayed for more than an hour.

It would be the last occasion on which the two boys would do anything with both parents. That evening, a row flared, finally convincing O'Reilly that he should kill his wife as soon as possible to resolve any difficulties she presented for him.

At 8.58 a.m., two minutes after the last call, Quearney attempted to phone O'Reilly again, but the call was aborted. The communication was picked up by a mast in north Co. Dublin, halfway between Swords and The Naul. Joe O'Reilly was less than ten minutes from home. At 9.03 a.m., Rachel's grey Renault Scénic passed the entrance to Murphy's Quarry, near the family home. She was on her way to the crèche with Adam.

Seven minutes later, a dark estate car, believed to be O'Reilly's Fiat Marea, passed the same spot heading in the opposite direction, to Lambay View. He received another call from Quearney at 9.25 a.m., which lasted just over two minutes. By then, according to the CCTV and phone records, he was at home, awaiting his wife's return. At that exact time, Rachel had just dropped Adam off at the crèche. At the door, she spoke briefly to another young mother, Kathy Henry, who remembered Rachel wearing grey tracksuit bottoms and a dark top.

At 9.41 a.m., Rachel's car passed the entrance to Murphy's Quarry, returning from her drop.

At 9.59 a.m., O'Reilly's car passed, going in the opposite direction, away from the house. Within the space of eighteen minutes, Joe O'Reilly had murdered his wife, using extreme violence.

Her body was discovered in her bedroom, her car keys under it, implying the attack had happened very soon after she entered the house. Pathology and forensic evidence of the blood patterns suggested she was subjected to a sustained attack with a blunt object. A dumbbell missing from the spare room in the house is believed to have been the weapon.

"She was violently beaten over a sustained period while she lay on the ground," Dr Diane Daly, a forensic scientist, testified in court. "The assailant was at some point during the assault crouching or kneeling in this position [next to where the body was found]."

Rachel received between four and nine blows to the head. An injury to her wrist suggests she was held down as some of the blows were administered. An injury to her arm showed she had probably taken a defensive stance. If this was so, she suffered a few moments of terror, aware that her attacker was intent on killing her. State pathologist Marie Cassidy concluded that she may have lived for a few hours after the attack, until she choked on her own blood.

At 10.07 a.m., on his way back to the city, O'Reilly sent a text to Rachel: "Hope you and the boys slept ok. Wish Jackie happy birthday from me. xx."

The affectionate tone was at variance with the contempt he had shown in the emails to his sister a few months previously.

In other correspondence – a letter and a phone message – with Rachel in the months that followed, the same affectionate tone was present.

By 10.38 a.m., O'Reilly's phone was bouncing off a mast in the North Inner City. Soon after, his car and Derek Quearney's were caught on CCTV leaving Broadstone bus garage. He travelled from there to his office in the Bluebell industrial estate.

The alibi he had constructed was that he had been in the Broadstone bus garage for the whole morning. He was now returning to work having completed the inspection of the work there.

As he entered Viacom, the receptionist Michelle Slattery noticed him. "His face was puffy, blotchy red, his eyes were the same," she told the court. "He looked like he had been crying. I said, 'You look like shit.' He shrugged his shoulders and said, 'Ah, Jesus.'"

At 1.10 p.m., while he was eating his lunch at his desk, he took a call on his mobile from Helen Moore, proprietor of the crèche Tots United. Rachel hadn't collected Adam at 12.30 a.m. as arranged. O'Reilly said he didn't know what the matter could be.

He told Moore he'd be out to pick up his son. He dialled Rachel's number and left a message that was not for her ears but for those of the gardaí who would soon be investigating a murder. "Hiya, Rach. It's only me. I just got a call from Helen in Montessori. She says you haven't picked up Adam. Give us a shout. I'm going to try the home number. You've no doubt left your phone at home or in the back of the car or something . . ."

A few minutes later, he rang his mother-in-law. Had she seen Rachel? There might be something up.

Rose Callaly was making lunch for her husband and son when O'Reilly rang. Instinct told her that something beyond the casual had happened. She got into her car and drove north to Baldarragh. She arrived at the house around 2 p.m.

The patio door was open, which was unusual. "And the curtains were drawn. I had never seen that before," Rose Callaly told the court.

Inside, the sink tap was running quite strongly. There were clothes folded on the kitchen table. Other items looked as if they had been "placed on the floor", she testified. She walked through the house, calling her daughter's name. She looked in the boys' room. She came out and noticed something at the door to Rachel's room. "As soon as I saw her I knew that she was dead and I knew she was murdered," Rose Callaly said.

She knelt down beside her daughter. Forensic evidence would show that the knees of her trousers were stained in Rachel's blood. "I talked to her. I felt her arm but it was hard," she remembered.

Within minutes, O'Reilly's Fiat Marea pulled up outside. En route, he had rung Rachel at 1.45 p.m. and left a message. "Me again, I spoke to your mother. I've been crying, you have me worried. I'm just coming on to the M1 now." It is unclear as to why he would be crying, just half an hour after hearing that Rachel hadn't collected Luke. In retrospect, if his tears were genuine, they can be attributed to the realisation of what he had done, rather than to any concern for Rachel.

At 2.05 p.m., he arrived at Tots United. The proprietor, Helen Moore, was waiting patiently with Adam. O'Reilly appeared a little flushed in the face to her but otherwise he seemed fine. She reminded him that Luke would now be finished in Hedgetown National School, and he might want to pick him up.

O'Reilly and his son drove the few miles to Hedgetown, just outside Lusk. There is some suggestion that he lingered at the school. Luke had already been collected by another parent, in accordance with an ongoing arrangement Rachel had made. If O'Reilly had gone directly home – it's unclear whether he knew that Luke would be collected – he would have been the first person on the scene. A killer who had planned to any degree would prefer to avoid such a scenario.

Instead, better that somebody else discover the body. And if that person was the mother who had raised Rachel, so be it.

At the house, O'Reilly came running to Rachel's room, where Rose Callaly knelt over the body. He got down on his knees. He moved a box that was near the body; later, he said to a garda that he hoped he hadn't ruined the crime scene. Rose told him that Rachel was dead. She got up and walked back to the kitchen. She put her hands under the running tap to wash away her daughter's blood.

The house began to fill. A neighbour, Sarah Harmon, arrived. An ambulance turned up. The paramedics quickly established there was nothing they could do. The gardaí drove up. By the time Rachel's father and brother Paul pulled in, the gardaí had cordoned off the crime scene. Rachel's youngest brother, Anthony, arrived soon after.

"I tried to run in to see Rachel but the gardaí stopped me," he said. "They [his parents] were there with Joe, everyone was very emotional . . . all crying." Soon after, the Callalys gathered and headed south to their home in Collins Avenue to begin the long process of grieving. O'Reilly put the two children into his car and drove to his mother's house in Dunleer.

At around 7 p.m. that evening, there was a knock on the door of Ann O'Reilly's home. Three gardaí introduced themselves. There was Detective Superintendent Michael Hoare, Detective Sergeant Pat

Marry and Garda Aaron Gormley. They were invited in. They sympathised with the bereaved husband.

Hoare told him they wanted to establish a few things about Rachel's background and his whereabouts that day. It would be an informal interview.

O'Reilly told them of his early start. He retraced his journey to Bluebell and then to the Broadstone garage. He told the cops that he and Derek Quearney travelled in separate cars to avail themselves of their mileage allowances. He was back in the office at midday, around an hour before he was alerted that Rachel hadn't turned up at the crèche.

Marry asked him about his marriage. There were rocky patches, O'Reilly said, but that had been behind them. There had been a complaint to social services about Rachel's treatment of the children a few months previously. They had dealt with it together. He had supported her all the way.

Was either of them having an affair? "No," said O'Reilly. He wasn't, and he was fairly sure that neither was Rachel. Twenty minutes or so later in the interview, the issue of an affair was revisited.

This time, O'Reilly conceded that he had been involved with somebody, a Nikki Pelley, but it was now over. When was the last time he had talked to her? "Around midday today," O'Reilly replied.

In the course of the interview, his sister Ann burst into the room. She was in a distressed state, having apparently just heard the news. She hugged O'Reilly and appeared as upset as any close in-law might be on hearing of a violent death. Soon after 8 p.m., the gardaí left.

Over the following days, the investigation veered towards the possibility that Rachel had been murdered in the course of a burglary gone wrong. The early indications were that O'Reilly's alibi checked out. Quearney confirmed much of what he had told the gardaí.

The forensic examination of the house threw up an interesting detail. There was nothing that might be attributed to the murder, nothing to suggest that somebody other than the occupants of the house – and Rose Callaly – had been there on the fateful day. There was no trail of blood leading from the bedroom where Rachel's body was found. There was no other blood, which might have belonged to the killer. There were none of the fibres that the forensics team would have expected to find following a struggle. No DNA samples. Whoever had killed Rachel O'Reilly had been extremely careful. There were none of the clues that should have been present if the crime had been committed in the midst of panic, or in the interruption of a burglary.

The only forensic detail of note was spots of blood taken from a washing machine in the kitchen. In time, they would be identified as belonging to Rachel's half-brother, Thomas Lowe. Briefly, he was under suspicion. He told the gardaí that he presumed the blood related to an incident that had taken place two months previously when he had offered to build a deck at the rear of Lambay View. During the work, he cut his finger and went to put it under the tap in the sink. Spots of blood had fallen on to the washing-machine and had gone undetected in the O'Reilly home until it was forensically examined.

Thomas Lowe had an alibi for the day of the murder, but it was hardly watertight. He had been due to go to work with his brother who called in sick. Thomas went back to bed. He didn't emerge until the afternoon. After careful examination of his story and the evidence, and with their enquiries increasingly pointing elsewhere, the gardaí soon eliminated him. That he was in the frame at all was down to nothing more than genuine coincidence.

Two days after the killing, the spectre of a robbery gone wrong was raised again. In a culvert, about a third of a mile from the house, a search yielded a brown camera bag. O'Reilly identified it as Rachel's. He said it had been in the house on the day of the murder.

The obvious conclusion was that the panic-stricken thief/killer had thrown the bag into the culvert after fleeing the house. The gardaí who discovered the bag weren't so sure. Its positioning suggested that it had been placed in the culvert, rather than thrown there from a car window or even the road. The theory of a robbery gone wrong was fast losing currency. Apart from anything else, why would a thief leave behind the €840 in cash that Rachel had in the kitchen, the proceeds of her cosmetics sales?

Meanwhile, the bereaved prepared for Rachel's funeral. On the night of the wake in the Callaly home, somebody suggested it would be a nice gesture for those who had been close to Rachel to leave a note in the coffin for her. Rachel's parents and her sister Anne settled down to compose theirs. O'Reilly went into another room to put together his final words for his departed wife.

The tone of the letter is heavy with the pain of bereavement. Only one line gives any hint that the dead woman and her surviving husband might be the only two people who knew exactly how her life had ended.

Rachel, I love you so very, very much. I cannot think what I will ever do without you and I don't want to think. You are the best thing that ever happened to me and you will never be replaced.

This is the hardest letter I've ever had to write for reasons only we know. Rachel, forgive me. Two words, one sentence, but I will say them forever.

I look at Luke and I see you and hear you and smell you. I remember you. You have touched the lives of so many and made us better people. You made me laugh, you always did. Everyone loves you now and they always will.

You were a smoker. You kept that quiet fair play to you. I am sorry about your mum finding out about Teresa, Thomas and co. But please don't blame me, it wasn't my fault.

I miss you so much Rachie. Please, please remember that. You went away from this world so very young. The world will remember how very beautiful you were. Like Peter Pan you will never grow old.

Softball misses you, hockey is after naming a trophy after you. Everyone misses your mad personality and can-do attitude.

Liam is heartbroken, your family, my family, everybody. Please look out for Jackie, your family and our boys. I need you as well.

Happy 31st birthday. You're no doubt having the best wine, the best coffee, the best ciggies.

Rachel I love you and miss you and I will mourn you forever.

XXX

Your hubby wubby Jofes.

Love you mammy, Luke XXX

Love you mammy, Adam XXX

The lines that would come to be regarded as significant in the subsequent trial was: "This is the hardest letter I've ever had to write for reasons only we know. Rachel, forgive me. Two words, one sentence, but I will say them forever."

Eighteen months after the funeral, Rachel's body was exhumed, and the letters retrieved from the coffin.

O'Reilly's missive was subsequently used in evidence against him.

The funeral mass took place at the Holy Child Church in Whitehall. As is the custom, an oration was given at the end of the Mass. Naturally, the best person to deliver it was the bereaved husband. He spoke of their times together, of Rachel's bubbly and loving personality, and how everybody would miss her. Then, in conclusion, he said he had a few words for "the person who is responsible for her death": "Unlike you, she is at peace; unlike you, she is sleeping. She forgives you and I hope she gives me the strength to some day forgive you." Even in the context of a brutal murder for which a perpetrator had not yet been identified, it was an unusual statement to make at the victim's funeral.

Later that day, O'Reilly had more disconcerting things to say. After the burial, the funeral party repaired to the Regency Hotel in Whitehall for a meal. In the course of the evening, he fell into conversation with one of Rachel's friends, Fiona Slevin. "There was a discussion about the murder weapon," she later testified. "He said: 'I don't know why they're searching the fields, it's in the water.' I was shocked and his reaction then was like he'd said something wrong. And he said: 'If I'd done it that's where it would be, because there's water all around and it would get rid of DNA and all that sort of stuff.'"

His utterances on the day of the funeral were typical of much that he said and did in the aftermath of the murder. Prior to the funeral, he told Rachel's parents there would be rumours that he had been having an affair and that they had abused their daughter. Speaking to a neighbour, James Flynn, whose farm was across the road from Lambay View, O'Reilly said: "You're a suspect. I'm a suspect. We're all suspects."

He had no compunction in pointing the gardaí in the direction of Thomas Lowe after the blood spots were found on the washing machine. Early on, he mentioned the men whom he had fired at work. In many ways, he was spreading muck.

Then there was Naomi Gargan, whose daughter attended the same crèche as Adam. She met O'Reilly at Rachel's funeral and offered to help with collecting the kids. He accepted. Three weeks after the killing, he invited her to a birthday party he was throwing for Adam at the Leisureplex in Coolock. While there, Naomi was introduced to a friend of O'Reilly's, Nikki. She also noticed that none of the Callaly family appeared to be in attendance.

A week or so later, she reciprocated with an invitation to her daughter's birthday party at her home. When O'Reilly called to pick up his sons, she got chatting to him. "I was complaining about pains in my arms. He said: 'I have some dumbbells you could use.' To be honest I was taken aback because there was speculation in the newspapers that it [the murder weapon] was a dumbbell. It was a bit of a shock."

On 9 November, he asked Naomi to meet him in the Little Chef car park in Swords. "I'm going to be arrested," he told her. "Don't worry, you didn't have a murderer in your house. They're saying I had an affair and you could be the one I'm having the affair with. Don't be surprised if you're brought in for questioning. You might be targeted."

Everybody could be targeted in O'Reilly's mind. Everybody was a suspect. Everybody, including the Callaly parents, could be victimised along with him. There was safety in numbers.

By then, Naomi Gargan was losing faith in the idea that O'Reilly was a bereaved husband, left to raise two boys on his own. She told her husband she just couldn't continue collecting the O'Reilly boys. Their father was giving her the creeps.

Jackie Connor, Rachel's friend, also found herself drawn in by O'Reilly. At the birthday party in the Leisureplex, he asked her to come back to his mother's house in Dunleer with him. "He said he was afraid he was going to be framed for the murder," she told the murder trial. He said: "You're going to have to help me prove my innocence."

She asked him whether he had an alibi.

"There are a few hours that are not accounted for where Rachel was."

In the aftermath of Rachel's death, O'Reilly said and did other disconcerting things. On 4 November, exactly a month after the murder, he left a message on his wife's mobile. "Hi, Rach, it's me, Joe. I'm very sorry for the early-morning call. This time a month ago you were probably doing what I'm doing now, getting the kids ready for school. Now, you're so cold. The sun was out. It was a normal day. You had less than two hours to live. I don't want to live without you and that's the truth. I miss you and love you. I just want to go back in time and say I love you. Sleep well and rest in peace. I have to get the boys ready. I love you. I miss you. Chat later. 'Bye."

It is impossible to know whether he left the message for the benefit of the gardaí, or whether it was the product of a mind experiencing regret, whether that regret was for his actions, or because the investigation was not going as he might have wished.

The most disconcerting behaviour he displayed was in re-enacting how he reckoned Rachel had died at the hands of her assailant.

On 12 October, the gardaí returned possession of the house to O'Reilly. The blood splatters in Rachel's and the boys' bedrooms and the bathroom had not been washed away. O'Reilly slept in the house that night. The following morning, he invited Rachel's family, the Callalys, up to the house, saying he had felt a great sense of peace there, and it might be helpful for them to come.

Jim, Rose, their son Paul and his wife Denise travelled to Baldarragh. "Joe brought us down to the room," Rose recalled. "It was still in the same state [as the day of the murder], there was blood everywhere. Joe was looking at the blood splatters and passing remarks. He was making movements with his hands as to how she was hit.

"Then he got down on his hunkers and said, 'When he [the killer] got her down, he wasn't going to let her up again.' The movements were imitating blows. He kept talking . . . 'He [the killer] must have done this and that.' Then he moved to the bathroom. He was seemingly going through the way she was murdered."

Jim Callaly said: "He said, 'This was the way she must have been murdered.' I nearly got sick, I was going to pass out."

Paul Callaly watched O'Reilly continue the re-enactment. "He moved to the bathroom. There was a drop of blood on the floor. He [O'Reilly] said, 'He [the killer] must have stopped here and heard her making a noise, groaning.' Then he moved back to outside the bedroom and dropped on one knee and enacted another blow."

Denise Callaly had been outside. She came to the bedroom. "He was on one knee, with his fist clenched, and he hit down into the ground, like he was hitting Rachel on the ground."

Jackie Connor gave similar evidence to the murder trial. On 25 October, she was at Adam's birthday at O'Reilly's mother's house in Dunleer. There, O'Reilly told her Rachel came to him in a dream and said, "Why are you doing this?"

Two days later, at the house in Baldarragh, Jackie went to Rachel's bedroom. "I was trying to make sense of it. Joe was in the hall. He said in the dream it was like he was doing it. He enacted two or three whacks. He turned towards the bathroom, and said, 'They heard gurgling, came back and gave her another whack at the door [of the bedroom].' He said they held her down."

He performed re-enactments for Rachel's friends, Fidelma Geraghty and Sarah Harmon, too. O'Reilly never admitted to killing his wife, but the re-enactments, including his professed knowledge of how the murder must have happened, provided an insight into how exactly Rachel may have died.

In particular, his suggestion that the killer had left Rachel in a battered state, gone to the bathroom and returned to finish her off, coincided with forensic evidence compiled by the gardaí – and unknown to O'Reilly at the time he performed the re-enactments – but which was ultimately deemed too inconclusive to present as evidence in court. An analysis of one of the blood splatters suggested that two layers of blood were present, the second having fallen a few minutes after the first. A second attack, some minutes after the first, would be consistent with the results of the analysis.

The re-enactments were a shocking display by a bereaved husband, particularly as those closest to Rachel had to watch them. But on their own they did not constitute evidence that he was a killer. None of what he said or did was in itself blatantly incriminating. In a criminal trial, it would be useful only as corroborative rather than primary evidence.

The real evidence being collated was the mobile-phone traffic and CCTV footage at various times of the morning on which Rachel had died.

O'Reilly's behaviour that Monday morning suggests he gave some consideration to the possibility of being snared by his phone, but he wasn't as clever as he thought. The email he sent to his friend Kieron Gallagher just after 8 a.m. illustrates his thinking. He didn't cancel a lunch appointment he knew he wouldn't keep. That might leave a trail. He told Gallagher that he would be "out and about most of the morning and in poor phone coverage areas".

He didn't want to contacted by phone, yet he obviously didn't know the extent to which phones could be mapped. At 9.52 a.m., Gallagher texted O'Reilly with a reply. The text was routed through the Murphy's Quarry mast near the O'Reilly home, putting him in the vicinity of the crime.

He had been obviously reluctant to use his phone that morning. Between 7.30 a.m. and 1.15 p.m. he made only one outward call (to Quearney at 10.04 a.m. for seven seconds) while receiving eleven. It was as if he thought refraining from initiating a call would be sufficient to eliminate his phone use as incriminating.

He told Pelley to minimise their affair. Yet on the day in question there were eighteen communications between the pair. Despite all the thought he had put into the crime, he left a trail for the guards with his phone, as clear as if his car had been pumping out bright red exhaust fumes all the way up to his home and back down to Broadstone, where he had attempted to construct an alibi.

The media played a major role in the fallout from the violent death of Rachel O'Reilly. Whether that role and its influence were positive or negative in terms of the pursuit of the killer and of justice remains a matter for debate.

Apart from reporting the violent death, the first media input of note was an appearance on television by O'Reilly with Rachel's parents, Rose and Jim. Just over a week after the killing, the three appeared on RTÉ Television's *News at One* to appeal for help in tracing the killer.

The Callalys looked uncomfortable, as befitting bereaved parents exposed to the glare of the media. O'Reilly was composed, offering insights that would have been more typical of your average barstool detective than a confused, heartbroken husband. However, the three appeared to be sharing their burden. They sat close together on the sofa at the Callaly family home.

Quite often following a violent death like Rachel O'Reilly's, the gardaí encourage the spouse, partner or person closest to the deceased to appear on TV. The tactic is most often used if somebody close to the dead person is hovering into the orbit of suspicion. Seeing them on TV might spark recollection in a viewer who hadn't yet come forward, or the suspect's manner might betray him.

By the time of the news broadcast, O'Reilly was in the frame but wasn't the sole focus of gardaí investigation. They didn't suggest that O'Reilly appear on TV, but neither did they discourage him. O'Reilly had already indicated his eagerness to engage with the media. On the night before the funeral, he told Rachel's friend Michelle Mulligan that he was advising the gardaí on how best to handle the media in relation to the case: "Joe said he'd suggested a number of things to the guards, like going to the media and telling his story as long as it was needed," Mulligan later said. Some relatives of victims of homicide find it cathartic to bare their soul to a media outlet. Other people do so in a genuine attempt to ensure their pain is not visited on others who may be in danger. O'Reilly had no problems in baring his soul. For a while, he couldn't get enough of the media. And while he may have embarked on this course in a strategic attempt to shield himself, it seems more likely that he simply loved the idea of being in the spotlight.

On 22 October, Rose Callaly and O'Reilly made their second appearance on TV. They were guests on *The Late Late Show*, while Jim, the remaining Callaly siblings and some friends of Rachel were in the studio audience.

The physical closeness that was evident in the news programme now appeared to be gone. The bereaved husband and mother did not sit together. There were no supportive glances as had been evident in their previous appearance. Rose directed all her answers to the show's host, Pat Kenny.

When O'Reilly was speaking, Rose looked out stonily at the audience. Her body language spoke volumes about the deteriorating relationship between O'Reilly and his wife's family.

O'Reilly remained composed when Kenny asked him the question that must have been on the tip of many tongues. Did he think that Rachel knew her killer?

"Yes, I think so," O'Reilly replied. "Where the murder happened was in the bedroom which is the very last room in the house, so it's the room you're least likely to bring someone you don't know because you're cornered.

"It's not a police theory, it's just my own personal belief that she knew the person, because why else would you kill her? If it's a violent robbery why go to the extreme of murdering the person unless they can identify you?

"There was a lot of blood and therefore there would have been a lot of blood on this person."

Towards the end of the interview, he expounded on possible suspects. "Everyone, including myself, is a suspect until this is resolved," he said. Once again, he had made a point of drawing as many as possible into the orbit of suspicion.

Apart from his TV appearance, O'Reilly did a telephone interview with Newstalk presenter Ger Gilroy on the Hallowe'en bank holiday Monday, 1 November. Already, he was finding that the media were turning against him. Gilroy asked him about the mounting speculation that he was the main suspect.

"Yeah, one of the tabloids had a nice front page last Sunday. 'I didn't do it, says Rachel's husband.' Well, the context used was they asked me were there any suspects and I said, 'Until the killer is caught everybody is a suspect.' I just have to learn to be more careful what I say. The gardaí did warn me about the media and they have questioned me. As Pat Kenny said the other night, eight out of ten times it's somebody who knew the victim. People are putting two and two together and getting seven."

Gilroy asked him how he was coping with the whole thing.

"I've two small kids and they've lost a mother. The last thing they need is to lose a father as well in a strait-jacket. No matter how hard this is on me, I have to remember I'm their sole parent and I can't let these things get to me."

Then Gilroy broached the other story that was current. There were towels missing from the house. Did O'Reilly think the person who did it had a shower afterwards?

"I suspect if the person had a shower they would have left their DNA on something and that will be found in the bathtub or around. The gardaí did have the house for eight days and the forensic people went through everything. So if they had a shower the guards will know that."

214

From the perspective of media professionals, O'Reilly was something of a coup. He was by then definitely a suspect, and yet he was willing to come on air to protest his innocence and offer his insight into who the killer might be. As with his re-enactments, he was either highly confident that he would get away with it or just plain stupid.

The print media also had a major input into the unfolding investigation. Within days, the *Evening Herald* was running front-page exclusives on the progress of the investigation into the crime.

For much of the remainder of a long investigation, the *Herald* would lead coverage in this manner. When the finger of suspicion pointed to O'Reilly, the newspaper appeared to have an inside track on the garda investigation. Time after time, the paper ran stories, declaring that O'Reilly was the "self-confessed chief suspect". The tone and content was leaning heavily towards the presumed garda view that O'Reilly had murdered his wife. For some, it amounted to a "trial by media" in which the evening newspaper had already convicted O'Reilly in the court of public opinion.

Yet, despite much comment around the coverage, and at a time when media intrusion is increasingly cited in the criminal-justice process, the defence hardly mentioned it in the trial. Any problem that O'Reilly had about the coverage would come with one major drawback: he himself had run to embrace the media after the killing.

*

O'Reilly was arrested twice, a month after the murder and again in March 2006. On both occasions he exercised, for the greater part, his right to silence. On 19 October 2006, he was charged with his wife's murder. After a week on remand, he secured bail.

The trial began on 25 June 2007 in Court Two in the Round Hall of the Four Courts. The court was packed for the first day of the trial, and the crowds grew as it dragged on. The queue for entry usually began forming soon after 9.30 a.m., ninety minutes before the scheduled start of the day's proceedings. Whether it was the media coverage surrounding Rachel's death, the wet summer or the trial itself, the public imagination had been fired.

Each day, O'Reilly came to court accompanied by his mother. She sat at the rear of the public gallery, alone more often than not. She would declare later that she always believed her son was innocent of the charge.

She had reason to be suspicious of the criminal-justice system. In 1976, when O'Reilly was barely a teenager, her brother Christy Lynch was jailed for murder. A former soldier, Lynch had been working as a painter-decorator on a house in Sandymount, where the body of a fifty-one-year-old woman, Vera Cooney, was found. Lynch was dragged in for questioning and made a statement under highly controversial circumstances. He was convicted of murder in the Central Criminal Court and jailed for life. Over the following four years, Lynch's case went through the appeal process.

Finally, in December 1980, the Supreme Court ruled that he should never have been convicted, and he was acquitted. The episode, naturally, left a scar on Lynch's extended family.

In the latter stages of the trial, Ann O'Reilly was joined by Joe's brother, Derek, who had been mentioned in the emails exchanged between Joe and his sister, Ann, who wasn't in court until the jury had retired to deliberate. The emails would provide some of the most dramatic and damning evidence in the trial.

Each day, Rachel's birth-mother, Teresa Lowe, sat in the front row of the public gallery. She was often accompanied by her son Thomas and other family members. The Callalys sat further forward, on a bench reserved for witnesses, lawyers and close family. Rachel's parents and four siblings were present every day and found much of the evidence upsetting.

Two hitches nearly scuppered the proceedings in the early stages. On the first day, the judge revealed it had been brought to his attention that one of the female jurors had had a conversation with a jury panel member in which she had mentioned the case and said something to the effect that this was the one where the man had killed his wife. Judge Barry White dismissed the juror, saying that justice didn't just have to be done, it had to be seen to be done.

Six days into the trial, the judge revealed that a copy of the book of evidence had been located in the jury room. Usually, the jury will not get to hear its entire content, so if any of the remaining eleven members had accessed it, the trial would have to be aborted. All jury members assured him that they hadn't opened it.

O'Reilly showed little emotion throughout the proceedings. During the opening of the prosecution case, senior counsel Denis Vaughan Buckley read an extract from the letter O'Reilly had left in Rachel's coffin. The defendant bowed his head and began to sob. That was the only time he showed any overt emotion over the death of his wife, or his role in it.

The first week was largely taken up with technical evidence and testimony from friends of Rachel about the comments O'Reilly had made in the aftermath of the killing. During the second week, the jury was sent out while a trial within a trial was conducted to evaluate whether certain evidence could be put before it. The crucial evidence was the mobile-phone mapping and the re-enactments O'Reilly had performed for the Callalys and some of Rachel's friends.

The re-enactment evidence was particularly difficult for the Callalys. Paul's wife, Denise, broke down in the box as she remembered the day when O'Reilly had shown them how he thought the killer had acted. Rose Callaly retained her composure, as she had earlier when she had testified about how she had discovered her daughter's body.

The prosecution argued that the re-enactments should be put before the jury because they displayed secret knowledge that only the killer could have had. Judge White disagreed. He couldn't find any secret knowledge in O'Reilly's actions. He ruled it would be unsafe to put the evidence before the jury. In legal terms, the re-enactment evidence was deemed to be potentially prejudicial rather than probative.

The mobile-phone evidence was a different matter. Engineer Oliver Farrell told the judge how he had tracked the use of O'Reilly's mobile phone on 4 October 2004 using records. He explained to the court how phones are normally routed through the nearest available masts, which make up the telecommunications network.

The results of his call-tracking were exhibited to the court on a graphic that showed the phone signal bouncing off masts on a route from the Bluebell industrial estate around 8 a.m., up to the M50 and into north Co. Dublin. In two communications at 9.25 a.m. and 9.52 a.m., the signal bounced off a mast in Murphy's Quarry, just down the road from the O'Reilly family home. Following that, the communications suggested a journey back south to Broadstone in the north inner city.

Farrell was asked whether his analysis of the location of the phone from around 8 a.m. until soon after 10 a.m. corresponded with Mr O'Reilly's account that he had travelled from his place of work in Bluebell industrial estate to Phibsboro-Broadstone bus garage. "It does not correspond," Farrell said.

A later batch of calls from 10.38 a.m. until 11.05 a.m.

was analysed. Farrell was asked whether these corresponded to O'Reilly's account of being at Phibsboro at that time. "They are consistent with that description," he said.

The journey mapped by the calls gave a timeline and tracking for O'Reilly's journey to Baldarragh at a time when he said he was at the bus garage in Broadstone.

An engineer employed by O2, Kareem Benabdullagh, was asked whether it was possible for a person to make a call in Phibsboro or Broadstone and have it routed through the Murphy's Quarry mast. "Impossible," he replied.

The evidence was devastating, putting O'Reilly near the scene of the murder at a time when he had said he was twenty miles away. Judge White ruled that it was admissible.

O'Reilly's alibi, Derek Quearney, was shaky on the time he had first seen O'Reilly at Broadstone that morning.

O'Reilly had said he arrived at the bus garage at 9 a.m. He couldn't locate the man he said was working there, Damien Tully, but he did locate Tully's van and mobile phone. As it turned out, Tully had been reassigned to another job that day. His replacement, Noel Paget, told the court he arrived at the garage between 10 and 10.15 a.m.

By that account, O'Reilly was hanging around for an hour without attempting to track an employee he suspected of dossing on the job. O'Reilly provided a street-by-street guide to his journey to work that morning. He didn't specify any street on the route he says he took to Broadstone.

The email exchanges with his sister the previous June showed a convincing motive. The prosecution also suggested that money had played a part. The couple's home was insured against the mortgage in a standard manner. In the event of one dying, the other would receive roughly the cost of the remaining mortgage, around €216,000 at the time of Rachel's death.

O'Reilly's defence counsel Patrick Gageby, in a well-thought-out speech, pointed out that his client's guilt simply hadn't been proved beyond reasonable doubt. He told the jury to be wary of the inexact nature of science, citing the cases of the Birmingham Six and Guildford Four. He blamed the media for creating a climate of suspicion against his client. The prosecution, he said, were trying to "marry a little science with a lot of suspicion".

The jury retired on the afternoon of Friday, 20 July. As soon as they had left, Judge White was told that the gardaí wanted to make an application to revoke O'Reilly's bail while the jury were deliberating.

Superintendent Joe Kelly told the judge that O'Reilly's two children were outside the jurisdiction and there were fears that O'Reilly might flee. The boys were staying in their uncle's home in Derry. The superintendent also claimed that O'Reilly had made comments to the effect that he would commit suicide if he was convicted.

O'Reilly and his brother were visibly agitated that the gardaí were going down this route. Judge White refused the request. O'Reilly would remain free at least until the jury had decided whether or not he was a murderer.

The jury was sent to a hotel for the night and resumed its deliberations on Saturday. At 6.40 p.m. that evening, minutes before the judge was due to send them out for a second night, the knock came on the door to the court: a verdict had been reached.

Despite it being the height of the weekend, when the rest of the Four Courts complex was deserted, the court was packed within minutes. The jury foreman handed the charge sheet to the registrar. "Guilty." The remainder of the registrar's function was drowned as the courtroom erupted in a roar more suited to a sporting arena. The confined environment amplified the sound.

A number of the Callalys jumped to their feet. Rachel's brothers, Paul and Declan, punched the air. Other members of the family hugged each other. A few of the gardaí who had been involved in the investigation were in tears. At the front of the public gallery, Teresa Lowe stood up and shouted, "Justice, justice." Two prison officers, apparently rattled by the reaction, moved closer to O'Reilly, as if to protect him if matters got out of control. When the noise died down, sobs could be heard coming from the Callaly and Lowe families.

The scenes were unprecedented for a trial in modern

times, a response of triumphal joy in the conviction of a murderer. But it represented a release of tension on the part of the victim's families and friends. For a long time, many had believed that O'Reilly was going to get away with murdering his wife.

Judge White asked O'Reilly to stand and imposed the mandatory life sentence. Then he was told that Rose Callaly wished to read a victim-impact statement.

She stepped into the witness box. "It's almost three years since Rachel kissed her beloved Luke and Adam goodbye, and for the next twenty minutes she was subjected to the most horrific, violent and barbaric attack that no human being should ever have to go through.

"We are haunted by the thought of what happened to our beautiful sister and daughter that morning. From that moment on, the lives of everybody who knew Rachel and loved her were thrown into turmoil.

"Even though justice has been done, our grief and distress will never diminish. Rachel was a truly beautiful, loving, caring and capable girl who has left so many memories, and she meant so much to so many – her aunts, uncles, cousins, niece and nephews and many friends.

"Each one of us has been traumatised by feelings of helplessness, shock, grief, and the horrific reality is that we can do nothing to bring her back. This is the hardest part of our pain.

"Not only did Rachel leave without saying goodbye, she also left her beloved sons, Luke and Adam, confused, scared and angry. We feel heartbroken as the biggest damage will surely be left at their door as they live their lives without the guidance and counselling of their best friend.

"Rachel was never away from their side, and her harrowing loss has left a huge void in both the boys' lives and in our lives.

"Every day we find it so difficult to accept the devastation of her death. We struggle to come to terms with the fact she is now gone for ever. There are days when we feel overwhelmed with grief. Sleepless nights, nightmares and panic attacks have become the norm for us. We often wake traumatised with fear by the images of terror, violence and brutality, and we wonder if we will ever return to some sense of normal life.

"We lost Rachel at the young age of thirty years, and we are devastated knowing we will never be able to share with her the enjoyment of all the milestones she was so looking forward to in her life and the possibility of one day sharing with her the enjoyment of seeing her own grandchildren. As a parent, it is devastating to lose a child, but under these circumstances it is unbearable.

"Rachel, if I could have given my life for you on that awful day I would have. You are such a big part of our life. Thank you for the short lifetime, which should have been so much longer and full of so many more happy memories. We treasure the memories of shared times with you. We miss you and love you so much, and not a day passes without you being remembered so lovingly."

She folded her piece of paper, got up and walked past O'Reilly. The room erupted again, this time in a resounding round of applause. As Rose Callaly passed Sergeant Pat Marry, the pair hugged.

The court emptied soon after, and the prison officers moved in to handcuff O'Reilly.

Outside, as the prison van left the Four Courts, there was cheering and jeering at the gates. Then the Callaly family emerged, walking in a line, arms raised in triumph for the photographers. Their supporters cheered as they came towards the gate, but there were also tears for Rachel and the violent and pre-meditated manner in which she had been killed.

6. AN INSANE TRAGEDY

The Case of Edward Hayes

Edward Hayes could relate to the Buddhist monks who engaged in the ultimate self-sacrifice for the sake of justice. Their grievance bore no relation to his, but he knew what it felt like to be helpless in the face of powerful dark forces. In June 1963, the Buddhist monk Thích Quang Duc sat down in the central market square in Saigon, poured petrol over himself and lit a match in protest at the treatment of the monks under the South Vietnamese regime. His self-immolation was photographed and broadcast around the world. He was followed by a number of other monks. The photographs of burning bodies sitting calmly on the street were to be one of the most prominent images of the Vietnam War.

Edward Hayes could see where the monks were coming from. He knew the burden of labouring in the wilderness under a burning grievance, as the world carries on in its merry way. Early in 1965, he considered following the monks' example. If he were to sit down in Limerick city and set himself alight, people might finally wake up to what was going on.

After pause for thought, he decided against self-immolation. If he were to do that, then nobody would know the detail of the injustice to which he was being subjected. And everyone might just ignore him, as they had been doing for a number of years.

By 1965, Hayes was suffering from a full-blown psychiatric condition. His physical health was also poor, although he was only forty-eight. That year he suffered a heart attack and had to cut back on the work he did on his farm, in the townland of Clonconane, in the North Liberties, a few miles from Limerick city. Before the year was out, he would take a life in the ultimate act of protest, but not his own.

The first manifestation of Hayes's illness could be traced back seven years to an incident involving one of his six children. There was some bullying at school, in which another boy assaulted his son. Hayes had a conversation with the other boy's father. When he saw the boy one day on the road, he gave the youth a clip on the ear. A court case resulted in which Hayes was bound over to keep the peace. He was of the opinion that witnesses had perjured themselves in the proceedings to get at him and his family.

His sense of grievance was heightened by a belief that his children were now being treated as outcasts or undesirables in school. Later, two teachers would testify that the Hayes children were very satisfactory pupils and popular among their peers. Their father didn't see it that way.

His troubles spread to his working life. A few land deals went sour. In one, he had wanted to sell land, but not to the person who had earlier secured an option to buy. There was another problem with land for which he had acquired planning permission. It was assigned for residential use, but Hayes wanted to build a factory on it.

Small things ballooned in significance. A number of horses belonging to an itinerant – as travellers were then known – strayed onto his land. He issued a civil summons against the itinerant. The case was adjourned a number of times, leading Hayes to believe that those who were intent on doing him down now included the judiciary. When the case came to court, he shouted from the back of the room that he was withdrawing the summons.

One group that preyed greatly on his mind were solicitors, who were collectively ranged against him and led by one of the most influential politicians of the time, Donogh O'Malley.

O'Malley was the local Fianna Fáil TD in Limerick. In the 1960s, he was Minister for Health, and subsequently education, where he introduced free secondary-school education, heralded as one of the most socially progressive moves of the past half-century.

Hayes knew O'Malley. He delivered milk to the politician's home. But as Hayes's problems mounted, he saw O'Malley's hand in the forces ranged against him. Over time, he became convinced that O'Malley was frustrating his efforts to sell the land. O'Malley must be intimidating solicitors whom Hayes had retained and controlling solicitors acting for other parties. He was using his powerful position in the government to stifle Hayes in other ways.

Hayes wrote to agriculture minister Charles Haughey about his problems with the land, but Haughey wrote back saying there was little he could do. Hayes was convinced that Haughey's drinking buddy O'Malley was pulling Haughey's strings.

O'Malley's influence was everywhere. In his court case over the trespass, the itinerant was represented by O'Malley's nephew, Des, who, twenty years later, would establish the Progressive Democrats. In those proceedings, Hayes was convinced the younger O'Malley had intimidated his solicitor.

Of course, there was no truth in any of it. No evidence was ever elicited to suggest that Donogh O'Malley or anybody associated with him ever attempted to do any wrong to Edward Hayes. Issues over land, particularly inheritance issues, touch the most primal instinct of farmers, and when the law does not converge with their implacably held beliefs, solicitors, the law officers, are often held to blame. In the case of Edward Hayes, this tendency was immeasurably amplified by his psychiatric condition, which had developed into a pathological state of paranoia.

At home, he felt his wife Bridget was giving him little support. Every time he mentioned the forces ranged against him, her reply was the same: "Leave those people to God," she would say.

By 1964, he had some intimation that he was ill. He felt like killing somebody, preferably "one of the O'Malley clan". He took down a shotgun he owned, considered what he should do, and in the end decided to try to save himself and anybody else from the turmoil that was haunting him.

He presented himself at Limerick city garda station, where he told Inspector John Reynolds that he had a murderous impulse and should be locked up. The garda suggested that he admit himself to St Joseph's psychiatric hospital. Hayes agreed it was for the best.

He admitted himself and stayed for four days. The doctor told him to put the worries at the back of his mind, not to dwell on the sharp practice and to go home. The intervention provided him with a brief respite. For the next few months, he managed to avoid slipping into deeper paranoia. Relations with his wife improved. Everything was on a relatively even keel.

But the following year, he was back in the blues. He suffered a heart attack. His wife's lack of support for him in his battles, as he saw it, led to a serious deterioration in their relationship. For most of the year, Hayes only spoke to her when absolutely necessary.

Above all, he became convinced that the only

recourse open to him was to get his story out to the wider world beyond the reach of O'Malley's influence. Then people would see the injustice being visited on him. He didn't renew his driving licence so that he would be brought to court. He was summonsed, and, on the appointed day when his case was called, he told the district justice he wished to read out a letter. The judge asked him what it concerned. Hayes said it was about prominent people in the area. The judge refused him permission to read it out and fined him ten shillings.

On 15 October 1965, Hayes left his home at 8.40 a.m. to drive five of his children to school. He returned a few minutes after 9 a.m. Bridget was bringing in the cows when he arrived back at the house. There was nobody else at home.

He went inside to the sitting room. Bridget came in from the farmyard to make his tea. While she was in the kitchen, Hayes went to one of the outhouses. He took a wrench from a toolbox and went back inside to the sitting room.

Within a minute or so, his wife came into the room with the tea. She put it down next to the fireplace. Hayes got up and hit her on the head with the wrench. Neither of them said anything. He hit her again, and at least two more times. She fell to the ground. He dropped the wrench to the floor. He walked out, got into his car and drove to Limerick city garda station, the same station he had visited the previous year to confess his impulse to kill.

At the station, he told Inspector John Reynolds that he had killed his wife. He asked that a doctor and a priest be sent to his home. Reynolds contacted the emergency services and drove out to Clonconane. When he entered the sitting room, he saw Bridget Hayes in a pool of blood. She was conscious. The garda asked her what happened.

"I can't remember," she replied. "Oh, my God, oh, my God."

Bridget Hayes was brought to a city hospital and died the following day.

At Limerick garda station, Hayes offered to make a statement. "I felt I had to do something that would not be suppressed in order to get a trial. My reason for hitting my wife was to get a trial to clear my children's name and their property. I intended to kill my wife as I'd felt I had to do something really desperate to get justice for my children.

"I felt there was a stigma on my children's names because of the perjury of a neighbour, and my business and my health were destroyed because of what I believe to be fraud perpetrated by Donogh O'Malley, minister for health, and his henchmen.

"I have done everything humanly possible to bring my grievance out and failed, so I had to do something desperate, and I felt, as I was not able to earn my living by working because of my health, both from nervous strain and because of a heart attack, I was in my children's way and was nothing more than a bad example.

"Instead of attempting to kill my wife I would have attempted to kill one of the O'Malley element, only I felt that if I did so they would take my children's property and leave them destitute.

"My wife's attitude to all this seemed to be as if I was to blame. I had not been on speaking terms with my wife for almost a year. We only spoke to each other when absolutely necessary because she had been nagging me over the land.

"When I hit my wife this morning, I didn't wait to see if she was dead. I thought she was when she fell."

When he finished the statement, he was crying. He asked one of the gardaí how his wife was.

Two days later, Hayes was charged with murder. He was remanded to Mountjoy Prison, where a doctor examined him. Later, he was released and sent to the Central Mental Hospital in Dundrum.

Immediately, the gardaí knew they were dealing with a case that required sensitivity rather than dogged investigation. Hayes's visit to the station the previous year, interviews with doctors and family, a cursory examination of his business affairs all pointed to a serious psychiatric condition. The man had never been violent towards his wife previously, and the motive he offered suggested a mind beyond any rational reasoning.

The violent death of Bridget Hayes occurred at a time in which homicide was rare. In 1965, seven murders were committed in the state and five other fatalities were classified as manslaughter.

The case dragged on through the following year without resolution. In February 1967, a hearing in the High Court was convened to determine whether Hayes was fit to stand trial. At the end of the hearing, the jury voted unanimously that he was.

The murder trial opened in the Central Criminal Court in Dublin on Monday, 27 November 1967. Hayes told the trial judge, Seamus Henchy, that he had dispensed with the services of a counsel, and he wanted to represent himself. He was pleading not guilty.

The judge invited him to take his place on the bench reserved for lawyers at the top of the court. Hayes came forward and sat in beside the gowned and bewigged prosecuting barristers.

Opening the case, the state's lawyer, Anthony Hederman, told the jury that there would be medical evidence that at the time of the killing the defendant was suffering from insane thinking and from a persecution complex. Under these circumstances, and in the twilight of a sick mind, he should not be branded a murderer. He told the members that this was the first time a jury was being asked to decide on an issue like this.

The prosecution was asking the jury for a guilty but insane verdict. This in itself was highly unusual. In 1964, a new Criminal Justice Act modernised much of the law, including the definition of murder to that which is still used today. One of the new provisions was effectively to abolish the death penalty for murder, except for a few specific types of cases.

Before the new provision, defendants on a murder charge sometimes pleaded guilty but insane in an attempt to avoid the death penalty. And sometimes juries, who were reluctant to condemn a person to death, were willing to accept such a plea.

The Hayes case was different. Here the prosecution accepted totally that the defendant was legally insane at the time of the killing. The only reason the trial was going ahead at all was because Hayes wanted it. He was finally getting a chance to air the grievances that were haunting him.

One of the first witnesses for the prosecution was psychiatrist Michael Reynolds of the Central Mental Hospital. He told the court that Hayes had come under his care on 1 November 1965. His troubles appeared to have begun about eight years prior to that when he became obsessed with the idea that his children were being treated as outcasts.

The doctor was of the opinion that Hayes's state became pathological around 1960. He was consumed by the idea that he was being done down, and this absorbed much of his consciousness, day after day.

Hayes cross-examined the witness. He referred to the High Court hearing to determine whether he was fit to stand trial. "Isn't it true the decision of the jury was that I was not of unsound mind and not incapable of managing my affairs?"

"That is true," Reynolds replied.

"Did you get the impression that what I wanted was to be put on trial?"

"Yes."

"Would you agree that it would be very hard for a man to act normally in the circumstances that you are aware of in my case?"

"It depends on the man," Reynolds said. "A reasonable man with grievances like yours would reach a stage where he cuts his losses and decides that he can do nothing more about them. A reasonable man would not be so tenacious or determined that he would have to do some grievous wrong to somebody else."

Two other doctors were called to confirm Hayes's paranoid condition.

A number of solicitors against whom Hayes held a grievance were also called. Some of them, including a Dermot O'Donovan, had acted for Hayes. O'Donovan was cross-examined closely by Hayes, who kept referring to Donogh O'Malley.

At one point, O'Donovan said to Hayes: "It might be of interest to the jury to know when you fell out with Donogh O'Malley."

"I never fell in or out with him," Hayes replied.

"Why did you stop delivering his milk?" the witness asked the defendant, who was supposed to be questioning the witness.

"I stopped delivering milk generally because I was worried about this deal and got a heart-attack. I delivered milk for two weeks longer to Donogh O'Malley than anybody else to facilitate him."

Later in the cross-examination, Hayes referred to a document he had signed in O'Donovan's office, relating to his land. "Did you tell me before I signed the document that Charles Haughey was a director of the company?"

"It was you who told me that," the witness replied.

"I expected that answer. I did not tell you that," Hayes retorted.

The examination of the other witnesses went on in the same vein. When it came to the defence case, Hayes went into the witness box himself.

"I felt that I could not give in to being walked on. I drove the children to school. I came home. I felt I would have to force myself to be put on trial. I got a wrench and when my wife came in I struck her three or four times. I did not mean to kill her.

"I felt my wife would be looked after and I would be put on trial. I was suppressed by these people, but I felt they could not suppress murder, no matter how much influence they had in the country.

"I know I have done a terrible thing. I was not being treated fairly. My wife used to say to me, 'Knock it off, leave those people to God, good does not go with bad.' It was like a red rag to a bull.

"My wife was not nagging me. I tried to get myself into trouble so that I could come to trial and clear all this thing up. What I did was to put myself in the worst possible position so that I could get a trial. When it was put to me what did I hope to get from a trial, I say now that I believe that I should get a state inquiry into the whole affair. Whatever your decision on me is, I ask you to recommend an inquiry by the attorney-general. That is what I expect to get out of this trial."

Hederman, for the prosecution, put it to him that he was fabricating some of his grievances in order to attack certain people in Limerick.

"I don't look on it that way. I had a fear limited to a few people in Limerick," he replied.

Why did he pick his wife to kill?

"I felt that if I interfered with other people they would take away the children's money and property from them."

"Do you think that the attack on your wife and all that happened since has cleared their names?"

"Not now. Things have got so bad I've done more harm than good."

"The main reason you selected your wife as a victim was because you resented her charitable disposition?"

"It could be part of it," Edward Hayes replied.

At the conclusion of the evidence, Hayes was asked whether he would like to address the jury. He said he had nothing to say.

Hederman told the jury that criticism had been made by the defendant of a number of Limerick solicitors. There was no truth in the criticism made against any of these people.

Hayes thought his wife was "too Christian" and she was not prepared to go along with him in building certain grievances against certain people. His attitude towards her in 1965 was that he resented her goodness, in the sense of her attitude to life, and of putting things in their proper perspective.

The prosecution had opened the case on the basis that a proper verdict would be that the crime had been committed by a person who should not be branded a murderer and that was the note on which it closed.

The judge's final remarks were in a similar tone: "He may have been under the delusion that he was a public executioner and would not know the moral nature of what he was doing. I think you can agree that he is medically insane as the reasons given for killing are so irrational, motiveless and perverted that it is very hard to see that they came from the working of a normal mind."

The judge added that it had been a hard and distressing trial for everybody involved. The jury retired on the fourth day of the trial and returned a "guilty but insane" verdict after fifteen minutes. Judge Henchy remanded Hayes to the Central Mental Hospital at the pleasure of the minister for justice.

The case had been handled with commendable sensitivity for the time. The man who killed his wife was himself a victim. He had attempted to seek help, but the seriousness of his condition was not recognised. The evolution of psychiatric medicine was such in the mid-sixties that it would have been difficult to identify him as a real danger to others.

While the prosecution made known its wish not to brand Edward Hayes a murderer, the "guilty but insane" verdict that was available at the time classified him as such in the technical sense. It would be another forty years, until the Criminal Law Insanity Act 2006, before the law would accommodate a verdict of "not guilty by reason of insanity".

Edward Hayes died in October 1981 while still a patient in the Central Mental Hospital.

7. THE MAN WHO RAN
OUT OF ROAD

The Case of James Lehman

Winnie O'Callaghan was worried that the electricity was going to be cut off. It was already clocking in at a hundred units in excess of her ration. Wartime rules stipulated that if you breached your ration, you might well have to do without electricity. There was little tolerance of any rule-flouting. Everything was rationed during the Emergency: although the country was officially neutral between 1939 and 1945, it was impossible to ignore what was going on beyond the shores and borders of the Free State.

Winnie was in a bind. Her own family, which occupied the ground floor of her home at 11 Leinster Road in Rathmines, was careful with the amount of electricity they used. She was a widow and had instilled in her son and daughter the need to watch every penny.

The problem was her tenants, the Lehmans, who occupied the first floor of the house. They had moved in three months previously, on 7 January 1944. He was a Canadian, a good-looking man, always in a positive mood, who ran a business in Chelmsford Road, over in Ranelagh. His wife Margaret, or Peg, was from Co. Kildare, a pleasant woman who was pregnant with their third child. Her son Kevin and daughter Patricia were three and one respectively.

Winnie O'Callaghan had some sympathy for Margaret Lehman. She seemed to be having a difficult time coping with two children and her advanced pregnancy. She didn't know anybody in the locality. She had family in the city, but getting around with two small children wasn't easy. While Mr Lehman appeared to be a proper gentleman, he wasn't at home much.

When they had first arrived, Winnie had provided them with two electric rings and a strong box on which to place them. Mr Lehman assured her he would be getting a gas cooker, but there was no sign of it yet. He said he would buy it through his shop, but nothing had come of that. If they continued using the rings, there would be trouble. She also needed the box back as her son required a home for his guinea pigs. But she didn't want to hassle them about it, not with Margaret's condition.

On St Patrick's Day, Winnie brought Margaret the evening paper. She frequently went up to the young mother at that time of day. Her husband was usually out. His routine saw him leave at 9.30 a.m. to go to his shop. He returned for his dinner for an hour around 1 p.m., and then came home at 6.30 p.m. for supper. More often than not, he went out in the evening again and mightn't return until 11 p.m.

Margaret was left alone with the children. After supper, she usually bathed the pair and put them to bed. They slept in the same room as their parents. The other room had been fashioned into a small kitchenette. Often at night, Winnie would come up to keep Margaret company. They would sit in the kitchenette, while Winnie did her mending.

On St Patrick's night, Winnie didn't stay long. The following day – a Saturday – they met in the afternoon. Margaret had developed a cold. She was now, by Winnie's calculations, a few weeks short of full term, but despite the cold she was in top form.

On Sunday morning, Winnie O'Callaghan went to church and returned home at 1.30 p.m. She was at home for the rest of the day but didn't encounter the Lehmans. Margaret often came down for tea on a Sunday, but when she didn't appear Winnie presumed she was staying away because of her cold.

Winnie intended to travel across the city that evening to visit relatives. She was hoping to catch the number 16 bus at 7.45 p.m. At 7.20 p.m., she visited the bathroom. In there, she heard a noise overhead, a sort of commotion she couldn't really recognise.

The Lehmans' kitchenette was directly above her bathroom.

On returning to her own kitchen, she noticed a strange smell. She asked her daughter whether she could smell it. Her daughter pointed out that she was cleaning her shoes, which might be the source. Winnie didn't think any more about it.

A few minutes later, she went out the back to fetch turf, which was stored under a stone staircase leading to the first floor. Returning to the house, she met James Lehman going out, carrying the two electric rings and the box. "I'm getting the gas cooker tomorrow, you'll be glad to know," Lehman told her. "It's coming from the country."

Winnie was relieved. It felt like a small burden had been lifted from her. "How is Mrs Lehman?" she enquired.

"Not great. She's been complaining she feels giddy, and if she's not better in the morning, I think I'll call a doctor."

"And a nurse," Winnie reminded him. If Margaret was nearing full-term, it would be prudent to have a nurse or midwife on hand. Lehman nodded in response. He was dressed in his customary evening attire, a lounge suit. The two chatted for a few minutes. Winnie then realised she might miss her bus and hurried back inside to get ready.

Within a minute, Lehman came tearing down the stairs. "Come quickly," he pleaded. "My wife is terribly ill."

She followed Lehman up the stairs. She heard moans from the bedroom. The smell she had first noticed some minutes earlier was more pronounced. "I brought her in rum for her cold and she must have taken it," Lehman said.

The light was on in the bedroom. The curtains were drawn. Both of the children were in the single bed, dressed in their night clothes. Margaret Lehman was in the double bed. The blankets were pulled up to her chin. Her face was contorted, her eyes wide open and glassy. She was frothing at the mouth.

Winnie put her hand to Margaret's head. It was cold and clammy. She tried talking to her but there was no response. Lehman was pacing madly up and down the room, crying. Winnie turned to him and said she had never seen anything like this before in her life. Lehman continued crying, helpless in the face of an emergency.

Winnie hurried down and out her front door. The Rathmines chapel bell was ringing through the falling darkness as she walked two doors up to number seven, where her friend, Annie Byrne, lived. She told her of the emergency and suggested Annie telephone for a doctor from the kiosk next to the library at the bottom of Leinster Road. There was a Dr McCormick in Terenure. Winnie hurried back to her home and up to the Lehmans' quarters.

When she re-entered the bedroom, Margaret Lehman's eyes were closed. Her face was a bluish purple and she had stopped moaning. Winnie thought perhaps she was asleep.

"Mrs Byrne is gone to get a doctor," she told Lehman, who was still pacing the room. "I hope they're on time."

Within minutes, Annie Byrne arrived in, short of breath. Dr McCormick told her that Mrs Lehman sounded like an immediate case for hospital. Annie Byrne had phoned for an ambulance. They stood around and waited for help to arrive, in what must have been a forlorn scene. Margaret Lehman, young and pregnant, motionless in the bed, the covers pulled up to her chin, life apparently ebbing away from her; the two concerned neighbours standing over her; the hysterical husband pacing up and down the small room; and the couple's two children, awoken from their sleep to a scene of chaos and worry.

Margaret Hayden was born in 1915 and grew up in Narraghmore, a rural part of south Co. Kildare. She was one of seven children, four girls and three boys. Her family was among the majority poor in the country. Work was a privilege. Margaret's father eventually travelled to England to seek a job, leaving his family behind, a not uncommon feature of life in Ireland in the 1930s.

Margaret left home at fifteen to look for work in Dublin. She managed to secure a job as domestic help in the capital, but in 1937, when she was twenty-two, she emigrated to England with her sister, Julia. They followed work around the south of England for two years. In September 1939, England declared war on Germany. Investment in the war effort meant more work would be available around army bases. The Hayden sisters moved to Aldershot in October and quickly found jobs at the barracks in the town.

Early in January, Margaret was serving in a shop there when a young Canadian private passed her a five-dollar bill for a purchase. He was newly arrived in the country, unaware that a different currency was used in England. Margaret explained the difference to him. He introduced himself as James Lehman. The conversation led to a casual friendship, and, within weeks, the couple managed to get a weekend away in London, booking into a hotel as man and wife.

By the end of February they were married. They set up home in Aldershot, and later that year moved to Surrey. Lehman was still serving in the army and could have been called up to the front in France at any time. Julia came to live with them for a while. On Christmas Day 1940 Kevin was born.

Lehman managed to pull a medical discharge from the army. He tried his hand at a number of different jobs. For a while he kept poultry, but that was never going to make them rich. Then he worked for an engineering firm. The family kept moving around England, trying to keep their heads above water at a time when most economic activity was directed towards defeating Adolf Hitler.

Julia visited regularly. She noticed that once the initial passion had died down, her sister and brother-in-law were not getting on very well. Money was tight, but that was the way with everybody. It was as if James Lehman felt he deserved more, and when it wasn't forthcoming, his frustration began to reveal itself.

Julia observed that Margaret was often practically destitute, irrespective of whether or not her husband was working. In January 1943, a daughter, Patricia, was born. Within months, the couple were making plans to go to Ireland.

It is unclear who wanted to make the move. Lehman would later say that Margaret was particularly concerned about the nightly air raids over southern England. The German Luftwaffe was intent on pounding Britain into submission by crossing the English Channel each night on bombing expeditions. The moaning air-raid sirens were a constant feature of life.

Julia Hayden remembered things differently. In her opinion, later related in court, it was Lehman who wanted the family to move to Margaret's native country. He might himself have been fearful of the air raids or have expected to be called back to the army. Maybe he saw a possibility of making serious money so that he could elevate himself to the style he felt he deserved.

In March 1943, Julia looked after the children as the couple travelled to London to sort out a passport for Lehman. It was three years since the romantic weekend in the city, but relations between the pair were now in danger of souring irrevocably. Another move, this time to a different country, might give the marriage a chance.

The passport wasn't a problem, and by August the Lehman family boarded a ferry for Dublin. Since leaving in 1937, Margaret had only been home once, for a fortnight's holiday. Now she was returning with her family, which was still growing, as she was pregnant again.

Initially, the Lehmans moved in with Margaret's mother, also Margaret, in the small cottage in Narraghmore. With Lehman out of work, they had to survive on his army pension, £11.10 per month. The amount was small but manageable. For instance, jobs advertised in the *Irish Press* in the same year were offering £20 per month for the manager of a knitwear factory, and £42 per month for an accountant.

Within weeks of arriving back in Ireland, Lehman fell ill. He suffered recurring back pain. A visit to the doctor uncovered osteoarthritis of the spine, a degenerative condition that results in joint pain. The local GP told Lehman that he should be in hospital.

In early October, he was admitted to the Ministry of Pensions Hospital in Leopardstown, in south Co. Dublin. The condition did not necessitate confinement to bed, but it required him to receive ongoing treatment.

Annie McCaigue was a nurse at the hospital. She came from Carrigmacross in Co. Monaghan. She couldn't help liking the new patient, a tall, good-looking man with a full moustache, plenty of chat and a keen intelligence. He was also a good listener. He told her he was in the Canadian Air Force, a glamorous job in wartime Ireland.

The patient had been the victim of some bad luck. He told her he had been married to an Irishwoman, who turned out to be already married. He had been devastated. On the other hand, it might have been a blessing in disguise. "She was beneath me," Lehman told Annie McCaigue. "She brought me down to the gutter. Her people are in Kildare and they live like pigs. I've been down there and it's a terrible place."

Despite being duped, he didn't hold a grudge, so he and the bigamous woman had parted as friends. She had gone back to live with her first husband, a man named Stokes.

A friendship developed between the nurse and this grounded Canadian airman, as he styled himself. Over the weeks that followed, he filled her in a bit more on his background. He had been a solicitor before he entered the forces, but now he was intent on making his fortune in business.

In early December, he left the hospital. Later, he would claim that he discharged himself in response to a letter from his wife saying that there was trouble at the family home in Kildare, and she felt it was time to leave. He didn't immediately send word to Margaret and the children to join him in Dublin. Before leaving the hospital, he invited Annie McCaigue to the pictures. She told him she had a boyfriend in Dublin. He was unfazed by the competition. He brought her to a hotel or lodging house in Mount Street, in which he had rented a room. Annie McCaigue was swept off her feet. The other boyfriend fell by the wayside.

Pretty soon, he was moving things ahead full speed. He told her he had bought her a ring but didn't want to give it to her yet. He also outlined his major plan in business. He was going to open up a baby-food shop. Baby food was all the rage and nobody had yet tapped into the potential. By his calculation, he would soon have a chain of shops throughout the city, and when the war was over, the world was out there to be conquered.

Lehman told the young nurse he wanted their union to be all-encompassing. She should come aboard the business. He would make her a supervisor in his first shop, pay her £20 a month and give her the free use of a car. Annie McCaigue was cautious. She knew that in the Ireland of the 1940s she was fortunate to have a good job at the hospital, steady and uncomplicated, until such time as she married. But Lehman was persistent. "When are you going to put some money in my business?" he said to her on another occasion, half in jest, wholly in earnest. In the end, she relented. She wasn't giving up her job, but she was willing to invest £25 from her savings.

Meanwhile, back in Lehman's other life, Margaret and the children arrived in Dublin just before Christmas. Despite his subsequent claim that Margaret had had to get out of her mother's house, he showed no urgency in bringing them to Dublin.

The proprietor of the hotel in Mount Street was, like most who encountered Lehman, charmed by the Canadian. Gertrude Moores remembered him always talking about his wife, how he was locked into a bad marriage, and all that he had to do for her. In England, he related, they had had two maids but it was never enough for his wife. Moores considered that he talked like an American, referring to the widespread perception in Ireland at the time that everybody in America was wealthy.

"Oh, well, it was a war marriage, and you know what they are," he said. The mores of the time ensured that he didn't spell out exactly what he meant – that he had had to marry his wife because she was pregnant. In the edifice of fantasy he was constructing, not even that detail was true.

Much to Gertrude Moores' surprise, within a few weeks Lehman's wife and two children turned up. Lehman's new circumstances required more accommodation. Moores also owned an apartment in Upper Mount Street, to which Lehman now moved with his family.

It became obvious to the Lehmans' landlady that money was tight. Despite all James Lehman's talk and social graces, he seemed to be broke. That Christmas, he came to Gertrude Moores and explained that his pension hadn't come through. The family had no money to buy dinner for the big day. Was there any way she could help? Moores said of course she would. Lehman suggested that he and his son could join

Moores and her husband for Christmas dinner. At Gertrude Moores' suggestion, dinner was also sent up to Margaret and the baby Patricia in the apartment at the far end of the street. Lehman's anxiety to be fed at Christmas time didn't extend to any concern for his pregnant wife.

A few days after Christmas, the intrepid Canadian showed up at Gertrude Moores' again, this time laden with a turkey and a ham, which required cooking. He told her he'd got them from his brother-in-law. Later, he said he had sold some of his clothes so that his family might have a proper feed over the festive period.

In any event, he asked Moores to cook the meat for him. She obliged and sent it down to the apartment. He didn't offer any to his landlady in reciprocation for her generosity a few days earlier.

The year 1944 dawned bright and expectant for James Lehman. He was going into business. In early January, he decided it was high time to move on from the debts he had built up with his landlady and start out elsewhere with a clean slate. Quietly, the family left the apartment in Mount Street, after Lehman had located rooms for rent at 11 Leinster Road in Rathmines. With their meagre belongings, they headed across town.

Next up was getting his business off the ground. He put an advert in the *Evening Mail* seeking applicants for a job in his baby-food shop. A young woman named Anne Finucane answered the advert.

Lehman arranged to meet her in her home. He told her about the position and the endless possibilities on offer.

The salary was thirty shillings a week, but he would also require a deposit of £40, as he was offering a piece of the business. Anne Finucane jumped at the opportunity to work with a man who appeared to be going places fast.

He acquired premises on Chelmsford Road in Ranelagh. By mid-January, the place was renovated and a splash of paint added to brighten it up. Annie McCaigue wasn't the only one who invested in the business. In total, Lehman managed to find £250 as capital for the venture. Then, on 25 January, Sister Anne's Baby Saloon opened for business. Lehman would later mention to Anne Finucane that the Anne in the shop's name was his fiancée, Annie McCaigue.

McCaigue was an early visitor. Lehman introduced her to his trusty assistant, Finucane. Later that day, he told his employee: "This is the lady I intend to marry." He also told her that the lady in question was the real boss, and he had bought her a ring costing £300.

Meanwhile, back at Leinster Road, Margaret was struggling. After they moved in, she was effectively housebound for six weeks. With a three-year-old and a one-year-old, she needed some form of transport, but from what her new landlady, Winnie O'Callaghan, observed, she had nothing. In the middle of February, Winnie saw Margaret with a go-car for the younger child. After that, Margaret went out daily, taking the air, walking down to Rathmines village, where she looked at the shops.

Occasionally, she stopped into a café for a cup of tea, and it was there one day that Winnie bumped into her. From then on they met frequently, and often walked back to Leinster Road together. Margaret didn't give much away, but Winnie O'Callaghan could see that she was lonely.

Over on Chelmsford Road, Lehman was thinking big. As well as Anne Finucane to run the shop, he required the services of a nurse, who would advise the mothers about health matters and food. Winifred McMahon answered the job advert in the *Irish Independent* and accepted the offer of two hours' work, four days a week.

The mothers of Dublin weren't breaking down the door of Sister Anne's Baby Saloon. In fact, the first weeks of business brought very little custom. Lehman whiled away some idle hours by unburdening himself to his staff of the travails he was suffering in his private life. He spoke about the war and the grief it had brought him, specifically how the conflict had thrown him together with his wife. "I have only hated one person in my life and I have never hated anyone as I hate her," he told Finucane one day, without specifying the object of his hate.

"Do I know who you mean?" Finucane asked.

"Yes, you do," he replied.

He told Finucane that his wife was unbalanced and her mother was insane. He said his wife was living in

Harold's Cross and he was in digs. He hardly ever mentioned his wife's name, it was all "she" or "her".

On another occasion, he told Nurse McMahon that he had been wounded in France, then sent back to England. One night he had got drunk and had woken up in the morning next to this woman. The army had forced him to marry her.

McMahon was surprised that the army was empowered to force a soldier to marry against his will.

"The military are very strict," he told her, in a sombre tone.

The nurse was not impressed by her boss or his venture. She gave up her job after three weeks.

From the testimonies of a number of people who encountered Lehman, it was obvious that he despised his wife to the extent that he constantly spoke of her in anger. It may be that he was by nature such a talker that he couldn't help laying bare his life as he saw it. On the other hand, his tales of derring-do in the army, the history he invented for his marriage and his story that he was a grounded officer were the work of a fantasist.

Everything he poured out suggested that he felt weighed down by the burden of a wife and children, and, if set free from it, his potential to fulfil his dreams – or fantasies – would be realised.

Annie McCaigue was a frequent visitor to the shop, checking on her investment and her fiancé. During one of her visits, Lehman told her he had heard that his ex-wife had taken an overdose of Anadin and ended up in Naas Hospital. He wasn't worried, though – Stokes (the man Lehman claimed was married to Margaret) and his family could take care of her.

One day, Margaret Lehman went into the shop with Winnie O'Callaghan. The two women had met in Rathmines village and decided to have a peep at Lehman's business. To the best of the knowledge of the assistant, Anne Finucane, it was the first time that the proprietor's wife had shown up.

The two women were met by Lehman, and he spent a few minutes with them, although they didn't receive the attention they might have expected. After they left, Lehman told Finucane that the younger woman was his "ex-lady love".

Sister Anne's Baby Saloon didn't last the course. Most small businesses take at least a few months to get off the ground, but four weeks after the shop opened, Lehman had seen enough. The baby-food business wasn't all it was cracked up to be. He declared that he was going into another line instead: importing coffee. The shop was renamed Leigh's. New stock appeared on the shelves, but custom didn't improve. Lehman's hopes of setting the world alight with his business acumen began to dissipate.

The women who surrounded him still appeared to retain their trust in him. His wife had no idea that the business was going so badly. At that stage of the marriage, she was accustomed to having no money. Perhaps she comforted herself with the eternal hope that brighter days loomed on the horizon.

Anne Finucane had invested in the baby-food business, but Lehman's apparent self-confidence and his charm tempted her to hang in there until the new venture turned a corner. Later, she would say: "When I worked for him, I always found him to be very nice, thoughtful, kind and very intelligent."

Annie McCaigue had an even bigger investment in the dashing entrepreneur. Apart from her financial contribution, she had left another relationship and had thrown in her lot with the man and his big ideas.

For Lehman, time was running out. He was now in a level of debt from which it would be nigh on impossible to extract himself in the short term. He quite obviously felt trapped in his marriage, and even by his children. Annie McCaigue may have represented a passing interest, an escape from reality, or she may have meant something more to him, but he had also fed her lies that she would most likely find unforgivable. To top it all, there was another child on the way, another mouth to feed.

On 4 March, Lehman walked into Gilsenan's chemist at 220 Lower Rathmines Road. He told Sean Gilsenan he required some cyanide to use for testing the purity of coffee. The chemist asked whether he was aware that cyanide was a deadly poison. Lehman said he was. Gilsenan agreed to order a 2.5 gram crystal, which made up 150 grains of the poison.

A few days later, Lehman called to collect his order. He didn't sign the poison register, which documents the sale of restricted poisons.

The following week, Anne Finucane walked into the back room of the office and saw Lehman bent over a table. There was a brown bag spread out on the table, and he was opening a white paper packet. He took out a little lump of what looked like washing soda. He picked up a pair of scissors and began flaking the lump into a powder.

"What are you doing?" she asked.

"This is an acid that tests the coffee for purity," he told her. "You have to be careful, though. It's a deadly poison."

She asked him where he'd got it.

"There are ways," he told her, the ghost of a smile playing at the corners of his mouth. When he was done, he rolled up the brown bag and brought it out to the backyard where he put a match to it. Anne Finucane followed him. It was the first she had heard of testing coffee for purity. He turned and told her it was better to burn the paper because he wasn't sure whether the crystal gave off any poisonous fumes.

The following day, Anne slipped into the back room to make a pot of tea. Lehman stuck his head round the door just as she was about to open a tin of milk with the scissors. He told her sharply to put them down. She obliged, even though she had boiled the scissors after he had used them the previous day. She hadn't realised the substance was that dangerous.

On Saturday, 18 March, Lehman and his assistant prepared to close the shop for the weekend. Anne was due to take Monday off, so Lehman said he would take the cash for the weekend so that he had it when he opened on Monday morning. They left together. Anne closed the door between the shop and the back room, and when she came out on to the street, Lehman locked the outer door. They said goodnight and went their separate ways.

The following Monday, Anne Finucane would forfeit her planned day off due to the circumstances that would befall the Lehmans' on Sunday evening. When she opened the shop, she was to notice that the door leading to the back room was ajar, although she knew she had closed it on Saturday evening. There would also be cash in the till, even though she had seen Lehman empty it before they had left together two evenings previously.

Somebody had been in the shop since she left on Saturday. That there was cash in the till suggested it wasn't an intruder. It was far more likely that Lehman had come in some time on Sunday and left the cash. Why would he do that? Perhaps he knew he wouldn't be opening the shop on Monday as planned and that his assistant would require cash in the till to conduct the business. How could he have known that he wouldn't be opening the shop? Maybe he knew that something terrible was going to happen to his family on Sunday evening.

*

They milled around Margaret Lehman's still body for

a few minutes. Lehman couldn't stand in the one spot. He paced up and down with an air of hysteria. Presently, Winnie O'Callaghan concluded that this was no place for little children. She took Kevin and Patricia downstairs to her front room.

The ambulance crew arrived. The driver, James Quirke, wanted to check the patient for vital signs, but the husband was beside the body, whispering something. Quirke asked him to move aside. The body was exceptionally warm. The woman appeared to have been perspiring a lot. He looked at the distraught Lehman. "We should have been called long before now," he said.

"I've been hours trying to get a doctor," Lehman replied. Winnie O'Callaghan looked up in surprise when she heard the remark. Just before he had called her to help him not an hour previously, he had looked as if he hadn't a care in the world.

Margaret was carried out to the ambulance. Lehman got into the back of the vehicle, sidling up beside Margaret's head.

At the Rotunda Hospital, the stretcher was carried from the back of the ambulance. Nearby, a wardsmaid spotted James Lehman. Brigid Hayden was Margaret's sister. By coincidence, she was working when Margaret was taken inside. She recognised Lehman and ran over. "What's happened to Peg?" she asked her brother-in-law.

"She had dizzy spells, I don't know. What am I going to do – what am I going to do?" Lehman said.

Within half an hour, Margaret Lehman was pronounced dead. One of the medical staff was detailed with the task of informing her devastated husband.

Back at Leinster Road, Winnie O'Callaghan and Annie Byrne were trying to comfort the children. After settling them down in her front room, O'Callaghan went back upstairs to get some blankets and a bottle to hold warm milk. Outside the kitchenette upstairs, she noticed the strange smell again. On the landing, where there was a sink, the smell nearly overpowered her.

An hour so later, as the clock inched towards 9.30 p.m, Lehman arrived back. He flopped down into a chair in Winnie's front room.

"How is she?" Annie Byrne asked him.

Lehman began to cry. "She's dead, and twin boys have been taken dead from her," he said. After a while, he went out to phone Anne Finucane to tell her the news and ask could she forgo her day off as he wouldn't be in a position to open the shop in the morning.

When he returned, Winnie handed him a mug of cocoa, and he began relating a strange story about his deceased wife. "Poor Peg," he said. "I knew she had something on her mind." He told the startled women that his wife had in fact been married before when she was in England and her ex-husband had shown up in Dublin recently. He also said she had had a similar attack to tonight's a few months previously when they were down at her mother's house in Kildare. On that occasion, he had called the doctor, but she had recovered by the morning.

Winnie asked him what the doctor had said the problem was that time, but Lehman didn't answer. Now, he said, he didn't know what he was going to do with his children. He wouldn't be happy with them going to his in-laws. When Margaret was living there with them, her mother had locked the children into a room. Listening to his story, the two women were taken aback. They had never realised that poor Peg had had such a complicated and hard background.

The following morning, Anne Finucane opened up the shop. Lehman phoned at some stage and asked her to inform Annie McCaigue that there had been a death in his family. She was to ask Miss McCaigue to come to the shop at 2 p.m. and he would fill her in.

Anne Finucane rang and passed on her boss's message. The communication explained one thing for Annie McCaigue. The previous evening, Lehman had been due to meet her at a friend's house for dinner. A place had been set for him, but he hadn't come, causing her some embarrassment. Now she understood. Within hours, she would understand a lot more.

Lehman didn't keep the 2 p.m. appointment. Annie McCaigue turned up at the shop to be greeted by Anne Finucane. The two Annes knew each other slightly from Annie McCaigue's visits to the shop. Both women had a desire to talk about the man at the centre of their lives. Anne Finucane shut the shop, and they walked down to the soda fountain in Rathmines village. Over the course of a chat they filled in a few blanks for each other.

Margaret's body was removed from the Rotunda on Tuesday evening, for burial in her home place in Kildare. By then, the gardaí were highly suspicious. An apparently healthy young woman had died. Initial enquiries had merely raised further questions.

It took a while to determine the cause of death. Eventually the state pathologist, John McGrath, stated that Margaret Lehman had been poisoned with cyanide.

Later, in court, he laid out how a body would react to the ingestion or injection of cyanide: "There may be convulsive seizures, that is to say a sort of minor fit. The victim may froth at the mouth. There may be nausea and vomiting. The eyes become staring and fixed. There is cold sweat."

The description fitted Winnie O'Callaghan's account of Margaret Lehman's last minutes alive.

At the funeral, Lehman was distraught. In a quiet moment, he told Margaret's mother that he had had a row with her the previous Christmas over her taking drugs, which she had got from a man on Mount Street. Over the following days, he was up and down to Kildare, where Margaret's mother was taking care of the children. On Thursday evening, he arranged to meet Annie McCaigue at the home of mutual friends, the Cochranes.

Annie was upstairs when he arrived and refused to come down. She had been doing her research, prising apart her boyfriend's lies. After her conversation with Anne Finucane on Monday, she had begun to make enquiries.

Her friends persuaded her that she had to thrash things out with him. When she eventually walked into the sitting room, he said, "I suppose you heard what happened. Mrs Stokes died on the way to the Rotunda Hospital."

"As a matter of fact I heard that Mrs Lehman died on the way to the Rotunda."

"What are you getting into your head?" he said. "Did Miss Finucane say anything to upset you?"

"I got my information directly from the Rotunda," she replied.

Lehman told her things weren't as they seemed. Margaret had been married to a man called Stokes, as he had told her.

But this time the charm didn't work. She had glimpsed the truth and didn't like it.

He asked whether she was worried about the money. "The money doesn't matter," she said. She just wanted him out of her life. She didn't want to see him again.

Lehman made to leave, attempting to retain some of the front that had served him so well for so long. "Where is Stokes?" he muttered, as he was going out the door. "If I could only get my hands on him."

That evening, he returned to the shop, where he met Anne Finucane. The gardaí had already interviewed her. She asked would there be further enquiries from them. Lehman said there would.

"You don't know anything about me, whether I'm married or single or whatever," he told her. She asked about the poison she had seen him with a fortnight previously.

"You know nothing about that. I got rid of it ages ago," he said.

Over the following week, the gardaí cast their net wide and began hauling it in. They interviewed everybody in Lehman's wide circle. They studied the toxicology report and hit the jackpot when the chemist Gilsenan came forward. On 2 April, a statement was taken from Lehman in Kildare. He related the couple's background, how they had met and their decision to travel back to Ireland. He suggested again that it was suicide, a course of action that had come as a complete surprise to him: "I have no idea how my wife could have obtained poison and I know of no reason at the moment why she should take poison. My wife and I always lived very happily together. We were very united. She was a splendid wife and a good mother," he told the gardaí.

Although Lehman had passed up the opportunity to come clean, the investigation was progressing rapidly. The threshold of evidence required to bring charges was in sight.

On Friday, 7 April, Lehman returned to the house in Leinster Road to pick up his mail. He asked Winnie O'Callaghan whether she'd seen the story on his wife's death in the previous day's *Irish Press*. The story speculated that the gardaí were following a definite line of enquiry and were about to make an arrest. "If you'd read that wouldn't you think that I had done it?" Lehman asked.

Winnie was non-committal.

He told her that when he was packing up to leave her house the previous week, he had found a small bottle, a crucifix and a "terrible" letter. She wasn't the first person to whom he had revealed this astonishing discovery. For a week he had been peddling the theory that Margaret had committed suicide and left him a note detailing her troubles. In deference to her, he had destroyed it after reading it.

Winnie didn't say anything. Like a growing number of people close to the Lehmans, she had made up her mind about what had happened. She asked after the children. He told her that he had placed Kevin in a convent in Blackrock and the little girl was with his mother-in-law.

To Winnie's eyes that day, Lehman cut a pitiful sight. The man she had always taken to be a confident, gregarious individual was laid low. "As he was leaving, he said he was in a strange country and he had no friends, no money and no home . . . he was clinging to the railings. I thought he was going to fall down the steps [leading to her front door]."

Winnie O'Callaghan was the last person to see James Lehman before he went on the run. The following day, when Lehman didn't show up for an appointment, the gardaí realised he was gone. In wartime Ireland, there were many strange faces in the major cities, and particularly in border towns, with plenty of people spilling over from Northern Ireland, which was at war. Finding Lehman would be no easy task, particularly as he had no ties to the country, now that his children were being cared for.

The following day, Easter Saturday, a well-cut man booked into the Oriel Hotel in Monaghan town. He used the name James McCaigue and told the manager he was an airman who was on sick leave for a few weeks. He had relations in Castleblayney, he told her.

Over the next few days, the displaced airman socialised in the hotel and the town. In one pub, he met a local bus driver, Charles Scott. The two men got drinking. After a while, the airman asked Scott for a loan of ten shillings to get him up to Belfast where he was to hook up with his regiment. Scott said he didn't have that kind of money, but he did have a return bus ticket to Belfast, which he happily gave.

On the Wednesday, the airman went north. In Belfast, he made for the army recruitment centre in Clifton Street. He applied to join the RAF. He said he had come to Ireland from the United States with his sister in 1938. His only problem was he didn't have any identity papers on him. The recruiting officer told him to go and get his papers and he might be accepted.

Back in Monaghan that evening, the airman returned to doing what he did best, charming and cajoling.

One local woman socialising in the hotel was much taken with the dashingly handsome man who accompanied her to the door as she was leaving. He told Eileen Hazlett he would like to see her again, and she agreed to go to the pictures with him the following day.

However, despite the wooing of a new conquest, the evening hadn't been a total success for Lehman. His photograph was carried in all the national papers that day, as a man to whom the gardaí were desperately seeking to speak. Somebody spotted the airman in the hotel and found a great resemblance to the photograph. (Lehman's only concession to disguise was to shave off his moustache.) The local garda station was informed about the suspicious American airman.

On Thursday evening, Lehman kept his date with Miss Hazlett. By then, a detective was keeping tabs on him. The following morning, he ordered breakfast in his room. Before the meal could arrive, two detectives knocked on his door and let themselves in. Lehman was lying on the bed, his hands behind his head. They introduced themselves and asked was he James Lehman.

"My name is James McCaigue," he told them. "I am an American officer invalided from the air force. They kept my papers." The two cops showed him a photograph of himself from that morning's *Irish Independent*. Did he know this man? Absolutely not. The game was up, though. His charm had run its course.

He told the officers that he had never been to Dublin. A quick search of his pockets revealed a Dublin tram ticket. He was carrying two gold fillings. His financial situation had become so parlous that he had been hoping to pawn them. His arrest ensured that his worries took on a far greater magnitude.

The Central Criminal Court was packed for the murder trial of James Lehman in October 1944. Murder was a rare enough occurrence at the time. That year only twenty people had died as a result of homicide in the state. Seven of those killings were classified as murder. (To put this in context, the population of the state in 1944 was 2.9 million. By contrast, in 2006, when the population of the state was 4.2 million, sixty-six homicides were recorded, a more than three fold increase from the war years. While the increase is considerable, it is very much in line with international trends through the middle and latter decades of the twentieth century. Ireland's homicide rate remains low by Western standards.)

Apart from the rarity of a trial of this nature, the circumstances of Margaret Lehman's death and the fact that the Canadian had sparked off a manhunt the previous April cranked up the public imagination a few more notches. Among those in attendance was a young widow, Isolde Byrne. Since his arrest, she had visited Lehman eighty-three times in prison. It was to emerge that they had been intimate for a few months before the death of his wife. Despite all his travails at the time, and his professed love for Annie McCaigue, Lehman had also had time to conduct another affair.

His only defence was that his wife had committed suicide. The prosecution presented all the circumstantial evidence. The motive was his affair with Annie McCaigue and his worsening financial circumstances. His expression of hatred for Margaret was also a factor. With the purchase of cyanide from Gilsenan's chemist, he had had the means. The purpose for which he claimed he was buying the poison was demonstrated as bogus. His only defence regarding possession of the cyanide was advice from an unidentified man whom he had met a few times in a city café. This man, he claimed, was an expert on purifying coffee and had since, apparently, disappeared into thin air.

The evidence of Anne Finucane and Winnie O'Callaghan showed how he had behaved on the weekend of the killing, both before and after his wife's death. Winnie's evidence was particularly significant in relation to Lehman's movements at the time his wife went into convulsions. It was noted that Lehman had told her that evening he was getting a gas cooker delivered the following day, but it never actually arrived. That was another small piece in the jigsaw being assembled to determine Lehman's intentions. Also, Lehman had told the ambulance crew he had been trying to get a doctor for hours. Winnie knew this couldn't be true.

Margaret's mother had to sit through it all, including the evidence that Lehman had been going around suggesting to all and sundry that she and her family were the dregs of society.

There was psychiatric evidence from a doctor, Harry Lee Parker. He told the court that he had examined Lehman and found him to be unstable, a liar and a psychopath. However, the doctor added that Lehman was not insane and had been fully responsible for his actions.

Lehman tried the charm one more time, by giving evidence himself. He told the court that he and his wife were both morphine addicts, indicating that this might in some way explain why she had committed suicide.

Summing up the case, Judge Martin Maguire told the jury of twelve men: "If this be murder, it is indeed a dreadful crime, but you must leave aside in your deliberations all feelings of indignation and horror and approach consideration of the case.

"The accused was not charged with his approaches to the young women mentioned in the case or of obtaining money from them on the representations he made and that must not weigh against him.

"I feel that the sympathy of everybody must go out to that poor old lady Mrs Hayden in the affliction that has befallen her. Hard things have been said about her by the accused, about some members of her family and about her little home – the home where she sheltered his wife when she was a child and was good enough to shelter him and his children when he came here friendless to these shores. Leave that aside. You are not here for the purpose of sympathy. You are here to investigate a crime."

The jury found Lehman guilty of murder. The judge handed down the death sentence.

Lehman appealed, and a new trial was set for the following January. After a nine-day hearing, the jury returned a guilty verdict on 24 January. Judge A. K. Overend said: "I do not see how the jury could arrive at any other verdict than they have done on the evidence put before them."

The court registrar asked Lehman had he anything to say. "I am satisfied that on my second trial there has been a small degree of fairness. I am innocent and my conscience is clear."

The judge then pronounced: "The sentence and judgement of the court are, and it is ordered and adjudged, that you, James Herbert Lehman, be taken from the bar of the court where you now stand to the prison from whence you last came, and that on Wednesday, the twenty-first day of February in the year of our Lord one thousand nine hundred and forty-five, you be taken to the common place of execution in the prison in which you shall be then confined, and that you be then and there hanged by the neck until you are dead, and that your body be buried within the walls of the prison in which the aforesaid judgement of death shall be executed upon you."

Lehman tried another appeal. The date of execution was put back again, but the leave to appeal was refused. A new date was set for 19 March, the first anniversary of his wife's death. When the appointed day arrived, there were between thirty and forty people gathered outside the prison to be present for the event. Early in the morning, a prison officer emerged and posted the notice of execution, informing the public that James Herbert Lehman had been put to death an hour previously for the murder of his wife.

The death penalty remained on the statute books for another forty-five years. In 1963, it was abolished for all but capital offences, which included the murder of a policeman, head of state or leader of government, as well as the crime of treason.

In 1990, it was finally abolished. The last execution took place in 1954.

8. THE WOMAN WHO DISAPPEARED

The Case of Gary McCrea

Gary McCrea and Dolores McGroary grew up within a few miles of each other, outside the village of Ballintra in south Co. Donegal. The village is located between Donegal town and Ballyshannon and practically straddles the border with Co. Fermanagh. They came from rural farming families. The McCreas were among the large Protestant population in the area. The McGroarys were Catholic.

Each attended their own faith's local primary school, then went on to the Abbey Vocational School in Donegal town, eight miles away. McCrea completed the Group Certificate in 1979 after two years. On leaving, he served his time as an apprentice mechanic. He and Dolores began dating when they were teenagers.

They were married before either had reached their twenty-third birthday.

Soon after the wedding, Dolores converted to the Protestant faith – not unusual in border counties like Donegal. At the time, her family and friends interpreted the conversion as an expression of love for her husband. That assessment would eventually be reviewed in the light of what transpired.

The McCreas set up home in Ballybulgin, a townland that consists of a laneway a few miles outside Ballintra. The construction of the N15 national route, which sweeps up into the county from Sligo, would render the laneway little more than an awkward connection between the national route and the village. Even today, Ballybulgin remains a distinctly rural area, despite a ribbon of new bungalows along the lane. Grass still grows in the centre of the road, and vehicles can only pass each other by pulling up tight to the ditch where briars scrape at car windows.

The McCreas lived in a two-storey house with a large garden and a rising drumlin to the rear. A construction of sheds with whitewashed walls and corrugated-iron roofs still stands beside the house.

Sharon was born in 1985. She was followed by Laura four years later. The two younger girls, Tanya and Leona, were born in 1996 and 1998. The expansion of the family put a gloss on relations between McCrea and Dolores. Their personalities suggested that the union was one in which opposites had attracted.

She was extremely sociable, and popular with those who encountered her. Over the years of her marriage she worked in a number of bars in Ballintra, Laghey and the nearby townland of Ballinakilley. Everybody had time for her. She was an enthusiastic member of the darts team in the Bay Bush bar in Ballintra.

McCrea also drank locally, but he was of a quiet disposition, even sullen, according to some local people. In 2003, he showed up at a reunion for pupils of the Abbey Vocational School. Such reunions are generally a time for reflection. All those in attendance swapped stories about where they were in life. Some had moved to Galway or Dublin, many others had remained in the locality. Having made it through the worst of the eighties' economic slump, most were now enjoying life.

Many of those present had families. Gary was his customary quiet self. He told of his four daughters and how he was proud of them. He didn't share much else. There was certainly no talk of how life really was behind the brown pebbledashed walls of his home.

By then, Dolores was working in the Country Inn at Ballinakilley. Occasionally, she would come to work with her face obviously bruised. She brushed off any enquiries. There was nothing to it, she insisted. Other times, she avoided any mention of the bruises, as if by not talking about them the injuries might disappear.

The snippets that leaked out from behind the walls of their home after the killing suggested that McCrea was a control freak, if not a tyrant. He expected his wife and four daughters to wait on him hand and foot. His every whim had to be indulged. When he arrived home from work, his dinner had to be ready, and any change of clothes laid out for his inspection. He wore false teeth, which the older daughters were ordered to clean each day.

The bluster and tyranny were also informed by insecurity. He knew he was king in his own home, but his obsessive fear was that Dolores might seek affection elsewhere. Over the final years of their marriage, he often accused her of involvement with other men. The accusations ranged from silly to bizarre. At one stage, he got it into his head that Dolores was having an affair with her cousin. There was no basis for this and no evidence to suggest that Dolores sought affection outside the home.

On another occasion, the couple were socialising in the Country Inn. There was music playing and the dance-floor was buzzing. One of the patrons, who was well known to Dolores, asked her to dance. It was nothing more than having a laugh, but McCrea didn't see it that way. He got it into his head that this man was interested in his wife, approached him and punched him in the face. The night ended in tears.

Another night, on New Year's Eve 2002, he gave her a beating as she was getting out of the car outside their home. Snow was lying on the ground, their breath visible in the chilled air. Something innocuous had set him off, as it often did – a perceived slight, a comment he found offensive. Gary McCrea got out of the car and went round to Dolores' side. As his wife was emerging, he punched her, then again and again. She fell onto the snow.

That incident might have been what prompted her to escape. Equally, it might have been the cumulative effect of the beatings and terror she and her daughters had endured over the previous few years. McCrea had never been the easiest, but in the last three years of their marriage, his obsessions and habits had grown steadily worse.

She had to get out. The beating she received that night was worse than before. She knew that to stay was to put her life at risk. She was losing weight – it was falling off her, with all the worry and stress.

Despite the evidence that would eventually come out about the violence he perpetrated against her, Dolores didn't once report him to the gardaí, which was not uncommon among victims of domestic abuse.

She left in April, having prepared to do so with military precision. If McCrea had known what was afoot, he would have done everything in his power to stop her. After eighteen years of marriage, she had reason to fear him. She didn't want confrontation, or worse. She knew she had to slip out furtively, escaping the prison that her home and marriage had become.

On the quiet, Dolores arranged to rent a bungalow in an isolated area, around two miles from Ballintra and the same distance from the family home in Ballybulgin.

She began moving her belongings by stealth. Then, on the appointed day, when she was sure McCrea would be gone from the house for a prolonged stretch, she left with the children.

That evening, McCrea returned to his home to find everybody gone. Rage took hold of him. At its core was the impulse to kill his wife. If he wasn't going to have her, nobody else would. He held on to the rage and dragged it around with him for the next eight months.

In the weeks immediately after their departure, McCrea did everything to entice his daughters home. He rang them several times a day. Laura, the second eldest, appears to have come in for particular attention from her father. "He would tell me if I moved in with him I would have a better life," she would later tell a court. McCrea told Laura that her mother was only using her, that she only wanted Laura so she would do the cleaning and tidying and look after the younger girls. "He used to tell me that I wasn't wanted there. I heard it so much that I believed him."

In his quest to have his daughters return, McCrea didn't spare them the more lurid aspects of his obsession. "He used to go on about other men, that she [Dolores] was a whore. He used to call her names, he used to say she was riding people, that she was a tramp and walking disease," Laura said.

McCrea was particularly obsessed about one man whom he believed was having a relationship with Dolores. "He told me that if I stayed with my mum and sisters, a man called Willie Armstrong would become my new father."

Over the course of the months following Dolores' departure, the couple attempted to cut a deal about access to the children. Dolores initially had custody, but this was eventually modified to give McCrea joint custody. For the greater part, the four girls stayed with their mother, but McCrea kept on at Laura, saying she would enjoy a far better life if she returned to him and their home in Ballybulgin.

Eventually, in early August, Laura agreed to move back in with her father. For the first few days, everything was fine, but then her father began to voice his obsession in every conversation. "He was calling my mother a tramp and said she was having relationships with different men," Laura recalled.

Dolores settled into her new life, out from under the yoke of her husband. While the freedom was welcome, the fear didn't leave her. Her new home was on an isolated road in the townland of Glasbolie, a few miles out from Ballintra. The bungalow was set back from the road and at the base of a hollow. Once darkness fell, each set of headlights coming along the road might signal the approach of her husband and his violence.

She persevered. By then, Dolores was working in the Bush Bar in Ballintra. She was managing to keep her head above water. After McCrea's initial rage had died down, they tried to talk over the financial details of the termination of the marriage. Eventually, he offered her €20,000 in settlement, but Dolores considered the offer derisory.

That summer, Dolores began to go out into the world again, free and still relatively young. Willie Armstrong, the man about whom McCrea obsessed, formed a friendship with her. There is nothing to suggest that the couple were on more intimate terms.

In August, they attended the Galway races together, although Armstrong would later say they slept in separate rooms at a B & B. Dolores was, most likely, just enjoying not being answerable to her husband.

Whether McCrea got wind of her trip to Galway is not known, but the same month he rang Dolores' mother in one of his customary fits of rage. "She isn't a fit mother," McCrea told Kathleen McGroary of her daughter. "If I had my way I'd fucking kill her and stab her."

Later in August, McCrea called on a neighbour for a hand with a little job he required doing. George Hammond helped him to dismantle an old caravan that was lying behind the sheds at the side of the house. The caravan was later burned, but its chassis survived.

The following month, Hammond lent a hand again. This time, there were bushes to be cleared around the house. The two men cut them and dragged some over to the chassis. The scene would eventually become central to solving the disappearance of Dolores McCrea.

Some time in the autumn, McCrea taped a programme

from the BBC's *Trail of Guilt* series. It consisted of reconstructions of significant crimes that had occurred in Britain. The programme McCrea taped involved a man named Simon Carter from Swansea. He had been murdered in the city by a number of men with whom he had been in dispute. The culprits buried his body initially, but subseq-uently dug it up and encased it in recently poured concrete. They then decided to move the body again. Jackhammers were used to extract it from the concrete. At this point, they began to burn it, in an attempt to leave no trace whatsoever. The operation involved using diesel and keeping a fire alight for more than a day. The culprits were eventually detected by the police. The taped video would be used in evidence against Gary McCrea.

Through the months, the rage never left him. Whenever he had the chance, he let his daughters know exactly how he felt about their mother. "He always maintained that Mum didn't care about any of the children, that he wanted to get full custody," Sharon would say later. "He said that he was going to keep fighting in the courts for full custody. He said he'd fight and that if he didn't get it he'd kill her. He'd be able to do time for her, that he'd be out in no time and that he'd get his family back."

By December, Dolores wanted to move into Ballintra. The isolation was too much for her, and, at the back of her mind, she didn't want to live with the prospect of McCrea showing up one night. She heard about a first-floor apartment on the main street in the village. The living quarters were smaller than she had in the bungalow, but at least she would feel safer.

The McCrea mother and daughters moved in, and with the help of her father Jimmy, Dolores got the new home into habitable shape. The apartment was opposite Jamie's public house. Her own place of work, the Bush Bar, was the only other pub in the village, a short walk down the main street. Her parents' home in the townland of Ballinaranny, outside the village, was also nearer. Her life on the far side of the marriage was now taking shape. She began to relax.

Gary McCrea was far from relaxed. Whatever turmoil occupied his mind is unknown, but the glimpses he gave, to friends or just people he met in bars, painted a dark picture. He was now adrift in middle age, cast off from the anchor of family life to which he had been moored since early adulthood. His daughters, apart from Laura, were gone. There was the public reaction to his failed marriage, too. The people of Laghey and Ballintra now knew of his circumstances. More importantly, in his mind they looked on him as a cuckold.

Over Christmas, McCrea went drinking in Carolan's Bar in Laghey. It was the first festive season he was to spend without the company of his children. At one stage of the night, a local man, Alastair McClay, came in. The two men had known each other for decades. Over the previous eight months, McClay had often been given an earful by McCrea about how Dolores had ruined his life. That night, despite his better judgement, McClay fell into company with McCrea. Inevitably, the conversation turned to his wife and children.

"He was very bitter. He never used her name. It was 'bitch' and 'whore'," McClay said later. He listened and attempted to talk sense. Things had gone far beyond that stage for Gary McCrea.

"He made a comment that he was going to sort it out," McClay remembered. "He more or less said he was going to take matters into his own hands." At this, McClay got annoyed. "Would you ever cop yourself on?" he said.

McCrea looked at him. "I'll do time for her," he said.

In the first weeks of 2004, McCrea contacted Dolores. He told her he was interested in buying her car, a red 1997 Peugeot 306. He told her he could get value from redoing the vehicle, and he was willing to pay her €1,000 for it.

Dolores was taken aback. The offer was generous. She hadn't kept the six-year-old vehicle in good nick, and while she was thinking of trading it in, she expected it to fetch no more than €700 or €800. She agreed to sell and told him she would drop the car out one evening.

On the weekend of 17–18 January, McCrea bought twenty quad tyres from a local man, Brendan Kearn.

He told Kearn he wanted them to burn bushes in the fields behind his home.

He called into the apartment in Ballintra one evening that weekend. Sharon, who hadn't seen her father over the holiday period, was minding her younger sisters. Dolores was out at work. There was a brief conversation. McCrea told his eldest daughter that she should "tell the health board" about the conditions their mother had them living under. It was typical of the remarks he had made over the previous eight months, but, for some reason, Sharon was particularly hurt by this. Her father left soon after.

On Tuesday, 20 January, McCrea drove the short distance to E&J Oil outside the village. The company CCTV recorded him buying two twenty-two litre drums of diesel.

In the afternoon, he attended to some chores. He drove to the depot of a local waste-disposal company to pay his wheelie-bin charge. Inside, Hillary Rooney, who knew McCrea, processed the bill. The docket included Dolores' name, and McCrea asked that it be removed. "It doesn't live here any more," he told Rooney.

Laura, despite her growing reservations, was still living with her father. He arranged for her to go to his parents' house after school, a trip she often made. Then he waited.

Inside, in Ballintra, Dolores was getting ready for a night out. The Bay Bush darts team was travelling to the Blue Stack bar in Donegal town to play in a tournament. She was going to drop the car out to

McCrea and then either he would give her a lift back to the village, or, more likely, she would hitch one. The extra money was going to come in handy.

Around 6 p.m., her father Jimmy arrived at the flat with four chairs, his latest contribution to the family's efforts to kit out the place. He stayed, and they drank some tea. The younger girls were still up when Dolores left, bidding her father and daughters farewell for the night.

She drove along the northern half of the village street, out past St Bridget's Catholic church where she was baptised, past the Church of Ireland school where her children were being educated. She turned left on to the lane leading to her former home. As she drove slowly along it, the darkness was broken only by lights from a bungalow here and there. Dolores McCrea had driven this way practically daily for twenty years, going to and from her home. Now she was planning to sever one more connection to the marriage she wanted to put behind her.

At the house, a friend of McCrea's, Martin McGrath, had unexpectedly visited. McCrea went out to meet him in the driveway at the front of the house. A naked bulb mounted on the gable end of the house flooded the driveway with light. McGrath rolled down the window, and McCrea spoke to him. He didn't invite his visitor in.

At 7.25 p.m., the headlights of Dolores' red Peugeot turned into the McCrea drive. McCrea looked up from his conversation with McGrath. He was now in a dilemma. This friend, who knew of his extreme marital distress, was present when his wife arrived at the house.

McGrath spotted the red Peugeot in his rear-view mirror. He recognised Dolores. Knowing the circumstances, he decided to go. "I'll leave you to it," he told McCrea, who nodded. With that, McGrath reversed out and went on his way.

No evidence was ever uncovered to suggest that Dolores entered her former home that evening. A few days later, gardaí obtained a warrant and combed through the house, but there was no forensic detail that suggested Dolores had, even for the briefest period, been inside.

At around 8.15 p.m., Charlene Walls was driving down the lane at Ballybulgin. She noticed flames dancing above the roof of the whitewashed sheds to the side of the McCrea home. It wasn't just the extent of the flames, but the texture. They appeared white, as if a surfeit of fuel was intensifying the heat. She thought no more of it and drove on.

Some minutes later, further down the lane, Joe Walsh stepped out of his home into the cold January air. Immediately on leaving the house, he detected a foul smell. He looked down the road to McCrea's, and against the night sky he could see black smoke coming from the side of the house. He thought no more of it and went back inside.

Meanwhile, the darts team had departed Ballintra, en route to the Blue Stack in Donegal town. Initially, there was no panic about Dolores' failure to show up. She might have decided to make her own way to Donegal, or perhaps she had been delayed.

The darts match got under way. One of the team tried Dolores on her mobile. No connection was established. An attempt to text her resulted in the text being returned unsent. The women found it unusual but continued with the darts.

Soon after 9 p.m., Willie Doherty opened his door to Gary McCrea. Doherty, a haulage operator, lived in Laghey and had known McCrea most of his life. It wasn't unusual for him to call around. McCrea came in and sat down. In the course of the conversation, McCrea brought up the subject of Dolores. Doherty knew enough by then to switch off when McCrea got on to his wife, but that evening the expected tirade of abuse didn't materialise.

McCrea just mentioned that Dolores had called down earlier in the evening with the car, which he was buying for €1,000. He said she had been a bit on edge. As she was leaving, a car had pulled up, and she had got into it, heading off in the Bridgetown direction. McCrea told Doherty that Dolores had said she was "going away for a few days" and asked him to mind the girls.

Doherty didn't think too much about it. Anything was better than the usual abuse. Maybe it was a bit strange, but then McCrea had been behaving oddly for a while. Back at Ballybulgin, the flames subsided but the fire kept burning.

Early the following morning, Tanya got up for school. Her mother wasn't in her bed. Neither was she in the apartment. Tanya went into Sharon's room. "Mummy's not home," she told her sister. Sharon tried to ring their mother on her mobile, but there was no connection.

Around 10 a.m., Sharon rang her aunt, Carmel McGroary. They discussed what might have happened to Dolores. Sharon tried one of the women on the darts team. She confirmed that Dolores hadn't turned up for the tournament the night before.

Through the morning, the women grew increasingly worried. They got into Carmel McGroary's car at about midday and drove around the village. They decided to go out to Ballybulgin, as that was where Dolores had been heading the previous night.

When they arrived at the house, Carmel noticed that Dolores' red Peugeot was in behind the picket gate that bridged the gable end of the house to the sheds at the side. McCrea told Sharon not to worry about her mother. "She's probably whoring around with somebody," he said.

Carmel McGroary didn't need to hear this. She raised her arms as if to fend off a tirade of abuse about her sister. "I don't want to get involved in family matters but there is her car," she said, pointing to the Peugeot. McCrea didn't respond. Carmel asked him how Dolores had gone to her arranged appointment in Donegal without her car. McCrea said she took a lift from a car coming up the road. The women left, their unease growing. Carmel phoned her mother to tell her something was wrong.

At 1.45 p.m., the local postman, Joe O'Gorman, was driving along the lane at Ballybulgin. As he approached the McCrea house, he noticed what he would later describe as "a fireball in the sky": "There was thick, dense, black smoke, going up to forty foot high at the back of the sheds," he said.

At 5.30 p.m., Carmel McGroary phoned the gardaí in Ballyshannon to report her sister as a missing person.

At around 9 p.m., Detectives Tom Connolly and Tony Curnyn arrived at Ballybulgin. McCrea invited them in. They told him the nature of their enquiries. "She was here last night, aye," McCrea said. "She left her car." He told the officers that he had offered to buy the vehicle from her. Connolly explained that she hadn't shown up at home, which, he pointed out, McCrea knew.

"She's probably fucked off whoring somewhere," McCrea replied.

How did she travel to Donegal? Connolly asked. McCrea said a car came up the road and stopped to give her a lift. He reckoned it was a silver or grey Volkswagen Golf probably, but he wasn't sure. The guards weren't sure either. McCrea's demeanour was shifty. Something wasn't right. Out at the back of the house, across behind the sheds, not ten yards from where the detectives sat, the fire smouldered.

Travelling back to Ballyshannon, Connolly wondered to his partner about the car McCrea said had taken Dolores to Donegal. The man was a mechanic. He knew his way around cars, and he would know exactly what kind of car had come along the lane. His vagueness as to the model was curious. Things didn't add up.

Later that evening, Superintendent John McFadden called a conference of detectives at the Ballyshannon station. There had still been no sighting of Dolores. McFadden asked the assembled five detectives their opinion. The general consensus was that Dolores McCrea was in serious trouble and already fingers were pointing towards her husband.

The following day, an Aer Chór helicopter from Sligo was drafted in. Gardaí at Ballyshannon began planning for a major search of the area. In the early afternoon, local garda Brendan McMonagle called out to Ballybulgin. McCrea invited him in and put on the kettle. While waiting for the kettle to boil, McMonagle went out the back. He saw the fire to the rear of the sheds, a thin plume of dark smoke now twisting into the air. The fire was burning in the chassis of an old mobile home. McMonagle went closer to investigate. There was a smell of diesel from the fire. He could see some tyres thrown on, and a few bushes.

What he saw next startled him. There appeared to be a bone at the end of a ball, on the periphery of the fire. The bone was around six inches long. He looked closer and saw what he believed to be part of a spinal column. He wasn't sure whether it was human or animal, but the sight chilled him. McMonagle went to fetch McCrea and brought him outside. The garda pointed to the bone and asked McCrea what he thought it was.

"It could be an aul' dog or something," McCrea said.

McMonagle couldn't believe his ears. "Gary, you must know what it is," he said.

"I don't, but I know what you're thinking."

"What do you believe I'm thinking?"

"You think I put her in the fucking fire."

McMonagle contacted Ballyshannon and told McCrea to go back inside the house. Within an hour, the small lane was clogged with garda cars. The house was sealed off. A warrant to search the premises was obtained. McCrea was told he'd have to leave, and he made arrangements to go and stay with his parents on the far side of Ballintra.

Out the back, the gardaí examined the fire. A local doctor, Marie Drumgoole, was summoned to the scene and the state pathologist's office informed. Dr Drumgoole concluded that the piece of bone discovered was a shoulder blade from a human being.

Later that evening, Detective Sergeant Shane Henry and state pathologist Marie Cassidy got down on their hands and knees and began to remove the bones that were retrievable. Two power extinguishers were used to smother the flames. Then the garda and the scientist attempted to remove the rest of the bones although the fire was still smouldering.

A number of fragments were recovered. Pieces of skull were identifiable, as were fragmented parts of the lower jaw. There were also foot bones, the upper part of a thigh and multiple vertebrae. A few loose teeth were recovered. Two gold rings were also retrieved from the fire. Cassidy was able to conclude that the distribution of the remains suggested that the body had been dismembered before it was put into the fire.

Later, the remains were collated and brought to the mortuary in Dublin. A forensic pathologist, Laureen Buckley, assembled all the bones and fragments in autonomic order, attempting as best she could to reconstruct a full skeleton. Contrary to popular opinion, it is not possible to completely burn a body. Due to a chemical reaction, bones in a fire can actually become stronger. Eventually, the pathologist concluded that the body was that of a woman, most likely in her late thirties. In addition, highly carbonised teeth recovered from the fire would lead the state's forensic dental surgeon to conclude there was a "high probability" that the remains were those of Dolores McCrea.

All of that would be uncovered further down the line. In the days after the discovery in the fire, the gardaí undertook a forensic examination of the house and surrounding area. Little of any evidential value was recovered.

One item that would be of use to the gardaí was found in the sheds. A drum of diesel less than half full was identified as similar to the one McCrea had purchased at E&J Oil on the day that Dolores had disappeared. In time, the contents would be measured to reveal that there were seven litres present. In the few days between the purchase of the drum and the discovery by gardaí, forty-four litres of diesel had been used.

The only other item of interest was the *Trail of Guilt* programme, illustrating how the criminals in Wales had attempted to burn a body.

While the case might now appear to have been solved, the gardaí had to continue the painstaking work of collecting evidence. The remains in the fire had not been positively identified as those of Dolores McCrea. Therefore, all other avenues had to be explored.

The following Tuesday, 27 January, Chief Superintendent Noel White made a plea to the public for help. Speaking outside the McCrea family home in Ballybulgin, he appealed to any witnesses of a fire on the evening of 20 January to come forward. He also asked for anybody who had passed along the lane that evening to make themselves known. In particular, he said, the gardaí were looking for the driver of a grey or silver car, which may have used the lane between 7 and 8 p.m. on the evening in question. "That car travelled in the direction of Bridgetown – Laghey," he said. "The last reported sighting of Dolores was when she was seen getting into that car at approximately 7.30 p.m." He declined to say who had been the last person to see her, but the gardaí were checking out McCrea's story that he had seen her getting into a car.

Over the following week, various pieces of evidence were correlated. All of the neighbours were interviewed, and those who had seen the fire provided statements. The investigating officers compiled a background to the McCreas' marriage, relying heavily on information from the four daughters and family friends.

On one cold evening, the gardaí re-enacted events outside the McCrea home as related to them by Martin McGrath, the friend who had left once Dolores drove up on the fateful night. Fairly quickly, a case including motive, means and opportunity was put together and placed in context with the discovery of the body. Within eight days of the discovery, the gardaí felt they had enough information collated to interview Gary McCrea about what he knew.

On the morning of Friday, 30 January, five officers knocked on the door of the home of McCrea's parents. Gary McCrea was told that he was being arrested on suspicion of murdering his wife. He dressed and was taken by car to Letterkenny garda station, some thirty miles away. Through the hour-long journey, he barely spoke to the detectives in the car. He kept his eyes on the countryside and towns that were passing by, a life that, he must have mused, he might well be leaving behind.

Over the course of twelve hours, teams of detectives interviewed McCrea. He said nothing, made no admission. As the detention time drew to a close, a decision had to be made on whether or not the state had a strong enough case to prosecute the suspect. Chief Superintendent White was in contact with the DPP's office to discuss the evidence.

By then, the investigating gardaí were of the opinion that McCrea had most likely strangled Dolores within minutes of her arrival at his home. Forensic examination of the house had uncovered no evidence that she had been there that evening. No blood samples were found inside or outside.

The most likely scenario, as far as the guards were concerned, was that Dolores had got out of the car, and, within minutes, McCrea had assaulted her for the last time. Then he had dragged her body to the caravan chassis, which he had prepared for a fire. Any dismemberment of the body had probably taken place in the immediate vicinity of the fire.

With just ten minutes remaining on the clock before the detention period expired, word came back from the DPP: Charge him.

A special sitting of Donegal District Court was convened for that evening. Judge Mary Devins was contacted and travelled to Donegal town. By the time McCrea arrived down from Letterkenny in a garda convoy, an angry crowd had gathered outside the courthouse.

Throughout the day, word had spread around Ballintra and Laghey that McCrea had been arrested. The pent-up fury at such a violent death within the community began to find voice. When it was revealed that there would be a sitting of the court in Donegal, friends of the family made their way in to witness this significant step in the hunt for Dolores' killer.

By the time McCrea arrived, some two hundred people had gathered outside. When he emerged from the car, there were a few shouts and heckles. His life as a quiet and apparently inoffensive mechanic was now over. The people of Donegal had already decided on his guilt.

Inside, he was formally remanded in custody after the court heard that he had been charged a few hours previously in Letterkenny garda station. He had nothing to say in response.

As he was bundled into a garda car to be taken away, the crowd let fly. Abuse rained down on his head. The gardaí, who had been his pursuers, became his protectors. The car pulled out and drove past the nearby Blue Stack bar, where Dolores had been scheduled to play darts on the night of her death. The car left the town at speed.

The following month, McCrea was granted bail. One of the conditions was that he live at least three hours' drive away from Donegal until his trial. He relocated to Cork, where he undertook a Fás training course. By June, he had found a job working as a driver for Sexton Transport, a company based in Mallow.

It was six months before Dolores McCrea could be buried. The process of identification was drawn out, and it was mid-July 2004 before the remains were released to the family.

The McGroarys took the decision to bury her in the rites of the Catholic Church in which she was raised rather than the Protestant faith that she had joined in accordance with her husband's wishes.

On 16 July, St Brigid's Church was packed for the Requiem Mass. The local Church of Ireland rector, Reverend Brian Russell, spoke to the congregation about the deep love that had been extended to the four McCrea girls in the aftermath of their mother's death. "Their teachers are to be thanked for the compassion and sensitivity which they have showed to the girls. They have been comforted by both churches, which is very important," he said.

Following the Mass, the coffin was carried by members of the McGroary family to the adjoining cemetery. Gary McCrea did not request to have his bail altered to allow him travel for the funeral.

Down in Cork, he was putting in serious hours at work. He began driving each day at 3 a.m. and worked an eleven-hour day, seven days a week, collecting milk from farmers and delivering it to Dairygold plants in north Cork. He was regarded as an excellent employee, but while he was there he invented a different history for himself, telling fellow workers that he had two children and a few ongoing problems with his wife. He showed around photographs of his two youngest daughters, but he made no mention of their older sisters. Every once in a while, he cried off work for a few days to attend to what he said was family business. His colleagues assumed he was at custody hearings, but he was in fact meeting his legal advisers to prepare for his forthcoming trial.

In September 2005, he left the job, saying he was going on holiday. In reality, his time of reckoning had come.

The trial began on 17 October 2005. Opening the hearing, prosecution barrister Paul O'Higgins said the case was largely circumstantial, but, he said, when the jury had heard all the evidence, they would have "no reasonable doubt that Gary McCrea killed Dolores McCrea and then disposed of her body". His prediction proved correct. The trial dragged on for three weeks, most of which was taken up by the prosecution outlining the circumstantial evidence against McCrea. Crucial evidence was given by the two elder McCrea daughters as to their father's behaviour in the months before their mother's death. The defendant himself did not take the stand.

The jury retired to consider its verdict on Thursday, 4 November. The following day, after four and a half hours' deliberation, the jury reached a unanimous conclusion. McCrea gripped the bench in front of him as the guilty verdict was read. His elder daughters were soon in tears, as were members of the McGroary family. He received the mandatory life sentence.

Emerging from the Four Courts, Sharon McCrea read a brief statement. "The family and I are relieved that the trial has come to an end and that the jury has returned with a guilty verdict and that justice has been done," she said. "You must remember that there are two families here that are victims – both the McCreas and the McGroarys.

"My mother was a wonderful mother, daughter and sister and friend to us all, and she will never be forgotten. We want to thank the people of Ballintra who have been there for us since Mammy's death." She thanked the local gardaí for the professional manner in which they had carried out the investigation.

"We ask the media to let us return to Donegal to pick up our lives. I have three younger sisters who need to move on with their lives without the glare of publicity. No further statements or interviews will be given by the family."

On Tuesday, 22 May 2007, the Court of Criminal Appeal rejected McCrea's appeal against his conviction. It was brought on the grounds that the trial judge had erred in charging the jury, and the warrants obtained to search the McCrea home after Dolores' body was found were defective. The court rejected the appeal on all grounds.

The McCrea daughters continue to live in the Ballintra area where their mother was reared, lived and died at the hands of her estranged husband.

Between 1996 and 2006, the average time a convicted murderer spent in prison in the state was thirteen and a half years, according to the Law Reform Commission's 2006 report on homicide. If McCrea serves the average term, he will be eligible for parole in early 2019.

9. IN THE PSYCHIATRIST'S CHAIR

The Case of Anton Mulder

It was 11.10 a.m. on 17 December 2004 when the squad car pulled up in the Mael Duin estate in the village of Dunshaughlin, Co. Meath. Gardaí Derek Halligan and June Maguire got out of the car and walked towards number ninety-three, one of the large four-bedroom houses in the estate. They were responding to a call that an incident had occurred.

Five minutes earlier, a secretary working for a local solicitor had run into the garda station. She said her office had had a call from a client, an Anton Mulder. Something terrible had happened up at Mael Duin. The two officers left immediately.

Now they had arrived but, from the outside, all appeared to be quiet in number ninety-three. The front door was closed. Halligan took a peek through the window into the front room. A man was sitting on an armchair, a young child on his knee. Two other children were in the room.

Anton Mulder looked up and saw the two uniformed gardaí staring through the window. He took the child from his knee and went to open the door. "She's up there," he said, waving towards the carpeted stairs behind him. His eyes were puffy and red. Through the door into the sitting room, Maguire could hear a baby crying.

Anton Mulder identified himself. He said his wife's name was Colleen. Garda Maguire mounted the stairs and entered what appeared to be the main bedroom. There was one double and one single bed in the room. The curtains were pulled open. A woman was lying on the double bed. A duvet was pulled up over most of her body, but a pyjama top was visible. She was extremely pale. Maguire noticed there was bruising on her neck. Her eyes were half closed.

"Colleen," the garda called out. There was no response. The garda put a hand on the body. It was still warm. She looked for a pulse but couldn't find one.

She went back downstairs. The baby was still crying. Within a minute or so, the ambulance arrived. She directed the paramedics to the stairs. At that point, she realised that neither she nor Halligan had their notebooks, such was the haste with which they responded to an emergency call. She raced back to the station to fetch them. When she returned, her colleague was in a room at the rear of the house with

Anton Mulder. Garda Maguire went into the front room to comfort the three children and the baby, who had no idea of the enormity of the change that had just befallen them.

In the back room, Halligan was taking notes. At 11.29 a.m., he cautioned Mulder, interrupted only by Mulder's heaving sobs.

The man had no problem talking. "It was an argument," he said. "Verbal abuse. I grabbed her around the neck and told her to shut up and leave me alone. It was words, words, words."

Within two hours, Mulder had been arrested under suspicion of causing an offence and brought to Navan garda station. Eight miles away, in a branch of Kentucky Fried Chicken (KFC) at Blanchardstown, nineteen-year-old Clinton Mulder got a phone call to tell him to come home. His mother was dead. He contacted his brother Christopher with the news. Then he left work and caught the next bus heading north to Dunshaughlin.

The Mulder family had known upheaval before. When Clinton was eight, they had left South Africa to return to their mother's native Bangor in Co. Down. They went back and forth a few times. Then, two years previously, the family had moved down to Co. Meath, a different country again in the mind of many they knew in Bangor.

Now, though, the upheaval was of a completely different magnitude. Their mother was dead. The two boys would be separated from their four younger sisters.

But at least, in Clinton's mind, they would be out from under the iron rod his father wielded. For while Anton Mulder presented an agreeable face to the world at large, he was a different man behind the closed doors of his own home.

Colleen Pollock was just seven when her family emigrated to South Africa in 1970. The Troubles were exploding in Northern Ireland. The previous year, the British government had sent in troops to protect the nationalist population from attacks by some dominant Protestant loyalists. Tensions between the two communities had been raised to a level not seen in several generations. The IRA was suddenly active, and loyalist paramilitaries moved into a higher level of viciousness.

Against this background, Colleen's parents decided to leave Bangor for what was then the prosperous outpost of South Africa. The apartheid regime ensured that white Europeans were well placed to exploit economic opportunities.

Colleen was the second of three children. Her older sister Anne was seventeen when the family left Ireland, and her younger brother William was just five. The family settled in Durban, in the Natal province. They remained in the country through the good times of the seventies and into the upheavals of the following decade, as the apartheid edifice began to crumble.

In 1984, when Colleen had just reached the age of

majority, she met Anton Mulder, a native Afrikaner. He came from a wealthy family in Durban. After leaving boarding school, he had taken a job as a train driver and moved on from there to the traffic police in Natal.

In his late teens, Mulder had married a local girl who gave birth to a daughter, Tanya. The marriage didn't last. By the time he was twenty-two, he was single again and somewhat disillusioned by the ending of his marriage. Within eighteen months, he had met Colleen. The couple hit it off and were married in May 1985. Colleen was twenty-two, and Mulder, embarking on his second marriage, was a month shy of his twenty-fifth birthday. Their first son, Clinton, was born seven months later. Another, Christopher, followed. By then, the winds of change were blowing through the country. The clamour for an end to apartheid had reached fever pitch. Nelson Mandela, who had been jailed in the early sixties, was now a worldwide symbol of the oppression to which his people were being subjected. Sanctions were imposed on the country by the United Nations, leading to isolation and economic stagnation.

With his Afrikaner background, there was no doubting whose side Mulder was on. Later, when the family moved to Dunshaughlin, he would claim that he had been affiliated to a right-wing group in South Africa and had been involved in an attempt to blow up a dam. This may have been a product of what friends would describe as a fertile imagination.

By 1990, with work drying up, Colleen's brother William, with whom Mulder had become friendly, decided to return to the country he'd left when he was just five. Mulder followed soon after. The turn of the global wheel meant that while the outlook in South Africa was poor, in Northern Ireland the bad times might be ending.

Mulder, Colleen and the two boys moved back to Bangor, but all was not sweetness and light. Work was still hard to come by in the Co. Down town. In January 1991, Mulder and his brother-in-law William Pollock resorted to crime. They hooked up with another three men and got their hands on a few knives. On 7 January, the gang entered the Jubilee Stores in Bangor and threatened the staff before making off with around £400 in cash and cigarettes. Pollock and the rest of the gang were subsequently charged with a number of similar robberies over the following weeks, but there is no evidence that Mulder was involved in any but the Jubilee Store incident.

On 11 February, Mulder, Pollock and the other men were brought before a court in connection with the robberies. Mulder was charged with robbery using a knife on 7 January. In reply, he told the court: "I wasn't holding the knife or anything."

At the subsequent trial, he escaped jail, telling the court that instead he would return to South Africa. Pollock received a jail sentence.

Mulder did return briefly to South Africa but was back in Northern Ireland before the year was out.

The following year, he landed a job with KFC in Bangor. This time he planned to go straight. During the twelve years he was with the company, he displayed a huge appetite for work, which was quickly noted by a series of promotions. Three daughters were born to the Mulders through the nineties while they lived in Bangor. Roxanne, Samantha and Saskia arrived in quick succession. Yet the marriage does not appear to have been happy.

Later, there would be conflicting accusations of violence from both Colleen's family and from Mulder himself. Nobody ever saw him strike Colleen, and he subjected none of his daughters to any violence. The two sons had an entirely different experience. Clinton later told the gardaí, "My father used to treat us all like shit. He used to hit me until I was fifteen or sixteen when I could hit him back." Christopher put it another way: "It was his way, or the highway." He also described how his father dealt with a loss of temper. "He would go around the house hitting inanimate objects," Christopher said.

His sister-in-law Anne described him as "an extremely violent man, particularly with the two boys".

By the turn of the century, Mulder's hard work was paying dividends. In 2001, he was asked to open and manage a KFC branch in Blanchardstown, west Dublin. Once this was deemed a success, he was appointed regional manager over six branches in the Republic. He later told gardaí that all he was interested in outside his family was work.

In 2002, the whole family moved down from Bangor. After a brief period living in Dublin, they moved up to Dunshaughlin, which offered a large house at a reasonable rent and easy access to Northern Ireland, both for work and family reasons. A fourth daughter, Shannon, was born the following year.

Once Mulder had acquired his managerial role in Dublin, he put the family to work. Colleen worked at KFC part-time, and his two sons began their working lives serving fried chicken to the people of west Dublin. Mulder also employed a number of fellow South Africans. A neighbour in Dunshaughlin, Chris Koortzens, managed to persuade Mulder to give his wife and son part-time jobs in the Blanchardstown branch.

Another South African, Andries Loubser, got a job as a chef in the same branch. Johann De Wall, who would go on to have an affair with Colleen, also got a start in KFC until he found a better job, truck driving.

If a certain solidarity existed among exiled white South Africans, it didn't stop Mulder employing black and Asian workers. He may have been a supporter of the racist apartheid regime in his native country, but such discrimination didn't extend to his work or social environment in his adopted home of Ireland. Not only did he employ them, he brought them along to his cricket club in the Phoenix Park.

He joined the Civil Service Cricket Club in 2003 and presented a highly amenable face to members of the club. He also showed signs of an imagination that one of the members described as "a bit Walter Mitty". On arrival, Mulder told the club officials that he had kept wicket for Natal province. This indicated a very high level of achievement in cricket terms, equivalent, for instance, to having played rugby for Munster or one of the major English teams. He didn't live up to the claim, and most members filed it away with his equally sensational boast about attempting to blow up a dam.

The yarn-telling didn't affect his popularity. "He brought a lot of people into the club, Asians and Indians who were working in Kentucky Fried Chicken," one club official remembered. "And he was often helping out. We had a summer barbecue and he showed up with bucket loads of fried chicken. He worked hard. He might have to go up to Belfast in the evening, leave there in the early morning, home around four or five and get up later that morning to play a game. We found him fine."

He also brought his two sons along to the club, and Clinton in particular played a number of games. Whatever the trouble or violence that went on behind closed doors, the front presented to the outside world was of a well-adjusted, stable family. In 2004, Mulder's contribution to the club was recognised when he was named Clubman of the Year. After he had been arrested, at least one member offered to give him a character reference if called on to do so.

In July 2004, Colleen Mulder suffered a miscarriage. The misfortune would be the catalyst that brought the Mulders' marriage to an end. Afterwards, Colleen was prone to depression, although there is no evidence that her mood swings indicated a clinical pathology.

She got little support from her husband, who was away working most of the time. A marriage that had been turbulent was now heading for the rocks.

By September, Colleen was seeking affection elsewhere. Johann De Wall arrived in Ireland from his native South Africa in November 2002. Through the usual ex-pat contacts, he encountered Mulder at a get-together. They became friendly.

De Wall was trying to get off the ground in his new country. Mulder appeared to be doing well, so De Wall asked him for a loan of €6,000 to buy a car. Mulder agreed. After that, they met a number of times at parties.

In September 2004, the Mulders hosted a get-together to watch a rugby match involving South Africa. By that stage, De Wall was seeing Colleen, although they weren't yet involved in a sexual relationship. De Wall attended the party. Over the course of the evening, Mulder confided in him that he was sick of his family and thinking of doing a runner. He said he planned to max out his credit cards and remortgage the house the couple still owned in Bangor. "He said he was going to disappear, head back to South Africa with the money so he could show his father that he had made millions without any help from him," De Wall remembered later.

It was the last time they spoke. The following day, De Wall received a text from Mulder telling him their friendship was over. De Wall replied that he knew the reason why. Mulder had become aware – possibly from Colleen herself – that his wife was seeing the man he had befriended.

For Colleen, it was decision time. After nineteen years of marriage, she no longer wanted to go on with her husband. However, the six children meant that divorce wouldn't be easy. By the end of October, she couldn't persevere any more. She went to see her mother in Bangor, but the visit was to be a springboard to escape. She decided she would leave the children behind until she could investigate how best to handle the issue within the law. Taking the four girls – who were all under eighteen – back to Bangor might present legal difficulties as Northern Ireland is a separate jurisdiction from the Republic.

Down in Dunshaughlin, Mulder was finding it difficult to adjust to his new circumstances. The realisation that his wife had left him was painful. He travelled to Bangor with baby Shannon. Colleen was adamant that she had had enough. Mulder left Shannon with her – he wouldn't have been equipped to look after the baby as well as the three older girls – but he vowed that the others would stay with him.

The journey back south must have been filled with dread. He was thousands of miles from home, cast adrift from the one form of stability he had known over the previous nearly twenty years. He would later tell a psychiatrist that he didn't maintain much contact with South Africa, not even with his family. He carried baggage from his childhood, as he had expressed to his wife's lover, De Wall: he laboured in the belief that making an impression on his father required him to return home with a lot of money, demonstrating that he could be a success on his own out in the world.

His history of violence in the home suggests that self-analysis wasn't a strong point. As such, he would have placed the blame for his new circumstances exclusively at his wife's feet. She was the one who had left. She was the one who was seeing another man.

Mulder began to lose weight. His high standards at work slipped. It was noted that his performance was deteriorating. He remained firm about one issue: his three daughters weren't going anywhere.

Colleen came back from Bangor in late November for Saskia's birthday. Once the celebrations were over, she returned to the North with Shannon. In Bangor, she confided in her sister Anne, who had returned to the town after a few years in the USA, that her big worry was custody of the children. She was worried about the legal implications of bringing them across the border. Anne accompanied her to the local CAB to see if complications would arise. She was reassured that no legal barriers prevented the children coming with her as they had been born in Northern Ireland.

South of the border, Mulder was behaving out of character. His sons were finding him more amenable than at any time in their formative years. Where previously their father had discouraged them from bringing friends into the house, now he was urging them to invite them round for a beer. The boys were wrong-footed by this strange turn.

His sister-in-law Anne also found a different Mulder when she visited briefly that November. In the nineteen years he had been married to her sister, he had shown very little interest in Anne. When Anne's husband had died, he hadn't attended the funeral. Now he was the man of a thousand welcomes. He sat down with her in the house in Dunshaughlin and talked about Colleen. As far as he was concerned, she was still feeling down about the miscarriage. He was worried about her mental health. Anne returned to the North, disconcerted by his welcome and concern, which had never before featured in his character.

Elsewhere, he opened the valve on his inner feelings. At work, he spoke to his compatriot Andreis Loubser about his domestic travails. Loubser was somewhat confused. On one hand, Mulder was complaining that Colleen had left home to go and live with her mother, while on the other, she was supposed to have left him for another man.

"Why is she living with her mother if she went with

another man?" Loubser asked. Mulder was non-committal in his reply.

In early December, he called in next door to the Koortzens, to leave wages for Chris's wife and son. The two men got talking. Mulder was in a state about his marriage. Koortzens recalled that his wife Esmarine had mentioned that Mulder had lost a lot of weight.

Mulder said he suspected Colleen was having an affair. She had returned briefly and now she was back in Bangor.

In the course of the conversation, he lapsed into the two men's native tongue and said, in Afrikaans, "I feel I can pick up a knife and make ends of her." Koortzens was taken aback. He advised his friend to see a lawyer over any custody issue that might arise.

A few days later, Loubser was having a cigarette out at the back of the Blanchardstown KFC branch. Mulder came over for a chat. His wife was again the topic of conversation. "She's not back yet," Mulder said, referring to a previous hope that his wife would eventually return to the family home. "I'm going to kill her. I'm going up North, going to the house and I will kill her. It's easy in this country. You only have to do five or six years. I would still be a young man when I get out."

He told Loubser that Colleen wanted to bring the children up to Bangor. But he just wasn't going to let that happen.

Thursday 16 December was Clinton's nineteenth birthday. Colleen came down to be with her son on the big day. Later that evening, Mulder, Colleen and the three girls went to Peter's Restaurant in Dunshaughlin. The manager of the restaurant, Valerie Daly, recognised the family. The couple were vaguely familiar. She couldn't help noticing that there appeared to be an absence of family spirit around the table. She noticed that one of the little girls was doing all the talking. The woman was saying next to nothing. The man didn't appear happy.

That night, Colleen slept in the master bedroom with baby Shannon. Mulder slept in the girls' room, retiring at 10 p.m. By then, Clinton and Christopher were also in, watching TV downstairs. The boys were both in bed by 11.45 p.m. It was the last night that the Mulders slept under one roof as a family.

The following morning, the two boys rose early and headed off to work. Mulder got the girls up and brought them downstairs. Roxanne didn't want to go to school so he wrote a note for her teacher. In the sitting room, he played blocks with the two younger girls. Mulder was working on flexitime. There was no mad rush to be up and out the door.

At some stage, Colleen called him to change Shannon's nappy. Around 10 a.m, he got ready to leave. He went upstairs to wash his face and apply some deodorant. His toiletries were in the en-suite attached to the master bedroom. Colleen was still in bed, most likely sitting up.

On either entering the bedroom, en route to or emerging from the bathroom, an altercation developed. Mulder would later say it began with Colleen abusing him. It ended with him strangling his wife in the bed some minutes after 10 a.m.

Downstairs, the girls heard a commotion. One of them confirmed that she had heard her mother shouting, although it is unclear whether she was engaged in a verbal spat with her husband or trying to repel an attack. A few minutes later, Saskia came upstairs. She looked into the room and saw her father standing over the double bed in which her mother lay, apparently motionless.

After some minutes, Mulder came downstairs. He picked up the phone and rang local solicitor Fabien Cadden. The solicitor had previously told Mulder that if he ever had any legal worries to be in touch. The invitation was offered in a general sense. When the call came through, Cadden was shocked by what Mulder said. He told his secretary to hurry down to the garda station. Something terrible had happened up at Mael Duin.

The interviews began just before 3 p.m. Mulder, having been cautioned, opened up with little prompting. The gardaí in attendance, Detectives James O'Sullivan and Valentine Cross, noticed that he spoke with an accent and occasionally lapsed into broken English. As Mulder's first language was

Afrikaans, an interpreter was brought in. However, he had a very good command of English.

Early on in the interview, he asked how his wife was. He didn't react when told she was dead.

The picture he painted of life behind the closed doors of 93 Mael Duin differed greatly from the one that would emerge from other family members. He had felt threatened. His wife had been violent towards him. As evidence of this, he referred to AMEN, an organisation concerned with domestic violence against men. A leaflet detailing how to handle violence in the home was retrieved from the house.

He claimed to have been the one living in fear. He told the guards that he was terrified at night that Colleen's brother, William Pollock, or friends of hers, would come charging in to shoot him with an AK-47.

Although he and Pollock had been friends some years previously, the deterioration of Mulder's marriage had put paid to that. In an interview in 2006, Pollock would tell crime reporter Darren Boyle that early on in Colleen's marriage, when they were all living in South Africa, and he heard that Mulder had been violent towards her, he had put a grenade in Mulder's mouth. "My only regret is I didn't pull the pin," he said.

Pollock did not give evidence at the trial, and no evidence was canvassed as to whether he or anybody else ever produced an AK-47 in front of Mulder.

"It was getting to the stage where me and the girls were barricading ourselves in the room. You don't know what it's like. I got something, in case I got woken up and the door was kicked in, have to grab something. You'd get done with an AK-47 easily . . . when you barricade yourself in the room, at least you know when they're coming with an AK-47," he said in the interview.

His sons were also a problem, Mulder told the guards. They smoked cannabis in the house and invited all their friends in to party. Colleen had sanctioned this behaviour. "She allows the boys to smoke that shit."

He claimed that when he tried to intervene, she threatened him with being shot. "She asked me how I survived, had anyone come and shot me. She called me motherfucker. I even phoned the guards over the boys and dope. I would get done. She tried to provoke me to hit her and I wouldn't."

At his subsequent trial, Mulder's counsel didn't call any witnesses to back up these statements. The boys testified that their father had never spoken to them about smoking cannabis. Clinton also said that he had seen his mother hit his father once, when Mulder had cornered her during an argument.

On request, Mulder sketched out the layout upstairs in the family home. His account of what had happened that morning came out in a series of bursts, some in response to questions, others in a stream of consciousness. "Colleen called me to change Shannon's bum . . . I went upstairs to put on deodorant and wash my face. Colleen was in the bed.

She was saying you've never been a father, a lot of chirping, asked me how I survived during the night – 'Has anyone came and shot you?'

"I grabbed her – 'Why are you being so nasty?' She was sitting on the side of the bed then . . . stop talking to me, stop abusing me. I still love her. Why did I do it?

"Then I went downstairs . . . I thought she was OK. For once, I got the chance to do the talking. Don't ever abuse me again. Jesus, I love that woman. I went downstairs to phone Fabien to phone the guards to come and see if she was all right.

"I just grabbed her and said, 'Don't be so bad to me, don't say those things.' Around the neck, around the head, wherever I could grab her. I told her to stop all the words she throws at me all day long. I was just having my say . . . you got to realise, I didn't mean any of this. I love her."

He brought the detectives through the build-up to what had happened that morning. "We weren't getting on well for four or five months. Just verbal abuse . . . the two boys are into dope smoking. I wouldn't agree with it . . . six, seven fellas upstairs smoking shit . . . every kid between the ages of fifteen and eighteen in Dunshaughlin has been in the house.

"I'm a workaholic. The four girls, I look after them, feed them and take them to school. They're my pets. I would do anything for them.

"This morning, she said my days are numbered. I was going to get done over by her friends. This morning, I lost it."

The following day, Saturday, 18 December, Mulder was charged with assault under the Non-Fatal Offences Against the Person Act and brought before a special sitting of Navan District Court. During the brief hearing, he cried and held his head in his hands. He was denied bail on the grounds that he was a flight risk. Within a week, he was granted bail.

Over that Christmas, and into January 2005, the gardaí compiled enough evidence against Mulder to upgrade the charge against him. On 1 February, he was charged with murder and remanded in custody. By then, his family had moved back to live in Bangor with their grandmother.

Court One in the Round Hall of the Four Courts can resemble a cattle market on a Monday morning. This is swearing-in time for juries to be assigned to the Central Criminal Court. Usually, it is presided over by Judge Paul Carney, the senior judge.

Scores of potential jurors mill around until their names are called. The selection process takes place for that week's sittings. It is open to both prosecution and defence to object to up to seven candidates for a jury without giving a reason. As a result, a large panel is called in to ensure that there will be twelve acceptable jurors for each trial due to go on.

On 2 May 2006, a Tuesday after the bank holiday weekend, Anton Mulder was arraigned before the court. He was asked how he pleaded. "Not guilty to murder, guilty to manslaughter," he replied.

Suddenly, there was shouting from the public gallery. "He's a murderer," a male voice called. Judge Carney asked whether the person shouting could be identified, and, if so, he should be taken into custody and brought before the court at a later stage.

The judge turned his attention to swearing in the jury, but before this could get under way, an intrepid garda approached the bench, saying he had identified the shouting culprit. A tall man with swept-back hair and a beard, wearing a shirt and combat trousers, came forward. Judge Carney asked him in what capacity he was in the court.

"I'm a witness for my sister, so I do apologise for shouting. I hereby apologise in front of the court and I will stand outside in the foyer. It is just my reaction to seeing my sister's husband who strangled her, it just came out of me." William Pollock spoke with a distinctive South African accent.

The judge instructed a garda to take the man to the cells until he decided what to do with him. The jury was sworn in, and the case assigned a judge, Philip O'Sullivan, and pencilled in to begin the following morning. Later in the day, when Judge Carney felt that Mr Pollock's heels had cooled sufficiently, he was brought again before the court.

In recent years, the courts – and the criminal-justice system in general – have offered greater recognition to the victims of crime, particularly the bereaved. Although Pollock had made an affray in the court, potentially interfering with the selection of a jury, Judge Carney took a lenient view and freed him. That should have been that, an emotional outburst from a bereaved brother dealt with by the short, sharp shock of a few hours in the lock-up.

The trial began in Court Fifteen, upstairs in the Four Courts building, in a modern room with bulbous lamps and tall windows looking out over the Liffey. The small room is not generally used for murder trials.

Colleen's elder sister Anne Czerepowicz and her partner sat behind the lawyers with Anton Mulder a few feet away on the same bench.

In the early days of the trial, William Pollock and his wife Andrea were at the back of the court. The initial witnesses were processed, including the gardaí and the emergency-services personnel who had attended the scene on the day of the killing.

One of the early witnesses was Andrea Pollock. She told of coming down to Dunshaughlin to meet Colleen in the weeks before her death. She was pulled up by one of the defendant's lawyers for engaging in hearsay, relating something that somebody else had said, which could not be confirmed by the court. It was obvious she was no fan of the defendant. When she finished her evidence, she marched to the back of the court and out the door, slamming it behind her.

The following day, the deputy state pathologist Michael Curtis gave evidence. He had carried out the post-mortem on the body and detailed the injuries Colleen had sustained. There was bruising around her mouth, and a bone at the back of her neck was broken. "She would seem to have died as a result of manual strangulation," he told the court. However, he couldn't say for sure how violent an attack she had suffered. "It is impossible to determine the quantity or length of force applied to the neck," he said. What he could say was that the neck must have been compressed for several seconds. Beyond that he could not go and was only willing to commit himself to saying that the asphyxiation had involved "moderate" force.

The classification was something of a victory for the defence. If Mulder had applied only moderate force, then his story that he hadn't meant to kill his wife might be credible.

The doctor was cross-examined by Mulder's lawyer, Roderick O'Hanlon. The counsel told the witness that Mulder had described how he had intended to stop the woman talking and indicated the use of his hand on her neck and mouth. Would the injuries be consistent with that?

"Yes," Curtis replied.

"Could it [death] occur rapidly?" O'Hanlon asked.

"Consciousness could be lost quickly," Curtis said. "Ten to fifteen seconds, but it would be longer for brain death to occur due to loss of oxygen."

On Friday, the third day of the trial, things took an unexpected turn. When the session began, but before the jury was brought in, prosecuting counsel Gerard

Clarke told the judge that the gardaí had some concern about the behaviour of William and Andrea Pollock. Clarke was requesting an order to exclude them from the court.

Before listening to that application the judge introduced another piece of drama. "I will be drawing this to the attention of the jury but I may as well as we are dealing with the whole thing, I have a note from the foreman [of the jury] Mr Shortall, saying: 'Colleen Mulder's brother is making himself a small bit familiar with some members of the jury.'"

William Pollock was back centre-stage. He stood up and made himself known. After further discussion, Judge O'Sullivan said he was going to bring in the jury and ask what had happened to raise these concerns.

The jury foreman spelt it out: "I need to go back a little bit to Tuesday, to Mr Carney's court. When the indictment against the accused was read out there was a scuffle at the back and it turned out that the outburst was by the deceased's brother, a Mr William Pollock, and he was brought before Justice Carney," the foreman said.

"The next day, which was Wednesday, 3 May, we assembled on the corridor outside Court Fifteen when one of the jurors was asked by Mr William Pollock if he could borrow the newspaper of the day and he read out the article, referring to this trial, and made it clear that the reference to the person who gave the outburst was in fact himself.

"And there were other people in the neighbourhood in the courts who heard what he was reading out. But the feeling that the juror felt was that he was familiarising himself with the juror. At the end of the first session, which was Wednesday, 3 May, he greeted the said juror with a smile and a nod. The outcome of the whole thing is that the juror in question feels somewhat intimidated and uncomfortable. And that concludes what I have to say."

It took a few seconds for that to sink in. The jury was asked to leave. More legal argument followed as to whether or not the trial should continue. The jury was brought back again, and Judge O'Sullivan asked if the juror in question would identify him or herself. A Mr Paddy O'Brien put his hand up.

The judge asked him whether he felt intimidated or uncomfortable. He pointed out that the foreman had related him as being "somewhat" intimidated and uncomfortable. "I think the word I am using and stressing was, the familiarity was wrong," O'Brien said. "That is about the extent of it. I don't feel intimidated or . . . but the word I did use to the foreman was the familiarity that was drawn to me, I just felt that was wrong."

How did he feel about staying on in his role as a juror? "I feel it is probably OK to carry on as it stands," O'Brien said. After further discussion between the judge and the lawyers, it was decided that the case could go on. But without the Pollocks. The couple were banned, not just from the court but from the precincts of the Four Courts building for the duration of the trial.

The remainder of the trial passed without incident. Mulder's sons appeared in court sporadically. Anne Czerepowicz was in attendance every day, a dignified presence. Mulder's counsel relied on provocation as its defence. The jury didn't buy it. They returned a verdict, guilty of murder, after five hours' deliberation.

Anne Czerepowicz sobbed after the verdict was read out. Judge O'Sullivan asked Mulder to stand for sentencing. "This is a sad day for your family," the judge told him. A few yards behind Mulder, at the back of the court, his son Clinton had his arms raised in a victory salute.

Outside the court, Christopher said that if justice hadn't been done, he would have taken matters into his own hands. His aunt recoiled. As Anne Czerepowicz was talking about her memories of her sister, William Pollock and his wife appeared, freed from the banning order now that the trial was at an end.

Pollock hugged his nephew, Christopher. "Justice for the People," he said, his arm raised. He spoke a while about his love for his sister and how Mulder had treated her so badly. Johann De Wall, who had been in court most days, hove into view. It was time for a photograph. The Pollocks, De Wall, his brother and Christopher linked arms and began walking down the street for the cameras, in what might be described as a victory march.

The law, however, wasn't done with them yet. Mulder appealed the verdict alleging that the outcome of the the trial had been prejudiced by William Pollock's interventions, both on the day of jury selection and in making himself "familiar" to one member of the jury.

The three-judge court found that the trial judge had erred in continuing and that Mulder was entitled to another trial. He remained in custody to await the second round of his case versus the state.

The new trial began on 21 January 2008 with a few different elements. The Pollocks were nowhere to be seen, but the new trial judge, Kevin O'Higgins, revived the banning order against them.

One of the witnesses in the first trial, the neighbour Chris Koortzens, was unable to attend. He was ill and had returned to South Africa.

The most significant difference in the second trial was a new plank of defence. Mulder was claiming that at the time of the killing he had been suffering from diminished responsibility.

This defence opened up for him following the enactment in June 2006, a month after his first trial, of the Criminal Law Insanity Act, which was designed to bring the law into line with advances in medical science. Up until then, a defendant who was on trial for murder, but whom the jury found was suffering from a major mental disorder at the time, could only be found 'guilty but insane'. The person would then be held indefinitely in the Central Mental Hospital and could only be released by order of the Minister for Justice. The law, which originated in the nineteenth century, branded a medically insane person as a murderer and determined that his or her detention would ultimately be in the gift of the government, rather than at the behest of a medical authority.

Things had moved on since the nineteenth century. The 2006 Act was designed to reflect these advances. A person who was found to be medically insane could plead "not guilty by reason of insanity". If the plea was accepted, the person would be held at the Central Mental Hospital until such time as a medical authority deemed he or she was fit to be released.

Crucially for Anton Mulder, the act also included a provision dealing with defendants who were suffering from a disorder but not one that was severe enough to come under the insanity plea. This was, effectively, a half way house between a person being fully responsible for their actions and being legally insane.

Under the new Act, if a defendant is found to be suffering from a disorder that "substantially diminishes" their responsibility at the time of a killing, the offence is reduced from murder to manslaughter. If Mulder could prove that he was suffering from a mental disorder when he strangled his wife, the scale of his offence might be reduced. He wouldn't be facing a life sentence and might reasonably expect a relatively short term in prison.

In order for a defendant to prove that he or she was suffering from a disorder at the time of a killing, evidence would be required to that effect from a psychiatrist.

This time, Mulder didn't plead guilty to manslaughter. His only plea was "not guilty". Most of the evidence was a repeat of that produced in the first trial. The only new aspect was the expert evidence on whether or not Mulder was operating at a level of diminished responsibility when he had killed Colleen.

On the seventh day of the trial, Dr Conor O'Neill, a consultant forensic psychiatrist attached to the Central Mental Hospital, gave evidence for the defence. He had examined Mulder in Cloverhill prison over a twelve-month period. He had read the book of evidence from the first trial to corroborate Mulder's story. He had contacted Mulder's mother in South Africa.

The doctor had considered some biological symptoms of depression that Mulder had apparently displayed in the months before the killing. In the two months leading up to the "index offence", as it was described in court, Mulder had lost a lot of weight, up to two stone. This was corroborated by other witnesses. He was waking early in the morning. Nobody could corroborate that. He had suffered a loss of appetite. He lacked energy. At work, the diligence that had seen him rise swiftly through the ranks had been absent in the autumn of 2004. The deterioration in his work was corroborated by staff at KFC.

Having compiled the evidence for his report, Dr O'Neill then applied criteria defining a mental disorder as set out by both the World Health Organisation and the American Psychiatry Association. The doctor was asked what he considered to be Mulder's mental state at the time of the killing.

"I feel that he was mild to moderate [depressed], closer to moderate from his evidence and the combination [of evidence] from other witnesses," Dr O'Neill told the court. "And this had been present over the previous months and would come under the definition of mental disorder."

If the jury fully accepted Dr O'Neill's evidence, and it wasn't rebutted by other psychiatric testimony, they would be obliged to consider returning a verdict of manslaughter, due to diminished responsibility.

The prosecution wasn't buying the diminished-responsibility line. Dr O'Neill was cross-examined by the DPP's counsel, Gerard Clarke. The lawyer wanted to know whether psychiatry was an exact science.

"No, it is inexact," O'Neill replied. "But by using classification systems, it is as exact as it can become."

Clarke wondered about the weight loss. Colleen Mulder had left the family home six weeks prior to her death. With her gone, Clarke wanted to know, who had been cooking the evening meal? Maybe lack of nourishment rather than the onset of a mental disorder had contributed to Mulder's losing weight.

"The rapidity of his weight loss would have been extreme," O'Neill replied.

"Did you check out his eating habits?"

"No, not really."

"Then, Doctor, you shouldn't speculate about matters you don't know about," the senior counsel lectured the consultant psychiatrist.

When Dr O'Neill was finished, the prosecution produced their expert witness. Paul O'Connell was a colleague of O'Neill's in the Central Mental Hospital.

He had interviewed Mulder for five hours in the month before the trial. He had found the defendant to be "cunning, deceitful, manipulative and implausible". O'Connell told the court that Mulder showed no sign of fatigue over the lengthy interview, displaying a stamina that would be inconsistent in somebody suffering from depression.

The doctor said Mulder was "an unreliable historian", a lovely psychiatric term for a liar. O'Connell also had a theory about the weight loss: "The hypothesis I find more believable is that his lifestyle – because he became physically much busier [after Colleen had left] – affected his weight loss."

He was not suggesting that all had been fine and dandy with Mulder since his incarceration in February 2005. O'Connell believed the prisoner was suffering from "chronic adjustment condition", which means he was having trouble getting used to life in prison, a common enough problem for somebody facing a long stretch in middle age.

"I have come across situations like this," O'Connell told the court. "Some are ill, some have an adjustment reaction. They are in prison." Irrespective of what trouble Mulder might have been experiencing during the trial, this psychiatrist was in complete disagreement with his colleague as to Mulder's condition at the time of the killing.

The jury was left with two opposing expert psychiatric opinions on a matter of great importance.

In summing up for the prosecution, Gerard Clarke said that Dr O'Neill had been retained to "find something". This upset defence counsel Roddy O'Hanlon, and Judge Kevin O'Higgins agreed. "Mr Clarke said that Dr O'Neill was engaged to find something," the judge told the jury in his charge. "Mr O'Hanlon got cross at that, and in my view he was right to get cross. Dr O'Neill was engaged to conduct an examination."

In the end, the jury didn't accept the diminished responsibility or any other plank of the defence. After three hours' deliberation, they found Mulder guilty of murder by a majority verdict of 10–2. As far as they were concerned, he was bad rather than mad. He received the mandatory life sentence.

After the verdict, Mulder kept his head bowed. His sons Clinton and Christopher waved at him, smiling, as they left. Outside, Anne Czerepowicz and Clinton expressed their relief that the process was finally over. Anne said that to get the right verdict once had been a miracle but to get it twice left her speechless. "He was a very hard worker, but that was all he cared about, money. And he didn't give any to

Colleen or the children. He was a very violent man, particularly towards the two boys."

Clinton spoke next. As he did so, a tear rolled down his right cheek. "My mother was a very loving person, one of a kind. She did not hit people the way he said. He was a violent, angry man. At least now we've got justice for my mum, and for myself."

With that, Clinton Mulder left to make his way back to Bangor, to resume the latest chapter in a life that had been so violently interrupted on a December morning in 2004.

Colleen Mulder was one of thirty-seven murder victims in the state in 2004. A further six killings were classified as manslaughter.

EPILOGUE

The more things change, the more they stay the same. The crime of spousal murder is unlikely to recede come what may. Unlike other forms of crime, it is not really susceptible to societal or economic changes.

For example, there is nothing to suggest that the crime is less prevalent in Ireland since the introduction of divorce in the mid-nineties. Neither has the economic boom that followed offered any indications that wife killing (or the less prevalent but equally appalling crime of husband killing) is on the wane.

Research on crime in general shows that the fear of detection is the greatest deterrent. Yet, despite the obvious fact that the police are most likely to look closely at the husband in the wake of a woman's murder, a belief appears to persist that men who do kill their wives think they can get away with it.

The only real area where public policy can affect the frequency of spousal murders is in the area of domestic violence. Despite advances in recent years, much remains to be done in this area, both in terms of dealing with the immediate problem and in identifying the risk of fatal attacks.

But, as many of the cases in this book demonstrate, sometimes there are no danger signs, no signals to suggest that a man has murder on his mind. Sometimes, only luck or fate can intervene to prevent a killing within a union, which was originally formed by the two individuals as a means to love and honour each other.

ACKNOWLEDGEMENTS

A special word of thanks to Maureen Gillespie, Picture Editor of the *Sunday Tribune* for her advice, encouragement and valuable assistance over the course of this project.

Special gratitude is also due to Marian Leonard and her family for inviting me into their home and telling me their story of the life and death of Marian's sister, Esther.

Lifelong gratitude is due to my parents Aideen and John, who read early drafts of this book, just as they had my first efforts at composition in Cahirciveen thirty-five years ago.

Pauline Sweeney and Luke Clifford stood patiently on the shore and egged me on through the peaks and troughs of research and writing.

Advice and friendship from Ronnie Bellew, John Fitzgerald, The Coz and Una Clifford was much appreciated. Thanks are due to all in the *Sunday*

Tribune, particularly Editor Noirin Hegarty, Diarmuid Doyle and Shane Coleman.

At Hachette Books Ireland, my editor Ciara Considine was a valuable source of support and advice.

A number of people who were interviewed in connection with this book wish to remain anonymous. Their time and insight was greatly appreciated, as were the valued contributions from Tony Sourke, Tom Connolly (Kildare), Tom Connolly (Donegal), Pat Ryan, Billy Flynn, Stephen Ryan, Paul O'Meara, Abigail Reilly and the staff at the National Archive and the National Library.

The following publications were consulted:
Why Do They Kill? Men Who Murder Their Intimate Partners by David Adams (Nashville, Tenn. Vanderbilt University Press) 2007.
Crime and Punishment in Ireland 1922 to 2003 edited by Ian O'Donnell, Eoin O'Sullivan and Deirdre Healy (Dublin, Institute of Public Administration) 2005.
Homicide: Murder and Manslaughter in 21st Century Ireland by John Burke and Eoghan Rice (Dublin, Merlin Publishing) 2006.

Newspapers:
Irish Independent, Cork Examiner, Irish Press, Irish Times, Limerick Leader, Donegal Democrat.

Photo acknowledgements:
The publishers and author would like to thank the

following for kind permission to reproduce photographs in the book: Marian Leonard, Mark Condron and the *Sunday Tribune*, *Irish Examiner*, *Irish Times*, www.courtpix.ie (including *collect pic*), and the National Archive.